Alanatomy

The Inside Story

Alan Carr is one of Britain's most successful and best-loved comedians. His unique humour and effortless stage presence, both on screen and on tour, make him part of the backbone of British comedy.

His hugely successful chat show *Alan Carr: Chatty Man* is not only in its sixteenth series and shown all around the world, but has garnered him a whole host of awards including two National Television Awards, two Royal Television Awards, three National Comedy Awards and a BAFTA for Best Television Personality.

When Alan is off screen you will often find him on stage entertaining the world with his hilarious stand-up. His first two sell-out tours, *Tooth Fairy* and *Spexy Beast*, saw him playing to legions of fans across the UK and Ireland including impressive performances at the iconic O2 and Wembley arenas. His current tour *Yap Yap Yap!* has seen Alan perform over 350 shows to 250,000 fans, not only in the UK and Ireland, but all over the world including Scandinavia, the Middle East, Canada – at the prestigious 'Just For Laughs' Comedy Festival in Montreal – and more recently as far away as Australia and New Zealand.

After the success of his previous autobiography, the *Sunday Times* bestseller *Look Who It Is!*, which sold over half a million copies, Alan's new memoir *Alanatomy* is set to be this autumn's must-read.

Alanatomy

The Inside Story

ALAN CARR

MICHAEL JOSEPH
an imprint of
PENGUIN BOOKS

MICHAEL JOSEPH

UK | USA | Canada | Ireland | Australia
India | New Zealand | South Africa

Michael Joseph is part of the Penguin Random House group of companies
whose addresses can be found at global.penguinrandomhouse.com

Penguin
Random House
UK

First published 2016
001

Copyright © Alan Carr, 2016

The moral right of the author has been asserted

Set in 13.75/16.25 pt Garamond MT Std
Typeset by Jouve (UK), Milton Keynes
Printed in Great Britain by Clays Ltd, St Ives plc

'Work Bitch'. Words and Music by Britney Spears, William Adams, Ruth Cunningham, Otto Jettman &
Anthony Preston © Copyright Britney Spears Music/Universal Music Z-Songs/Refune Music Rights AB.
Universal Music Publishing Limited/Imagem Music.
All Rights Reserved. International Copyright Secured. Used by Permission of Music Sales Limited

A CIP catalogue record for this book is available from the British Library

HARDBACK ISBN: 978–0–718–18075–1
OM PAPERBACK ISBN: 978–0–718–18076–8

www.greenpenguin.co.uk

MIX
Paper from
responsible sources
FSC® C018179

Penguin Random House is committed to a
sustainable future for our business, our readers
and our planet. This book is made from Forest
Stewardship Council® certified paper.

For Max and Isla

Contents

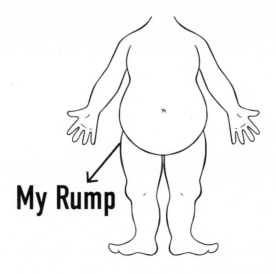

My Rump

I bent over the table submissively and felt the lady's calloused hand caress my cheeks through the fabric of my trousers. There was a contemplative pause – and a muffled giggle from the audience. Had she found something? 'You're struggling with the book, you are, but you must do it, don't give up on it.' I spun round – how did the rumpologist know this? No one even knew I was writing a book, let alone that the words weren't flowing as freely as I had hoped. The rumpologist smiled knowingly. Karl Pilkington looked unimpressed – mind you, he always looks unimpressed – and as for the *Chatty Man* audience, well, they were just waiting for One Direction to come out – they were the next guests and were waiting

1

backstage. But seriously, it was a revelation to me, it was as if she had looked into my soul – well, arse – and seen something. She said some other things too: that I was going on holiday next month – I was, Barbados – and that I was on the cusp of something big – but then they always say that, don't they, it's the law.

Sometimes you have to humour these people. I remember when Justin Lee Collins and I went on *This Morning* and they asked us if we wouldn't mind having our fortunes read live on air. I love that type of thing and immediately said yes. Would she be using runes, tarot, Ouija board? I enquired. No – asparagus. By throwing sprigs of asparagus on the studio floor and seeing where they landed she could tell our future – a bit like if Nostradamus worked in Whole Foods. Justin immediately backed out: 'No way, no way – what if she says that we're all going to die?' What – with asparagus? That asparagus would have to land pretty violently to predict a death. Anyway, seeing the fear in Justin's eyes I went ahead with it regardless and it was vintage *This Morning* – bonkers and yet fun.

So I had some history in dealing with nutjobs telling me what life had in store for me. Still, the comment the rumpologist made about the book rattled me – maybe I had given up too soon, maybe I should put finger to keyboard one more time and see what happened – but then, even if I did finally finish the book, most authors thank their mums, dads, kids . . . God, how could I thank a woman who reads arses for a living? What kind of an idiot would actually believe something like that? Well, you're reading this now, so I guess – me!

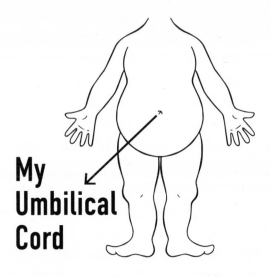

My Umbilical Cord

As some of you lovely readers might know, this is my second book. My first book, *Look Who It Is*, covered my childhood and feral youth, and this book picks up where that book left off, just as I was about to embark on my first-ever presenting job on *The Friday Night Project*. So there I was all alone, living in Holloway. I'd moved down to London for work, leaving my friends up in Manchester. I'd been travelling up and down that M6 for the past three years and driving three and a half hours plus to get home was taking its toll. I was off my face on energy drinks and 'Percy Pigs' and on first-name terms with the canteen ladies in the service station caffs – 'Hi, Val!' 'Hi,

Alan! Who was you with on *8 Out of 10 Cats* tonight, love?' over a stale *pain aux raisins*.

So I had decided to take the plunge and move to the Big Smoke, through gritted teeth I hasten to add. I loved Manchester – I had a wonderful network of friends, had my favourite pub, my favourite bar, my favourite curry house – and I so wanted to resist moving, but you have to go where the work is. If the M6 was the umbilical cord for me, nourishing me, keeping me attached to my Mancunian womb, then the Brent Cross shopping centre was the vagina from which I was sprung. The umbilical cord had to be snipped at some point, so I left Manchester and moved to Holloway. Why Holloway? Well, it sounded like Hollywood (shallow, I know), and the estate agent said the area was Crouch End Borders – apparently if you stepped over the mattress and turned left at the dead cat you would be in Crouch End. They must have seen me coming, but I wasn't to know. I remember ringing up to pay my council tax and correcting the bloke when he said 'Holloway' –'Oh no, Crouch End Borders,' I said, and he suppressed a laugh. He must have thought I was one of those deluded Hyacinth Bucket characters who names their two-up two-down 'Hedgehog Cottage' or their bedsit 'Downton'. I can imagine the postman coming through the gate muttering under his breath, 'Who does he think he is?'

As always when you move to a new area, you start finding your feet – you discover your nice neighbour, your not-so-nice neighbour, your favourite local baker, your favourite local newsagent and, in my case, your favourite local halfway house two doors along. A group of men

4

would always be sitting outside leaning nonchalantly on the wall in various states of delirium, making comments to all the passers-by and watching the world go by. It got to the point where I could gauge my level of fame by the amount of money they would ask for when I passed. When I first arrived in Holloway it was a gruff 'lend us a quid' but by the time I left three years later it had gone up to a grand! 'C'mon, you know you got it,' they pleaded – with an air of desperation and cider.

In the early days, though, feeling isolated, miserable and out on a limb, I decided to fill the void by getting off my arse and earning some cold hard cash. As Britney so eloquently put it, 'You want a Lamborghini, sip Martinis, look hot in a bikini, you better work, bitch!' and that's exactly what I did. I threw myself wholeheartedly into work mode. Corporates, stand-up gigs, you name it, I did it, but for the most part I loitered on the outskirts of terrestrial television and flirted with the burgeoning new satellite channels that were multiplying before my very eyes. There seemed to be a new channel appearing every day and although it was all very exciting I don't think anyone really understood that they had to actually fill the channel with, err, umm, something? Some content perhaps? You can't just have that test card with the girl holding a piece of chalk and a blackboard and a sinister-looking puppet. They were desperate and when people are desperate they call me. I shamelessly popped up on anything and everything.

My particular forte was those awful talking heads programmes – two hundred and fifty quid for a couple of hours' work – I'll pop that in my bumbag, thank you very much. Look, money was money, and I was mercenary. I would talk about anything if the price was right – well, if the price was two hundred and fifty quid. Women's rights, the sixties, international terrorism, Spandau Ballet – you name it, I would appear and hold forth on these and other subjects till the cows came home. It didn't matter if I wasn't even born when the actual event happened – I would still say I was there, and put in my two penny-worth: 'Emily Davison told me she was going to throw herself in front of the king's horse at the Derby, I told her not to but she wouldn't listen – typical Emily.' Who cares? I didn't, neither did the producers and neither did the four stoners watching at quarter past three in the morning.

Like the way stand-up comedy had exploded in Manchester in the early 2000s, all of a sudden the growth of satellite channels had mushroomed and there was this need for all the dead air to be filled. I guess I was in the right time at the right place – or maybe the wrong time and wrong place depending on whether you want to make a living filling dead air.

Now, we've all watched those 'before they were famous' shows and thought 'Really?' Shaking our heads and laughing as pre-celebrities down on their luck dressed up as chickens for pasta sauce adverts or were pulled out of a canal as a dead prostitute in *Taggart*, but the truth of the matter is that it pays the bills. It's only the snootiness of hindsight that makes you cringe. I was once a sperm on roller skates for a segment on teenage pregnancy. Sadly, I got cut from the montage as I couldn't roller-skate and kept hanging on to one of the other sperm's tails – if we'd gone into an egg we would have had twins. Of course, that would be looked back on now with an arched eyebrow and a grabbing of pearls but I got paid more for that afternoon than I would have got working four days in the factory packing shampoo.

Channel 4 had obviously seen something in me because they started using me more and more frequently and I was often to be found on *8 Out of 10 Cats* with my brother Jimmy (ha ha – well, everyone else says that to me at least eight times a day so I might as well use it to top up my word count). The exposure from *8 out of 10 Cats* did wonders for my career. I started getting noticed in the street and my stand-up ticket sales got a hearty boost too, all thanks to the wonders of television. Plus it was a lot of fun to film even though Sean Lock scared me.

One night on the show I ended up sharing the panel with the comedy legend that was Joan Rivers. In the dressing room as I plonked myself down in the adjacent make-up chair I was in awe as I was a huge fan of hers. I was expecting an acerbic barrage of one-liners slagging off my cork wedges and cut-off denims but instead I found a woman who was really sweet and supportive, almost motherly. Sadly, that was the only time I got to work with her. I would have loved to have had her on *Chatty Man* and we had been making genuine inroads into getting her to appear on the sofa (well, when I say inroads, we kept pushing the fee up!) but she died before this appearance would come to fruition.

Come to think of it, 2016 is turning out to be one of those awful years; we've already lost David Bowie, Sir Terry Wogan, Ronnie Corbett, Victoria Wood, Prince and Caroline Aherne at the time of me writing this and summer is barely over. I don't know about you, but losing Victoria Wood and Prince on successive days hit me really hard and by the time that gorilla was shot at that zoo for protecting that child I was up to my eyeballs in muscle relaxants screaming 'Stop the world I want to get off!' Just as I'd managed to process Victoria's death, here it was: breaking news that Prince has been found dead at Paisley Park – and I burst into tears again. If you've read my previous autobiography you'll know I was a huge fan of both of theirs, especially Prince.

I think my dad always saw my fixation with Prince as rubbing salt into the wound. Not only would I rather stay in my room and listen to music than be outside kicking a football around but my favourite musician was someone who sang in falsetto, wore stillies and had a penchant for bumless trousers – *Really?* My poor father would come into my bedroom with a morning cuppa and see Prince on the wall, *Lovesexy* era, naked astride a very phallic-looking orchid . . . well, it must have been hard. Oh, Prince will be sadly missed, I genuinely was a HUGE fan. I didn't just listen to 'Purple Rain' on Smooth FM, I'm talking *Dirty Mind*, *Lovesexy*, *Parade*, *Sign O' The Times* – I even listened to the rubbish ones like *Graffiti Bridge*. It's hard to explain to people who haven't seen him live just how magical it was – it was like a religious experience. I had seen him only last year at an intimate gig in Koko with my friend Melissa – also a huge fan. I rang her up on the day he died and we reminisced about the mind-blowing evening we'd experienced.

'I really wish I'd taken a photo of him,' she said dolefully.

'You did,' I replied, 'but you got hit with a stick.'

'Oh yeah,' she said and we both laughed.

Prince notoriously hated being filmed at his gigs and his people would shine lasers into the lenses of cameras or hit you with a stick, as Melissa found out to her dismay. Melissa had whipped out her iPhone and had been tantalizingly close to getting a photo when she was rapped on the knuckles by what can only be described as a cane – the kind you find holding up tomato plants in garden centres. With a yelp she'd dropped her phone.

I will treasure that night now, I'm so glad I saw him and took it all in through sober eyes. Me and Justin had seen him on his '21 Nights' residency at the O2 years back and we'd finished off three bottles of rosé before he even came on. I cannot remember a thing – can't even remember him coming on stage. The only thing I remember about the night is getting home – a white van pulling up outside my house, the door sliding open and me being thrown out on to the pavement by a gang of men. I have no recollection of who drove the van, who threw me out, what had happened in the van. No idea. Mind you, Justin fared even worse. He said he remembered being sick and getting the bus home – he lived in Bristol!! Anyway, at least I got to see Prince again and this time it was civilized and very mature, and you'll be pleased for my kneecaps to hear that I got an Uber home rather than being slung out on to the pavement, so overall a decidedly more memorable night.

Anyway, I digress – back to those early Channel 4 days. It seemed like everyone suddenly wanted a piece of me and I lapped it up. Soon I was appearing on all sorts of things. I was offered the role of team captain on *Would I Lie To You?* but I was so bad at lying that I had to pull out. Secretly, they must have been relieved because I was ruining the whole show. I just couldn't lie. At best I would go red, at worst I would come out in hives. Sometimes I would get myself in such a tizz I would forget what actually was the truth and just say anything to get me out of the lie, and that's why I've never been used as a drugs mule. How can those people on *Jeremy Kyle* just sit there, silent, stony-faced, when they are being given a lie-detector test? Oh, I know – heroin. But anyway, *Would I Lie To You?* was not for me and I was eventually replaced by Lee Mack, who is just perfect for that role – not that I'm calling him a bare-faced liar but you know what I mean.

Of all the television programmes and pilots I did, two that definitely bear mentioning are *Flipside* and *FAQ U –* not because they were particularly good or groundbreaking but because they were presented by my future co-host Justin Lee Collins. *Flipside* was very simple – we would all sit on chairs watching telly whilst commenting on what we were watching whilst being filmed. Basically, it was a precursor to *Gogglebox* – yes, Justin and I were the Sandy and Sandra of the noughties. *FAQ U* was a discussion show filmed in Bristol, which was a bit of a schlep, and once you'd paid your petrol out of the fee it was more or less charity work, but it was exciting to be on the telly. We all sat round on some sofas and discussed certain subjects and topics, some random, some topical, and just hoped what came out of our mouths was funny.

An awful lot has happened and a lot has been said about Justin in the years since we worked together on those early shows. All I can do is talk about my experiences with him. Me and Justin instantly hit it off. We had the same sense of humour and would bounce effortlessly off each other. He made what could have been some real slogs into a lot of fun and we went on to enjoy four years together in a TV partnership. You see, now here's the dilemma. In 2012 I got the shock of my life, as I'm sure you did too, when Justin was convicted of harassing an ex-girlfriend. The details of the case, and the taped recordings of his abuse, were difficult to listen to – at some points they were like the rantings of a madman, both alarming and creepy – and yet totally alien to the person I'd shared a whole chunk of my TV life with. I wanted to go over to him and shake him and say 'What the hell are you playing at, Justin?' It really is hard to imagine that this is the same guy. So I am in a quandary when writing this. What do I do? Do I cut out all the laughter, the fun times and the adventures? Or do I pretend I knew all along that something wasn't quite right and that I had my suspicions? It would be convenient for my story but then life isn't convenient and sometimes good people lose their way. I can't deny that he made me laugh and that he was one of the most generous, kindliest people you could ever meet, I can't, I can only tell it like it was. I could stick the boot in but I don't want to do that. Ironically, he used to do these really funny nostalgia shows, called *Bring Back . . . Star Wars* or *Bring Back . . . the*

A-Team – now I think he needs to bring himself back and find himself again.

The thing is when I knew him he had only love for the ladies and always seemed to be in a state of arousal. I remember him asking me out to meet an old school friend of his and this buxom blonde with huge breasts, considerably younger than him, was there propping up the bar; the next week, I got asked again, 'Will you come with me and meet my old school friend – she's waiting for me in a bar in Soho,' and yet again there was another buxom beauty, curvaceous and blonde. 'School friend? Really? Which school did you go to, St Trinian's?' Oh, I do miss Justin and his erections.

I was trying out material for a new stand-up show the other day – I've no plans to tour as such but it was a bit of a muck-about on stage, tentatively trying out new and very sketchy material that I'd thought up on my travels. It was an out-of-town venue and there was a write-up about it in their local newspaper. Well, I couldn't believe my eyes, there it was, bold as brass, in black and white: 'veteran comedian'. Veteran! The pince-nez nearly fell off my nose. I beg your pardon, *veteran comedian* – some people might be shocked at 'comedian', but as we all know, haters gonna hate. Anyhow, I was outraged – I'm a whippersnapper, I wear hoodies!! But after having a bit of a moment I realized that I've now been doing stand-up comedy for fifteen years and have been on television for eleven years. So although 'veteran' is maybe over-egging the pudding, I have been round the block.

When people ask me how I got into stand-up I politely

point them to my first autobiography, which is still available in all good bookstores. For those who are too tight or too thick to get the hint and who just stand there, I explain it to them instead. The first two or three years you don't get paid plus you have to pay for your own travel and you usually get back in the early hours of the morning. I never had a car in Manchester so would often have to get the night train, where it would just be me and a flasher chug-chug-chugging across the Pennines. Then you get up and go to work to do your proper job. The people I'm explaining this to soon glaze over and walk away. They always seem a bit despondent that there isn't an easier way – that someone doesn't just spot you, pluck you from obscurity and plonk you on the stage, microphone in hand, and TV comes a-calling, but sadly that isn't the case.

Trying to explain all this, it dawned on me that I don't even know how I got here – it does seem a hell of a lot of hard work. How did I, possibly the least ambitious person you could ever find, put up with the early days? It doesn't feel like me. It feels like I'm telling someone else's story. Really? The person who can't be arsed to go to the offie for a bottle of wine if it's raining – who will just drink something out of the cupboard that he nicked from the *Chatty Man* drinks globe – was the same person who would do a four-and-a-half-hour round trip to perform in Newark, get booed off, come home after earning no money and get up to go to the call centre and then go out the next night to perform again? Alan, was that you?

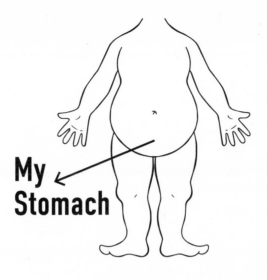

My Stomach

I'm in a wonderful position now where I get offered scripts and formats to read and I do always read them, reread them and scrutinize them. Will it work? Is it 'me'? Is it entertaining? These questions swim endlessly around my head, so it's strange to think that when I got offered the chance to co-host the *The Friday Night Project* in the late autumn of 2005 I just said 'yes'. Just 'yes, why not?' In for a penny, in for a pound. Simple. As. That. I hadn't even watched it when I agreed – can you believe it? Not that I was being deliberately offhand or blasé but I was riding high after a critically acclaimed Edinburgh, I got five stars and everything – there's no need to clap – and I was working every night, performing my stand-up all over the place. I didn't have time for telly, darlings, I had to whip an arts centre in Hull into a comedy frenzy. All I knew was that Justin Lee Collins and I were replacing Rob Rouse, Jimmy Carr and Sharon Horgan as hosts. I'd got very close to hosting my own telly show earlier when I'd got down to the last handful to host *Big Brother's Big Mouth* on Channel 4 and eventually lost out to Russell Brand, who in my opinion rightfully won – his mercurial mind and boundless energy was just perfect for that show. Sometimes, though, in my darker moments, as I'm sitting here on my couch, hungover, watching the rain pitter patter up against the window, sipping a cup-a-soup, I wonder if maybe I had got the job instead of Russell it would be me living as a vegan Buddhist in Hollywood, strutting up Sunset Boulevard in my skinny-fit jeans and trying to bring capitalism to its knees, but hey ho, it wasn't to be.

Initially we had some run-throughs at the Princess offices, the production company behind *The Friday Night Project*, which are bizarrely situated on the top floor of a shopping centre in west London – you'd go in for a meeting and come out with 'bits'. The run-throughs went well, the team were young and enthusiastic, bursting with fantastic fresh ideas as young people seem annoyingly able to do, and I got on with Princess. Most importantly, JLC and I gelled. Once all that was done, we were shown on a laptop a 3D mock-up of what the set would look like. I don't know if you remember those huge, eight-foot tall, dotted, almost Seurat-influenced portraits of me and Justin – they were behind us in the sofa area – well, when I saw them on the laptop screen all of a sudden the shit got real. We would do eight shows with us as the new hosts and then Channel 4 would either scrap the whole damn thing or recommission it.

It was all very exciting and the last thing I had to do that year before Christmas came was to have my clothes fitting with the stylist so they could all be ready, pressed and hanging on a rail in my dressing room ready for when we started filming in early January. The stylist normally dressed Girls Aloud and the Sugababes so God knows what he thought when he saw me waddle through the door – for a start my leg was the width of Nicola Roberts – but he never let on and foolishly took all my measurements down and hotfooted it to Oxford Street to shop till he dropped. Yes, you read right, I said foolishly, because the poor sod had no idea what Christmas does to my body. It's all right him jotting down in his notebook on 23 December 34-inch waist but by 4 January it'll be a whole different ball game – oh yes. Non-stop eating and no exercise, all washed down with gallons of red wine over the Christmas period will leave my buttons squeaking, my zips bursting and my belt chafing. And to add to the (cake) mix, unbeknownst to them I was going to Italy with my then flatmate Hayley for a cheeky break before the show got up and running. God, I love Italy – the women are fit, the men are fit, the wine is fit and what's more the food is fit, so as you can imagine Christmas plus Italy equalled Diabetes Type Duo. I came back literally huge. There is a photo in St Mark's Square that I must dig out of me wearing a pink tracksuit and looking like a pig – an actual pig that in some weird re-enactment of George Orwell's *Animal Farm* has got up on to his hind

17

legs and decided to go sightseeing. When I arrived back for the first show the stylist couldn't believe his eyes. The inevitable had happened and I couldn't fit into any of my clothes. The shirt that pre-Christmas had been loose and flappy now clung to my body like a fitted sheet. The trousers wouldn't even get over my thighs: one yank from the stylist and the zip burst and the legs ripped round my calves – I looked like David Banner at the start of one of his rages. I feel stupid retelling this, I feel ungrateful. What a wonderful opportunity I'd been given and I didn't even recognize it. Most presenters get match fit, get a personal trainer, hit the gym, cut out the carbs so they can look their best – and there's me on record day being smothered in Bertolli butter so I can squeeze into my trousers. Unsurprisingly, I looked like shit, a fat shit in fact.

Apart from looking like a Richmond sausage in a cardie, it didn't help that I had decided to get my hair cut while I was in Italy, all ready for the show. One extra thing to cross off the list for when I get back, I'd said to myself, patting myself on the back for my resourcefulness. Those black-and-white photos of serial killers from the seventies that they place in barber shop windows, I thought they were exclusive to British hairdressers. Well, apparently not – it's Italy too. The trouble was, I knew very little of the Italian language and the barber didn't know any English and instead of saying *scusa* and making a sharp exit I thought I'd grin and bear it. Over here, if you can't explain the hairstyle you desire there are normally a selection of celebrity magazines fanned out on a nearby coffee table that you can flick through to find an appropriate hairdo. There wasn't even that to guide him – all he had on his coffee table was a solitary property magazine with a Tuscan farmhouse and a couple of olive trees on the front. After trying to communicate 'a little trim', only for him to brandish a pair of clippers rather menacingly, I reached for the magazine and tried my best whilst doing the universal sign for short. I pointed to a hedge that if it was attached to the side of my head would be the kind of length that I was after. This charade went on until I eventually capitulated and let him 'do his worst'. Grinning, he carried on – *snip snip snip*. He cut everything short apart from the back of my head where he left a rat's tail. Just when I thought it couldn't get worse he emptied a tub of 'wet-look' gel on top of it. Can I just get this off my chest – why does anyone want 'wet look'? What's the appeal? Why do I want my hair to look like I'm really really sweaty or have just been caught in a downpour? Thank you. After emptying the tub, he then smiled some more and added insult to injury by moulding my hair into a point like a walnut whip. With a flourish, he removed the towel from round my neck. It was time to pay. Totally unhappy and yet totally British, I paid up and gave him a tip, and walked out of the hairdresser's with my head looking like a Tuscan villa – a fat Tuscan villa. So for my first ever *Friday Night Project*, let's just say that I wasn't looking my best. Thankfully, the make-up girl who was also a hairdresser was able to salvage my hair, freeing my rat's tail from the nape of my neck and releasing it into the pedal bin for a new life.

The first *Friday Night Project* I did was with guest host Billie Piper, who at that time was more famous for being the *Doctor Who* assistant rather than the high-class hooker

Belle de Jour in *Secret Diary of a Call Girl*, so we did 'Doctor Who on Ice' at an ice-skating rink on Hampstead Heath with her. Talk about easing yourself gently into a show. For a start, I was really nervous because it was my first piece for the new show; secondly, I'd never watched an episode of *Doctor Who* in my life; thirdly, I'd never ice-skated before; fourthly, it was all going to be filmed; fifthly – do I need a fifth example? – I was bricking it!! You know when you start a new job and it's your first day and the boss says 'You couldn't just nip to Pret and get me a crayfish and avocado salad could you?' And you have to walk twenty minutes out of your way but you smile and say yes even though you REALLY don't want to do it – well, television is like that. For the first few series me and Justin were their bitches, we wouldn't say boo to a goose and we sucked it up big time. Then as the show became more and more successful we felt more inclined to put our foot down.

A good example is the 'Coat of Cash'. For those readers not au fait with the 'Coat of Cash', basically Justin and I at the end of part one would put on a coat made entirely of five-pound notes, then we would run up the stairs through the centre of the audience whilst they would frantically try to grab a fiver off the coat. Now for the first few weeks this would be a surprise for the audience and people would quite tentatively grab a fiver here or there, but as the weeks went on, the coat of cash became legendary – not in the world of TV but on the streets. 'What? A coat you say of free money? In Studio One, ITV Studios? I'm there.' Soon we were attracting tramps and undesirables to the show, coming not to enjoy themselves but just to get free money. You could see people shamelessly turning up for Part One, grabbing a handful of money, shoving it in a carrier bag and then disappearing up the stairs and off home, leaving a smattering of empty seats for the remainder of the show. With the desire for free money increasing each week, so did the desperation, and it got to the point where the audience wasn't so much an audience as – a mob. We were getting punched, kicked and dragged down the stairs. One time I was dragged UP the stairs by the baying mob – all for a fiver!! And don't give me all this 'Ooh, a fiver's a lot of money' – this was before the recession and food banks. The final straw for me was when I was pushed down the stairs and got my head caught in the cable of one of the studio cameras. As the crowd were yanking my legs (I don't know why they were doing that, maybe they thought if they tugged my leg hard enough loose change might cascade down my trouser leg), I was slowly being garroted. The cameraman pushed the camera to one side and bent forward I thought to help me but instead picked a crisp five-pound note off my coat and popped it in his pocket – nothing, it seemed, was off limits when it came to tax-free wonga.

Me and Justin huddled together after the show. 'We cannot carry on with this,' we agreed.

'I nearly died,' I told the producer, showing the bite marks on my back. This is ten years ago and, sitting here writing it all down, sometimes I get little pricks from my conscience raising an eyebrow – 'Really? You nearly got killed?' – so it was very interesting when I recently went to the wedding of one of the researchers of *The Friday*

Night Project and I was on the same table as some of the other team who had worked on the show. It was great to see them all grown up, some of them married, some of them with kids, and it was so nice reminiscing about our time on the show, but the one thing that dominated the chat was the 'Coat of Cash'. Everyone said, 'Oh, Alan – it was so dangerous – why did you even say yes to doing it?' and I felt instant relief – I was right, it was bloody dangerous. One of them who still works in telly said that they were shown a health and safely video about what you can and can't do in television and there was a clip of me in the 'Coat of Cash' being mauled, exemplifying what NOT to do.

Anyway, Justin and me said that we didn't want to do it any more and the producers said that we could get a surprise masochist – er, sorry – guest to do the 'Coat of Cash'. Usually they would be contestants freshly evicted from the *Big Brother* house. I remember one week it was Charley Uchea to do it. She had come across as very feisty and moody in the *Big Brother* house, which had made her a great reality TV contestant but maybe not such a good 'Coat of Cash' contestant. For the first time ever in the history of the 'Coat of Cash' people in the audience were bypassing the chance of free money and were just walloping her; she still had money left on the coat by the time she'd got to the top of the stairs. The poor girl looked like she'd been dragged through a hedge backwards. People were waving their handfuls of fivers in the air triumphantly and then we noticed that someone had pulled part of her weave off and was waving that around – we had to remind the audience that it was 'Coat of Cash' not 'Coat of Weave'.

We had created a monster. Not only did people want money, they wanted more of it, and we started getting claims. One woman caught in the scrum had lost her 'Tiffany' necklace and wanted compensation – oh God, how awful, we thought – but what this claimant in the audience failed to understand was that in a TV studio you are more often than not being filmed by one camera or another and once we looked at the footage we discovered that she hadn't been wearing any necklace in the first place, let alone a Tiffany one. The claimant then decided not to pursue compensation – funny that.

One poor woman was trampled and needed to be pulled from the crowd and given oxygen at the side of the stage. She kept giving off hints that it was a health and safety nightmare and that, you know, it shouldn't really be allowed, and if she was that way inclined she could pursue litigation. When we watched the footage back we saw that, yes, the lady had been horribly crushed in the melee but not before she had thrown herself across three rows of chairs, basically crowd surfing, trying to grab a cheeky fiver. She too, once we showed her the footage, decided to let go of her dreams of a million-pound pay-out.

Slowly people's opinion of the show started to become more positive and we even got some nice things said in the press about us. One of the things they honed in on was mine and Justin's 'bromance'. We did have a chemistry and it shouldn't really have worked but it did. It wasn't only the media that noticed us – we were soon getting asked about our availability for corporate work. 'Do you have an act for corporate evenings?' we would get asked. Some people might say we didn't even have an act on the telly. Well, we didn't – our unique selling point was our ability to bounce off each other in an unforced, unscripted way. I think if we'd actually thought about it and written an 'act' something would have been lost. Needless to say we still took the jobs.

These corporate evenings can take many guises but normally it's where a company will pay for you to host their evening of entertainment and give awards out to their hard-working employees. These corporate events pay really well but sometimes you feel a bit dirty up there because you're only doing it for the money – yes, I can be ruthless too. You're often performing to a paralytic crowd who don't really care about you, or the night, or the awards, and are only there so they can drink the profits dry of their employers. They know that you are only there for the money, that you are mercenary and that you might as well be Princess Leia chained to the engorged corporate bulk that is Jabba the Hutt, dancing your little gold bikini off. They are a complete riot but not in the good sense of the word – they are literally a riot. Have you ever seen those westerns where people are being punched, having chairs smacked over their backs and being thrown along the length of the bar? Well, just picture that but in suits. I remember doing a corporate event for Eddie Stobart lorries and the image of an obese knickerless woman doing 'Oops Upside Your Head' by herself on the dance floor will stay with me for a long time. Every time I pass a sinkhole I shiver.

For this particular corporate do I was co-hosting with my TV husband Justin in a very lavish marquee in the middle of Battersea Park and I was so sure we could rekindle the magic we had on the telly. We'd think of something, wouldn't we? Well, in a word – no. We were screwed. The event was fast approaching and we didn't have two punchlines to rub together. Justin had heard me singing Tina Turner's 'Steamy Windows' through my dressing-room wall and it gave him an idea.

'Al, let's do "It Takes Two" – you do a great Tina Turner and I'll be Rod Stewart. We can dress up, sing the song, funny and upbeat – just perfect.'

'What a great idea! Everyone loves people dressing up. It's going to bring the house down,' I predicted.

So we rushed out to HMV to buy Rod Stewart's *Greatest Hits* CD, thanking the Comedy Gods on high for their divine guidance in picking us a classic, soon to be legendary, comedy performance. Those Comedy Gods, they can be right fuckers, you know. We died a death. Ask any comedian and they'll tell you that dying in front of an audience is the worst, but dying in drag is even worse; dying in front of an audience and in drag and having to carry on for the whole four minutes and seven seconds of the stupid song you've chosen is the epitomy of shit. We finished and no one clapped – no one! It was awful, plus the audience was full of famous people, and when I caught any of their eyes they did that pitiful look, where you half smile and roll your eyes. Me and Justin decided in the break to not take our wigs and outfits off – the twisted logic being that if we kept them on, the audience might think it was the genuine Tina Turner and Rod

Stewart doing a really shit job and our careers would go unscathed.

We really needed a drink after that, so once we peeled off our leopard skin we retired to a bar. Not only was my ego bruised but so was my neck, which was stiff and sore both from the nerves and dodging bread rolls. A woman comes over and sits with me, black thigh-high boots, low-cut top and a miniskirt – okay, okay, yes, yes, prostitute klaxon, prostitute klaxon, but you must remember I was naive back then, and besides, I obviously didn't live in the sleazy world you inhabit where a scantily clad woman milling around a hotel bar the wrong side of midnight is clearly a prostitute. I thought she'd missed the last bus home and someone had stolen all her clothes. 'Fancy some fun?' she said, fingering the complimentary nuts. Well, as soon as I opened my mouth and she heard my dulcet tones, her little face fell – she knew she wasn't going to be giving any hand jobs any time soon. She dismounted the bar stool like a jockey and strutted off looking for more suitable clients, leaving behind some flyers for a strip bar.

Now, I'd never ever been to a strip bar in my life (female strip bar, you understand – I'd been to male strip bars but only because it was raining and I needed a radiator to dry out my anorak). Feeling a flush of *why not?* I said to Justin, 'Let's go to this strip bar,' waving the flyers excitedly in the air like Charlie outside the chocolate factory. Justin thought about this for approximately one second and said 'yes'. We headed there.

Me and Justin, possibly two of the least hedonistic people you'd ever meet, never did this kind of thing. We would usually find a nice bar after the show, sit in a snug and just chat and giggle over one or four bottles of red wine. Thinking about it, we sort of lived out our hedonism on screen – there were very few episodes of *The Friday Night Project* where we weren't naked, wearing a gimp mask, tied up, cross-dressing, you name it – so I guess when we came off stage we were so sexually depleted that our idea of fantasy was wearing clothes that didn't chafe and eating a burger.

As we went into the strip bar off Tottenham Court Road we were instantly pounced upon by a gaggle of girls, like moths to a flame, or like flies around shit depending on your opinion of strip clubs. We must have had twelve young women stuck to us like glue, giggling at every word I uttered and playing with their hair a lot. The waitress came over and asked if we would like a drink. 'Ooh, I'd love a rosé,' I said. I was going through my rosé phase at the time, in fact I'm still going through my rosé phase – okay, let's just call it alcoholism. I wafted the drinks menu away as if it was an annoying wasp. 'Bring me rosé, bring me rosé,' I cried petulantly. When the woman returned – with twelve glasses, I hasten to add – the 'hostesses' dived in, snatching the glasses from under mine and Justin's noses. Another bottle was ordered, then another. I was gasping, I'd only had one sip. Every time I leant over to grab a glass a perfectly manicured hand would grab it away from me with a grating giggle. As we were the only people in there on a Tuesday night, these girls saw us as meal tickets. Having your wine stolen from you gets boring after a while. I'm sure it's quite cheeky and sweet if you are a horny businessman looking for light relief and hoping for sex on a Tuesday night, but all I wanted was a drink.

'Come on, Justin, let's get out of here,' I said. We asked for the bill and it came. Oh yes, it came all right – £3,000!! *You're having a laugh.* They had brought me Cristal Rosé at five hundred quid a bottle, basically working out at £1,500 a sip. Not only was I dry, I was parched and once my lips had been peeled from my gums I demanded to speak to the manager. The women, once so giggly, slowly disappeared into the background. I kicked off and the manager came over, refused to apologize and said that it was MY fault for not being specific. As you can imagine, I was horrified – I can't actually remember what I said but it was something along the lines of *I'm in a strip bar, I've spent three thousand pounds and I haven't even had a hard-on.* I kept it classy. He still would not budge but as a 'goodwill gesture' he would give me a complimentary lap dance in a booth. I thought okay, he's not the most handsome man I've met, but hey, in for a penny. He then clarified that it would be 'with one of the dancers'. My heart, like my semi, sank. Some menacing men had started walking over so I settled for the lap dance – me and Justin in adjacent booths, one of us thoroughly enjoying himself and the other scowling, arms folded, thinking to himself that there was more chance of them raising the *Titanic.*

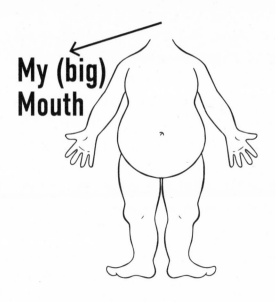

My (big) Mouth

The Friday Night Project was quite a huge show to produce each week. There was a lot going on: there were hidden camera skits, a quiz, musical performances, sketches, days out, you name it, and all these things need to be thought up and produced. This of course takes time, so me and Justin would spend ages with whoever the guest host was that week, just sitting around chatting, waiting. Not surprisingly, you find out more about the guest host from these moments of relaxed off-camera chit-chat then you ever do on a chat show or anything filmed in front of the cameras.

We'd been with Mariah all day at the studios. She was at the height of her fame then and had just found out that she had surpassed Elvis in America for number ones as

'Touch My Body' became her eighteenth chart-topper. She was in a good mood, I really liked her, and although her diva reputation went before her we often found that the demands weren't coming from her at all but from her entourage/hangers-on, depending on how you viewed the huge whispering throng who seemed to hover aimlessly in corridors. I remember one show we did, we had a star on who will remain nameless because I don't want to ridicule her, but she had a huge entourage and before she came on she did a twirl and said, 'How do I look, guys?' The entourage cooed their enthusiasm and clapped encouragingly and then when she disappeared back into her dressing room I saw them pulling faces, sniggering and muttering conspiratorially, 'She is a hot mess,' 'Ugh, did you see that dress – disgusting.' It struck me as so sad – I suspect we've all got frenemies, friends that probably haven't got your best interests at heart, coming along for the ride, but to be surrounded by these people all the time when you're away from home – and more importantly paying for them – has surely got to be bad for you!! You do wonder psychologically what effect that can have on your morale and self-esteem. I never saw any of that with Mariah's entourage, thankfully. I liked Mariah too much and it would have got right on my tits if I'd noticed any backbiting. They just tended to order things for Mariah, doughnuts, pizza, candy bars, and I began to wonder whether she was actually getting them or if she had worms.

'Did you enjoy your doughnuts, Mariah?' I asked mischievously like I was some kind of food detective.

'What doughnuts?' came the reply.

'Did you enjoy your Harrods speciality teabags flown all the way from China?'

'What Harrods speciality teabags flown all the way from China?' Okay, okay, you get the gist. Anyway, we had bigger things to worry about. The props lady had been pulling her hair out at the spoof video we had done because Mariah had asked for an ostrich feather to fan herself down as she was hot. Where were we supposed to find a fucking ostrich feather at that time of night? And on Regent Street. Apparently 'Ostrich Feathers R Us' had just shut down and been replaced by a trendy wine bar. Mariah has a few more curves now but I remember back then her body was smoking. Whilst we were waiting for the cameras to be set up Justin offered her a bit of his Scotch egg and she declined, saying that her personal trainer would 'kill her'. I look back with sadness sometimes and think Mariah would have loved to have had that Scotch egg.

On set she was fun and often sent her diva antics up, which made us all warm to her. When her stylist brought her clothes down for her to peruse she filled me with delight when she broke into the Faye Dunaway 'Wire hangers, Christina, wire hangers' line from *Mommie Dearest*, tongue firmly in cheek. It's one of my favourite films so I couldn't believe it. Saying that though, she did request that she only be filmed from the left side as that was her best side and that *The Friday Night Project* set would have to be rotated 180 degrees to accommodate this. We all laughed – I did my 'what are you like' face but her face remained the same. We didn't rotate it (I don't think we actually could rotate it) and to this day I still don't know if she was joking but she looked beautiful whichever side. And, unlike me, at least she's got a good side.

We all got along so well during the recording that she very sweetly invited us to Cipriani to celebrate with her. This kind of thing never ever happens to me. We were whisked to the restaurant after the show and escorted through the throng of fans who had already found out she was there. No scowly door attendant with a clipboard for me that night, no 'Alan who?' – I was straight in there like a rat up a drainpipe. We had champagne with Mariah and she was really chatty and funny. The champagne soon went to my head and before long awestruck Alan was replaced by overconfident Alan. As we sat round the table, someone tapped their glass with a teaspoon, calling, 'Speech, speech!' Mariah stood up and said what an amazing day it was, and how truly blessed she was to have had eighteen number ones. We all cooed and smiled amiably. 'But there is one person who I owe it all to . . .' she went on. Everyone looked to Benny, her then manager, who stood there with a smile. And that's when I stood up and went, 'Oh, don't, it was nothing.' There was a pause – not just a pause, but an awful pause, a pause filled with white noise. One of the entourage's mouths fell open, more pause, fear, more pause, more fear and then Mariah laughed. 'You're crazy!' she said, and then everyone laughed. 'Of course I'm talking about my manager, Benny.' Everyone cheered and air-kissed and I went to the toilet to rinse my pants under a cold tap.

Being a huge fan of *West Wing*, I got a double whammy when both Rob Lowe and Martin Sheen appeared on *The*

Friday Night Project. I had had a man crush on Rob Lowe since *St Elmo's Fire.* I thought I was over him until the sound guy tried to fit a microphone pack unsuccessfully on to Rob and Rob assisted by lifting up his crisp white box-fresh Ralph Lauren shirt to reveal a perfect set of bronzed abs – I had a funny turn and was whisked back to the eighties with my hands rummaging frantically under the duvet covers, 'Man in Motion' blaring in my ears from my portable television.

Rob was such a nice guy and Justin, whose forte was cult films of the eighties, was constantly surprising Rob with his obscure film trivia, so those two were in their element. We had a fun day out with him courtesy of *The Friday Night Project* – the brief was to show him a quintessentially British Day Out – but instead of going to Ikea or sitting in a traffic jam we decided to helicopter to Cambridge, where we went punting on the river Cam and even had a cream tea in a field. Throughout the day I was trying to block out Justin and the camera crew and pretend that it was just me and Rob on a date. He was so charming and I was smitten. He was a real sweetheart in the studio – though now I'm thinking back, was he a real sweetheart? Or was I just loved up? So intense was my desire for him that I think even if he'd spat scalding tea in my face or stubbed a fag out on my hand I would still have gazed at him, hand resting on chin, and whispered, 'Dreamboat!'

I remember him being really professional and worrying a bit too much about the David Beckham sketch, asking the producer to come down and see if he was doing it the best way, could it be done differently maybe to get more laughs – he just wanted it to be perfect (for me, probably, I gushed inside). Even through my love-filled eyes I thought he was giving too much of a shit – chill out, love, it's only a *Friday Night Project* sketch and I'm going to come on in a minute with massive tits and a wig, there'll be the sound of a swanee whistle and that's your punchline.

It was sweet, though, when these stars came over and put some effort in because it was one of those shows where the more you put in the more you got out of it. For every Rob Lowe or Kim Cattrall enquiring about which wig should be used or how you wanted the punchline delivered, there was a Lily Allen lying on a mattress in the corner of the studio recovering from a hangover. When Christian Slater guest-hosted *The Friday Night Project* he really didn't want to do it. He kept looking at me and Justin with a perplexed expression and you could see him thinking, I wonder if the money's gone into my account yet. The writers had written a *Brokeback Mountain* sketch and Christian didn't want to be in it. He refused to dress up as a cowboy, not because he didn't want to be cast as a homosexual but because the sketch was shit. Justin and I had no qualms about quality control and with or without Christian we soldiered through the sketch, me dressed as a lonesome cowboy and Justin dressed as a saloon wench – like I said, we had NO quality control.

After Rob left to go back to Hollywood, I said to Justin, 'Do you think he's had any work done?'

Justin looked at me disbelievingly. 'He's forty-six and he looks younger than us, of course he's had bloody work done.'

Martin Sheen was in the same freewheeling frame of mind as me and Justin – he wasn't phased by much and just got on with it, even when some of the stuff we got him to do was sailing close to the wind. Like you, I watch these nostalgia shows that seem to be back in vogue on television at the moment – the ones where opinionated, 'right on', youthful punters gasp and splutter outrage at those shows from the seventies, rolling their eyes at what passed as 'entertainment' back then. They are quietly smug, implying 'Haven't we come a long way?' (We haven't – but it's nice to think we have.) I watch these shows and laugh along too, shaking my head, muttering 'unbelievable', and then it dawns on me that we did things like that on *The Friday Night Project* and this wasn't even the seventies, this was ten years ago, and then it sinks in: I just know *The Friday Night Project* is going to end up on one of THOSE TV shows. It's a show ripe for ripping apart come 2050 – though thinking about it, people were ripping it apart in 2006! And when they do stick the knife in we'll be taking Martin Sheen with us. What an intelligent, articulate, wonderful man – I could have listened to him all day, and I did. He talked about politics, the environment, *West Wing* and his rough ride on the film *Apocalypse Now* – he had me and Justin mesmerized with his anecdotes about working with Marlon Brando. He was so progressive and enlightened in his views, which made it all the harder when we came to filming the sketches – they were so beneath him. I remember one sketch that still makes me squirm, where he was dressed in leather shorts, leather hat and a whip and turned up at the White House looking for Obumma (me). Not only was it a very cheap gay gag, I was also blacked up as Obama. Channel 4's stance on blacking-up would change weekly depending on which Channel 4 person had popped along to oversee the show – one week it would be perfectly acceptable and the next it would draw gasps of shock and I would dash off to the toilet with a wet wipe, it was a minefield. Anyway, just for the record, we never meant it to be offensive. But we are in an era of re-evaluation, where goodies become baddies, and social media has unleashed an army of Smug Sallys who are horrified at everything. Who knows, maybe history will be kind – more likely we'll end up being forgotten, but if not, when they're slagging us off in 2056 on *They Did What in the Noughties!!!?*, remember, we weren't being malicious, we were only trying to be funny!

Sometimes I had such a good time with the guest host that I ended up reciprocating and turning up on their show for shits and giggles. This was the case with Carol Vorderman – she was such a laugh and a good sport with a surprisingly naughty sense of humour. Carol has the best gossip ever, I swear half of London's ears are burning when we get together. Justin really fancied her – she is his ideal woman. I swear, when she said that she was up for 'Rear of the Year', Justin nearly shot his load. Carol and I hit it off so well that when she asked if I would consider being the celebrity guest in Dictionary Corner on *Countdown* I just had to say yes. I had been on it before but only in the audience as part of *The Friday Night Project* sketch. Sitting in the audience was like sitting in a sea of cotton wool with all those pensioners so you can imagine the shock I got when the floor manager came on the set and enquired of the audience, 'Has anyone here got AIDS . . .?' I looked around at the grey-haired, anoraked geriatric crowd – AIDS? They didn't look like they'd had sex for half a century, let alone caught a sexually transmitted disease. 'If you have got AIDS,' she then gestured to her ears, 'please turn them off.' Phew, hearing aids!

I was naturally worried about being in Dictionary Corner – I really didn't want to be exposed as a charlatan, so I watched the show religiously, thesaurus in hand, to try and expand my knowledge of the English language. I didn't really need to, as I later found out that they would tell you via an earpiece during the thirty-second countdown clock some longer words that maybe you hadn't got round to thinking of, ultimately saving you the embarrassment of looking like a knob. All the guests have this help and are not as intelligent as they like to make out – apparently Giles Brandreth is a borderline cretin in real life and speaks like Nell in that Jodie Foster film. (That last sentence is a lie – I don't want to end up on *Judge Rinder*.) It was terrifying each time the clock started its iconic countdown – being naturally apprehensive anyway I couldn't help thinking that if the people in my ear couldn't find a long word I'd be hung out to dry. For the first twenty-five seconds I would be in a blind panic staring down at the OR, ON, AS and AT scribbled on my notepad, then on the twenty-sixth second I would hear 'ABSORBATE' out of the blue. Wow, I thought, this must be what it's like to be clever.

I'm still friends with Carol and every Christmas without fail, me, my partner Paul, Carol, Gok, Paul O'Grady, Sally Lindsay and her husband, the drummer Steve

White, meet up for a very boozy Christmas lunch that more often than not spills over into the early evening and then turns into a pub crawl and at least one of us falling over and ending up in the *Daily Mail*'s sidebar of shame. It is the high point of my Christmas. Our diaries are always so chocka that it's a real treat when each of us finds a free day so that we can meet up. Whenever that evergreen question is put to me, 'Who would be your dream dinner-party guests?' I don't even have to think as I already know the answer – I have that dream dinner party every Christmas.

Carol is now a qualified pilot, and a very good one she is too. I know this first-hand because I have actually flown with her in a tiny plane. During my Yap Yap Yap tour I was performing near an air show that she happened to be flying to so I cadged a lift – well, why not, it beats being in a traffic jam, doesn't it? I'm not going to lie, I was dubious about Carol's flying ability – she said she was a pilot but then so had Deirdre Rachid's boyfriend and he only worked in Tie Rack. Luckily, she wasn't a fantasist and was in fact a brilliant pilot. I hadn't really got 'it' before, but being up there, if this makes sense, was both exhilarating and surprisingly serene. Sadly, there was no in-flight meal – not even complimentary nuts – but the gorgeous views of the English countryside took my mind off my belly. Carol is hoping to fly solo around the world and I wish her all the best, as long as she is back for Christmas with me, Paul, Paul O'Grady, Sally, Steve and Gok – our dinner wouldn't be the same without our own little Christmas Carol.

*

Browsing at the Weston Favell Shopping Centre one day with my family in Northampton, doing the sort of unadulterated mooching you can only do in a shopping centre, I got a phone call from the production office: *The Friday Night Project* had been recommissioned for a second series I got told in a jubilant voice. I could hear that everyone in the office was cock-a-hoop, and even I gave a little squeal outside Superdrug. Things were looking up – a smattering of other job offers were clogging up my inbox and I was what you could call 'in demand'. For the first time in my life I had security, albeit a tentative one, and with this new-found security came confidence. And guess what, don't tell Manchester but I was getting to love Holloway – I really was. I'd only just realized that if you went up the hill instead of down the hill you came to Highgate, and a further stroll onwards would bring you to Kenwood, and then there in front of you in all its green finery you had the delights of Hampstead Heath at your disposal.

My *Tooth Fairy* DVD had sold over half a million copies, more than I had ever expected. Bizarrely, it had even been sold to a Thai airline as part of their inflight entertainment package, plus – maybe more bizarrely – it had been nominated for a South Bank Show Award.

The South Bank Show Awards ceremony is a black-tie event that reads like a Who's Who of the arts, so as you can imagine I had no sodding idea who anyone was. All I remember thinking is I bet there'll be a lot of people in berets. I was so nervous about going, but anyway, I took a deep breath and walked into the art-deco fabulousness that is the Savoy Hotel on the Strand. I was dreading being cornered by some avant-garde sculptor who made statues out of dog poo or that bald husband and wife couple who used to be on that programme *Eurotrash*, do you remember? But the dread dissipated when I heard behind me, 'Oi-oi, Saveloy!' It was only Amy Winehouse, who came over and gave me a hug, bless her – well, that made me feel a bit more at home. I lost out to James Corden for *Gavin and Stacy* in the end but I still had a right laugh dancing the night away with such an arty crowd, who were surprisingly good at letting their hair down. I ended up doing shots with a ballerina and doing the lambada with an internationally renowned cellist.

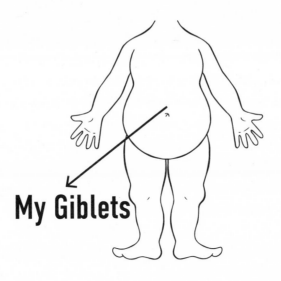

My Giblets

I didn't let not winning a South Bank Show Award get me down. I was still buzzing about the recommission and the accompanying financial security was a revelation. Money was coming in steadily and for once in my life I got a tantalizing taste of having savings and withdrawing money from the cashpoint without looking at the balance first, a whole new experience. And I was one of those people who was outraged when the banks stopped cashpoints issuing fivers! For the first time I could splash out on some nice furniture or objets d'art. I had always bought Ikea stuff – it looked good and, more importantly, it was cheap – but as we all know, the downside of Ikea is that it's so flimsy if you leave a window open by accident, one gust of wind and you've got a Billy Bookcase samba-ing around the living room – you at one end of the room, Billy Bookcase at the other, squaring up like two prize fighters in a boxing ring. So I started going upmarket and getting some bits from Habitat and on really, really special occasions from Heals, but then the ensuing days would be filled with shopper's guilt and I would end up sending it back. 'My chaise longue has Ribena on it – yes, it was like that when I bought it.'

Viewers actually got the opportunity to see my house for themselves on *The Friday Night Project* when we had Girls Aloud co-hosting. I threw a faux Christmas dinner at my house and the girls came round with Justin to celebrate Christmas with me. It was the best Christmas ever – the production company, Princess, decorated the house, erected the Christmas tree, bought all the food and did the washing-up. I know, just perfect. Filming started with all the girls arriving and we had to prepare the dinner. Me and the girls brought out the turkey and they filmed us putting it in the oven, then we did the usual television trick of getting the turkey out and replacing it with a pre-cooked one. Cheryl disapproved. 'This is so deceiving for the viewers,' she protested sullenly. I said, 'Well, if you want to sit here, love, watching a turkey brown for eight hours then be my guest but I'm off down the pub.' I didn't say that obviously, but I thought it. Bless her, I do get her point though – television is deceiving and we were all new to the game. It can be genuinely heartbreaking to find out that there is considerably less 'magic' involved than you think. That turkey being cooked was as authentic as Cheryl's 'judge's house' in Papua New Guinea or wherever it was last *X-Factor* series.

I remember once getting a real insight when we went to film with Barbara Windsor in Albert Square for an *Eastenders* sketch. The obscene graffiti written on the back of the flats that make up the Queen Vic wouldn't look out of place on the tiles of a public toilet in a working men's club. It even made me blush and I am filth. Well, some parts of the *Eastenders* set are like an Escher painting; the landing of the Queen Vic is on the same level as the downstairs, so the upstairs is next door to the downstairs, and the launderette isn't where you think the launderette is. Boy, as Danny Dyer would say, it really does your nut in. I couldn't have been more bamboozled if they'd told me Dr Legg wasn't an actual proper doctor – what?! But it was a real eye-opener for me and it's testament to how good the actors are on these soaps that they can act and put themselves in these situations with such brain-frazzling surroundings and obscene graffiti.

Anyway, back to Christmas dinner with Girls Aloud at my humble abode. It was going swimmingly and we just knew it was going to make a great VT for the show. The day was filled with laughter. To me, and hopefully to them, it didn't feel like work, but towards the end I wasn't feeling too great. I could feel a tightness in my head and I was finding it hard keeping my turkey down. I know me and Justin had had maybe a few too many wines but he didn't seem to be turning green and shivery and none of the girls did either. What could it have been? The Brussel sprouts? That sneaky mince pie I'd popped in my mouth when no one was looking? Or when me and Nadine pulled that cracker and the cheap toy plastic pair of lips that flew out had inadvertently gone down my throat? Then it suddenly came to me. When me and Sarah Harding had prepared the turkey she had told me to massage the flesh to make it more juicy – apparently it draws the flavours out. Inside I was thinking, who d'you think you are – Bernard Matthews? Now I had never heard of this – really, massaging a turkey? I'd heard of choking the chicken but that was something totally different. I gave in and allowed her to do what I thought was basically witch-craft and together we massaged the bird. As we were being filmed we started throwing in some orgasmic *oohs* and *ahhs* for the more discerning pervert. I'm sure if the turkey was alive he'd have been loving it. Once filming had stopped Sarah went to wash her hands and told me, 'Turkeys can carry salmonella so wash your hands good and proper.' I thought, here she goes again with more turkey talk bollocks, so out of spite I licked my fingers suggestively. That would show her – ha! Turkeys carry salmonella? Really? Whatever next! I tell you what next – the shits, vomiting and a headache so bad it felt like I was wearing a concrete sweatband. Oh my God, Sarah, I will never ignore your turkey advice again – you were so right. As soon as the last of the Girls Aloud left the house I went straight to bed with a bucket, less 'Something Kinda Ooooh' more 'Something Kinda Bluergh'.

The next day was a photo shoot that I couldn't get out of and it wasn't one of those nice photo shoots that other celebrities get – you know, subtle lighting, a rail of designer clothes to choose from, champagne on demand – no, I was re-enacting Britney Spears's breakdown for *Star* magazine, where she shaved her hair off and attacked that car with an umbrella. It was a freezing-cold day and the sky was the same colour as my skin – grey. Even if there had been a beautiful sunny cloudless sky I wouldn't have seen it as I was in an underground NCP car park in Blackfriars. The bald cap was pulled tightly over my already throbbing head, but I still don't know what was squeezing hardest, the bald cap or my buttocks. As I re-created Britney's attack, with every swing of the umbrella I was worrying about something getting dislodged. I had very little bum trust, you see, and let's face it – diarrhoea is unpleasant enough in trousers let alone a miniskirt. It was a very long day but as always with these things I survived it and after a good night's sleep recuperating I felt like myself again – or not Britney at least. So if any of you are planning to cook Christmas dinner this year, please – if you've learnt anything from this book – please do it with a member of Girls Aloud.

We often did hidden camera wind-ups on *The Friday Night Project* with varying results – one of my favourites, ironically, was the one that never ever got seen. It involved Pamela Anderson and when you read on you'll realize why the punter involved didn't want this particular wind-up aired. The punter, who was a plumber, had been told by a mate (in on the joke) that a lady needed her pipes lagged or something – could he go round and sort it out? No problem, he said, oblivious to the wind-up. Only when he arrived at the flat did he realize it was Pamela Anderson. Pamela was being outrageously flirty, with lots of biting on lips and playing with her platinum locks as he opened up his tool box. The comedy raison d'être of the sketch was to watch the plumber squirm and blush as this highly sexed screen goddess came on to him as only Pamela Anderson could. However, this didn't go according to plan because not only did the plumber start enjoying it, he whipped his wedding ring off and made a move on her! It was a fantastic TV moment, just not for the punter. His face was a picture when Pamela announced that he'd been wound up for *The Friday Night Project* and pointed jubilantly at the huge array of hidden cameras around her flat – he went ballistic! He did not (understandably) see the funny side whatsoever. When Pamela went to reveal something he was assuming it was her tuppence, not a handful of producers and a camera crew in a wardrobe. He was very angry and refused there and then to sign the release form, obviously once he'd slipped his wedding ring back on. We offered him a bottle of champagne – no; flowers – no; money – no. The money kept going up but still he would not yield, he point-blank refused – and there you have it, the best hidden camera prank never shown on television.

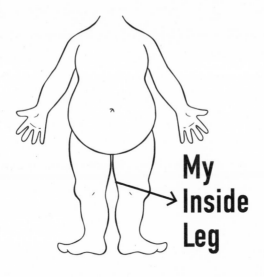

My Inside Leg

I hadn't realized it when I first moved in but there were a lot of celebrities in Crouch End and even though I worked in that business I still got a buzz from seeing a celebrity. Sometimes going in that Budgens in Crouch End was like flicking through *OK* magazine. There was always an All Saints in there and a smattering of *Eastenders* cast; sometimes I'd see Simon Pegg and I was told quite ominously by the local gossip that David Tennant lived 'up the hill', as they pointed 'up the hill' like it was the Bates Motel. I never went 'up the hill' to see David but I did work with him and I can vouch for the fact that he is one of the loveliest men you'll ever meet. I remember I'd done a bit at the BBC Centre for Children In Need and I was on my way to get to the car when I passed David and Catherine Tate in the corridor – 'Alan,' he said, 'we need some more people for this sketch – will you help us out?' Of course, I said, twirling on my already tired feet, and followed them. I went with them backstage and had to go through this hole in the backdrop that would bring you out on to the stage. David and Catherine went through and got a cheer from the excited Children In Need audience, followed by a Cyberman and other people who were vaguely *Doctor Who* related, and then the penny dropped and I saw we were entering through a Tardis! It was a homage to *Doctor Who* – shit! I haven't ever been in *Doctor Who*. I don't even like *Doctor Who*! I realized this as I came through the Tardis door – I got a cheer and then a bemused 'uhh?' from the audience. I shouldn't have been there and I knew it so I shuffled behind a large green thing – I don't know who the character was, I just needed to be out of shot.

We all know fame can be a fickle mistress but it doesn't necessarily stop you from making life-long friends. The curtains in my street were well and truly twitching when I filmed *Gok's Fashion Fix* – the man himself, Gok Wan, and his camera crew descended on Holloway to give my wardrobe a good old seeing-to. I do like Gok, we have the kind of celebrity friendship that you need in this business – a genuine one. I was naive about celebrity – when someone off the telly tells you, 'We must go to dinner, dahling, call me,' I just assume that they want me to go for dinner with them and that I must call them. Oh no. In Celebrity-ville it means something different and sometimes the complete opposite. Lady Gaga said to me in one of the *Chatty Man* ad breaks, 'Let's hang out, I'd love that.' My heart leapt, but you soon realize it's a minefield. Did she mean it? Should I ask for her number? If I did, say, just turn up at her house would she recognize me or, worse, would I get tasered? 'You said turn up!!' I'd scream as my body jolted, my skin being scorched with electricity. And then you don't want to appear rude, do you? The thought of her alone in a restaurant looking down at her phone every two minutes, eating breadsticks – 'Alan Carr said he'd phone – hope nothing's happened to him.'

Anyway, back to Gok. We first hit it off on *The Friday Night Project* where we all dressed up as him: he was Gok Wan, I was Gok Two and Justin was Gok Three – silly . . . a little bit racist, but still silly. After getting on fabulously (just so you know, this always happens when I mention or socialize with Gok, my language gets flowery and I start pontificating like a specky Anna Wintour – after a few G and Ts you can often hear me in bars talking nonsense like 'hems are coming down, darling' and 'ankles are the new black'), I decided to do *Fashion Fix* a) because I liked Gok and b) because if there was anyone's wardrobe that needed urgent attention it was mine. My clothing didn't need rejuvenating, it needed resuscitating; it was less autumn to winter, more wardrobe to bin bag. The show's premise was that Gok came round and sorted out all your fashion woes, which was a big step for me as I absolutely hate clothes! No, I'm not going to admit I'm a naturist so you can stop swallowing sick. Is it naturist or naturalist? I always get those two mixed up – which one is David Bellamy? I always get dressage and frottage mixed up too but that's a different story for a different time.

If I'm honest, my lack of interest in clothes is probably down to the dislike I have of my body. I wear my self-confidence like some people wear a snood – it just hangs there over my head. It seeps out of my pores and clings to my clothes like a depressing sweat. At times it's like the clothes don't even want to be there – they either hang off me limply or cling to parts of me you really don't want them to cling to. At the most inopportune moments my trousers slip over my non-existent arse and climb down the back of my thighs as if they want to do a runner. But I knew I was in safe hands with Gok. If there is ever a person you need to have around you to boost your confidence, it's Gok. That thoughtfulness and kindness and overall positivity that you experience when you watch him on screen is the same feeling you get from him away from the cameras.

It's so funny on a night out with him – he has this effect on women like I have never seen before. I bet even David Gandy doesn't get the reaction Gok gets. He is like catnip to the ladies, Messiah-like. Women will leave whatever they are doing and approach him with girdles, support tights, push-up bras, crying, 'Heal me! Cure us!' We were both working really hard in our televisual careers and one day, in one of those weird synchronicities, we both said to each other over a brew, 'Do you fancy a cheeky weekend break away?' Next thing you know we're in Venice, gliding majestically down the Grand Canal in a gondola swigging rosé wine (not very majestically), and women were STILL asking for advice from the canal-side – 'Gok, do these shoes go!?' We whizzed past so fast we didn't have time to ask 'With what?'

I remember one time, we were having a meal in Soho and a woman came up to the table and whipped up her top, revealing breasts wedged unforgivingly into an undersized bra. 'What do you think of this, Gok?' she asked, putting me right off my melon balls, I must say. He probably sees more breasts per day than most heterosexual men have in their whole entire lives. I did mischievously suspect in the early days that he wasn't gay in the slightest, and that he didn't really care about women's self-confidence at all, it was just one big ruse to get to see women's tits.

Needless to say, on *Fashion Fix* he worked his magic on me, picking things out of my wardrobe that had hung there unworn for years (admittedly stopping to take the piss out of a pony-motifed blouson – well I liked it), and with a scarf here and a safety pin there transforming it into something that was bloody gorgeous and filled me with confidence – what a gift that man has!

In May that year I got a confidence boost of another kind. We got our first BAFTA nomination for *The Friday Night Project*. It was in the Best Entertainment Show category and it was a complete shock, but a wonderful shock nevertheless. As it happened, that year was a watershed for the show: all the hard work was starting to pay off, we were getting noticed and it seemed appreciated. When we were also nominated for a Royal Television Society Award for Best Entertainment Show and won it, it slowly dawned on us that maybe the BAFTA nomination wasn't a fluke after all. Winning one was nice for a whole array of reasons. We had been nominated for a Royal Television Society Award the previous year and turned up only to be beaten by Simon Amstell for *Never Mind the Buzzcocks*. In his speech he sneered, 'Who actually voted for *The Friday Night Project*?' Deciding not to take the moral high ground, I shouted 'Fuck off!' and Justin threw a bread roll at him, which sadly missed Simon's face and hit an elderly woman in a shrug. Yes, Simon was being predictably catty but to be fair to him he was only echoing what some admittedly snooty people thought about the show. I think it was unfair: yes, the show was silly, there was a lot of dressing up and it worshipped at the altar of celebrity, but it was warm and its heart was in the right place and what's wrong with that? What's wrong with silly? What's wrong with being throwaway? I remember Henrietta, the head of Princess, the production company that made *The Friday Night Project*, coming into the studio whilst we were filming, saying that she'd had a call from another production company that was doing a programme called *TV Shows We Love to Hate* and could we send over a clip! Cheeky bastards – I wouldn't even send them a fart in an envelope. Quite rightly, she didn't send them a clip but it was a pretty good example of the sniffy attitude towards us at the time.

We never tried to be – that terrible word that gets bandied about on telly now – 'relevant'. Relevant to whom? Relevant to what? Who cares? If you aren't relevant then you get demoted to a 'guilty pleasure', an awful phrase that means you are so embarrassing as a concept that people can only enjoy you behind closed doors. I say embrace your guilty pleasure, don't let society tell you what you should or should not like. If you like a bit of cheese then go for it. If you love Crocs then go to the highest mountain and shout 'I love Crocs.' If you want to line-dance to Steps' '5,6,7,8' down Oxford Street, who gives a shit – do it!

So as you can imagine, getting a BAFTA nod came just at the right time. Not only was it a pat on the back, it was a two-fingered 'up yours' to all the naysayers. The show had actually won something back in 2006, a Rose d'Or. No, I hadn't heard of it either, but as it turns out it's a very prestigious award and not a high-end brand of ice cream, and we got flown to Switzerland no less to collect the prize. Once there I saw that past winners of Rose d'Ors had included *Ant and Dec's Saturday Night Takeaway*, *Little Britain* and *Strictly Come Dancing*, and I could have kicked myself for being so ignorant. Put up in a beautifully grand hotel overlooking the lake, sipping a celebratory glass of champagne with the likes of Stephen Fry and Ricky Gervais, I felt such a fraud– I mean this didn't happen to people like me.

The BAFTAs were on a Sunday and I was really looking forward to it. I'd hired a tux and everything. We were up against *QI*, *Harry Hill's TV Burp* and the *X-Factor* so an acceptance speech had not even crossed my mind, let alone been written down and slipped into the inside pocket of my tux for good luck. A friend of mine was having a birthday party on Saturday but thankfully it was just going to be 'quiet drinks'. Quiet Drinks. Have there ever been two words in the English language more misleading, more dangerously unassuming and more deadly than the two words 'Quiet' and 'Drinks'? The words are like a spell – every time I've turned up for Quiet Drinks I've ended up twatted, or I've lost a shoe, or got into a fight. If people instead dubbed their night of birthday celebration a one-way ticket to Sodom and Gomorrah I'd probably be in bed by half ten with a Horlicks and a Catherine Cookson. Needless to say the drinks were not quiet, I drank loads, I ended up at Walthamstow dogs for some reason and woke up at one o'clock the next day – at least in my own house. Well, I think it was my house, because whilst I'd been asleep someone had filmed a rap video in my lounge. Minging, I was. I climbed out of bed, tried to find my phone, couldn't find my phone. Damn, the curse of Quiet Drinks had struck again. Downhearted, but not too downhearted – I was a BAFTA nominee after all, albeit a hungover one – I went down my local. I'd checked the TV listings and the BAFTAs weren't on till 7.00 p.m. that night – six hours away, fine. I'd have a beer, have a nice Sunday roast, the puffiness would go down and hopefully the cat litter tray that was basically my mouth would start feeling a bit more fragrant.

Now, reader, you thought the BAFTAs were live, didn't you? When I used to watch them on the telly they always seemed live. So I'm sitting in the pub – I'd moved on to my second pint, was feeling much better thanks for asking, and was now perusing the dessert menu for a strudel. 'Alan! Alan!' I heard. Oh shit, I thought, I've started hallucinating. Shut up, voices in my head. Shut up! 'Alan!' It was the barman holding up the telephone receiver. 'It's your agent.' I went over and took the phone and, yes, it was my manager, Addison Cresswell.

Addison Cresswell was a legend in the comedy world. He passed away, sadly, in 2013 and I owe so much to him. He represented some of the biggest names in comedy, including Jonathan Ross, Lee Evans and Michael McIntyre. Basically, if you've laughed at them Addison has probably represented them.

'Hi – ooh, sorry, I sound a bit croaky . . .' I said.

'Where the fuck are you?!'

'What?'

'Where the fuck are you? The BAFTAS are about to start – where are you?'

'It's okay, they're not on till seven, I've got loads of time. It says in the TV listings—'

'Get your arse here now!'

Well, apparently the BAFTAs are pre-recorded. And when they say 'don't believe everything you read in the newspapers' I'd assumed it was the articles they meant, not what was in the TV listings.

I dashed home frantic, absolutely frantic. Most actors and actresses treat themselves to a mani, a pedi and a nice facial before their Jimmy Choos even skim the red carpet – my first big award ceremony and I was rifling through a succession of bags looking for the invite, running down the road, cuffs flapping pathetically in the wind whilst I tried to insert my cuff links. Eventually I flagged down a taxi and got to the Palladium. The red carpet had been rolled up and a solitary pap putting his camera away tapped his watch and said, 'You're late!'

I felt awful. The ceremony had started and the host Graham Norton had made a joke about 'If you do win, give it lots of eyes and teeth. Well, maybe not you, Alan Carr,' or something like that – I wasn't there, remember, Justin told me. Apparently the camera had panned to my empty seat with Justin shrugging next to it. I felt so bad, it was so disrespectful, but it was the TV listings that did it, honestly it was.

We didn't win, as predicted, which maybe was a blessing as I hardly felt like a winner. Plus I was sweating and hadn't showered and still had that stale smell from the night before. I knew I'd been at Walthamstow dogs but I didn't know I'd slept with them too. The rest of the night went smoothly, thank God, and although technically losers we had a great time meeting some of our television heroes and experiencing something in the flesh that I had only ever watched cross-legged on the floor in front of the telly.

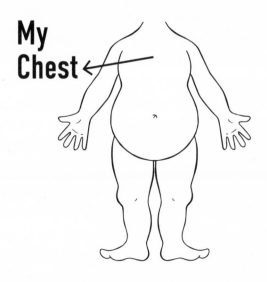

My Chest

We'd had the *Big Brother* lot on *The Friday Night Project* so the producers thought it would be a good idea for a sketch if me and Justin actually spent half a day in the *Big Brother* house. Firstly, and not surprisingly, it is very claustrophobic; and secondly, it is unbelievably dirty – of course, when you think about it, it's going to be. Fifteen people living in such a confined space for up to a month, well, there are going to be stains, hairs, smudges all over the place. I swear I saw a skid mark in the diary room. After being in there for even a short period a lot of the behaviour you witness on screen suddenly makes sense.

Interestingly, you do actually forget you're being watched and after an initial urge to fool around your self-awareness evaporates surprisingly quickly. When Justin and I watched the footage back, there I was picking my nose, adjusting myself and scratching my tit. At one stage, my face pressed up to the mirror, I was pulling my lip up to see if I'd got any food stuck between my teeth – it was only when I heard the whirr of the camera behind the mirror that I remembered I wasn't in the comfort of a brightly coloured, albeit filthy home but a CCTV-riddled Orwellian hell. That always freaks you out, knowing there is someone on the other side of the mirror just watching you – plus there was that quite unsavoury urban myth knocking around the corridors of Channel 4 that a cameraman had been axed as he was caught wanking behind the glass as a housemate was undressing. All of a sudden I felt relieved to hear just a cameraman's whirr behind the glass rather than the frantic flapping of wafer-thin ham and a groan of release.

I get asked to go on *Celebrity Big Brother* most years and I always decline, basically because I remember that surreal half-day in that house. It is dangerous. Sat on the sofa, I started a really bitchy anecdote about someone and it was only when I saw Justin's eyes widening that I realized, shit, Alan – you're being watched – again! The anecdote stuck in my throat and I clamped it shut like a Venus flytrap with a bluebottle. And just imagine unlimited alcohol being thrown into the mix – my God, I would either leave the *Big Brother* house as the best housemate ever or a complete social pariah. I think it's a lot safer to stay watching *Celebrity Big Brother* from my own sofa.

Watching the first couple of *Big Brother* series was an absolute joy, seeing these characters blossom organically as they found themselves and interacted with their housemates – who could forget lovely Anna the ex-nun or the charismatic Brian Dowling? But by the time series six came along, the genie was out of the bottle, the experiment had imploded and the people who auditioned were a motley crew of Mensa-dodging fame-hungry halfwits. Journalists always ask eagerly, 'Who was the worst guest on *The Friday Night Project?*' and you see them with their pens poised to write down Mariah or Lily Allen, both of whom were in fact great. Without a doubt, it was the *Big Brother* lot. So-and-so wouldn't speak to so-and-so; so-and-so had to be out of the room because they had slept with so-and-so's boyfriend. Oh, by the way, I'm not calling them 'so-and-so' because I'm disguising their identities and don't want to run the risk of defaming them but because I've forgotten their names and I'm not prepared to use my precious Wi-Fi data searching for them.

Of course, there was one *Big Brother* contestant we had on who was a delight and who had somehow managed to outgrow the *Big Brother* franchise/curse (delete as applicable), and that was Jade Goody. We had her on during her first 'National Treasure' phase just before we hated her again, but then fell in love with her again when she was sadly diagnosed with cervical cancer. I would love to say that the ditzy, 'fick with an f' persona was just that – a persona – and that when we met her she was halfway through James Joyce's *Ulysses*, but alas no. Then again, we didn't love her for her mind, we loved her because she was so down to earth, a laugh, a girl done good, and in that respect she didn't disappoint.

I actually met her at her beauty salon, Ugly's, in

Hertfordshire, where she was to give me a chest wax and a fake tan – all on camera, of course. The salon shut down soon after and press speculation was that the prices were too high. Well, I think otherwise and I have two good ideas why it closed down – my yellow and purple tits. With her trademark cackle, Jade ripped the wax strips off my chest with no warning and with no waxing cream. I had foolishly assumed you yanked the strips in the same direction as the follicle. Oh no, not at Ugly's it seemed – the strips were laid haphazardly on my chest and yanked off with the same ferocity that a Chippendale stripper removes those odd Velcro trousers they seem to wear. I cried, I actually cried. She thought it was hysterical. I looked down at my red chest – well, I say red, but I could see it slowly turning a delicious plum colour, like a mood stone. Surveying the carnage, I couldn't help saying a silent prayer for any lady going into that salon to have her bikini line done. Ouch! Their fannies must have looked like they'd been dipped in Ribena Toothkind.

I then went on to have a spray tan. 'Stand up straight, please,' she requested – I was still bent double from the waxing. As I was in Hertfordshire I was planning to pop up to Northampton after the filming to see my family and as I was staying over I specifically asked Jade, 'Is this fake tan going to run?'

'Oh no, don't be silly,' she laughed as I stood there in my paper pants, letting her do her worst. Hmm, let's just say I wasn't convinced. If my mum and dad had told me that they'd had a succession of religious pilgrims marching to Northampton and kneeling at their front door chanting, begging to be let in, I would not have been surprised as the next morning when I pulled back the sheets in my parents' spare room, lo and behold, there was a carbon copy of the shroud of Turin – well, the shroud of Essex. It was a smudged version of me – a bright satsuma outline – of my good self, prostrate. My actual body was patchy, part brown and part orange apart from the now mauve slash yellow expanse that used to be my hairy chest. I'm all for small businesses and for anyone trying to make a go of something and following their dream but I can say for certain that Jade was probably better sticking to being the nation's sweetheart than becoming a beauty therapist.

I was back at the *Big Brother* house the following year, this time thankfully outside, waiting for Michael Barrymore, who was to be the guest host on *The Friday Night Project* that week. Now, what people want to do with their lives is their own business and who am I to judge, but standing in the pissing-down rain in a Tesco car park in Borehamwood holding aloft an A4 piece of paper with 'MAGGOT OUT' written in crayon is not how I choose to spend my Friday nights. Me and Justin were plonked into the middle of this baying mob. We got quite into it and before you knew it we were booing if a contestant showed a side to them that was displeasing and cheering if they showed a side of their character we liked. I could fit quite easily into a mob, I thought as I jeered at a celebrity I'd never even heard of before as they flashed on the screen. I had grown up with Michael Barrymore – watching those popular family favourites such as *Strike It Lucky* and *My Kind of People* – and to finally meet him, let alone work with him, was going to be such a treat.

However, his time in the *Big Brother* house had revealed a man very different to the ebullient, over-the-top all-round entertainer that had been a staple of my 1980s TV diet. While presenting *The Friday Night Project* his mood swung pendulously from being unbelievably upbeat and really funny to being totally morose. At one point he read 'the dubious Michael Barrymore' from the autocue – 'Who wrote that?!' he demanded, pointing accusingly at the autocue. But there was nothing *on* the autocue – oh great, I thought, we've had people drunk and on drugs hosting the show but never anyone hallucinating. It was sad to see, and I feel guilty writing these things down because obviously he needed help and half of it might have been side effects from the prescription drugs (I assumed) he was taking. In fact, I probably would have omitted it from this book if he hadn't . . . well, I'm struggling to think of the word because it was an assault but it was so bizarre I don't think it could be classed as an assault. I'll try to explain.

The sketch was topical at the time and concerned the FIFA World Cup that was being held in Germany. Justin was dressed up as Sven-Göran Eriksson and me as Nancy Dell'Olio, and we had both supposedly arrived at a hotel, suitcases in hand. Michael Barrymore wanted to play his Hitler/Basil Fawlty character and pop up from behind the hotel reception. He said he wanted to put an unscripted joke in. Great, we thought – we loved it when the guest host used their initiative. He said he would just ad-lib it.

Me and Justin (Sven and Nancy) enter stage left and ring the bell.

Michael pops up, dressed as Hitler, goose-stepping and Heil Hitler-ing. He turns to me and says, 'Have you heard ze joke about ze Gestapo?'

'No,' I said.

'LIAR!' he screamed and slapped me hard round the face. The impact was so forceful that I completely forgot my line. Justin was standing silent next to me, open-mouthed. Awkwardness hung in the air. Cameramen were starting to look at one another and my face was starting to smart badly.

The producer came out to check if I was all right – I said I was fine and he said, 'It's a funny joke, would you mind doing it again?' I glared at him. Okay, anything for the show.

Michael said, 'Look, I'll do it again but I'll only mime slapping you so don't bother tensing your face.'

'Good idea,' I said, thankful – my face was really aching now.

We started the sketch again. Me and Justin approached the hotel's check-in desk and he popped up.

'Have you heard ze joke about ze Gestapo?'

'No,' I said. He hit me so hard across the face that I went flying. Justin stepped in – 'Whoa whoa whoa. C'mon now, Michael – that's not nice.'

The producer came out again and the look on his face was literally 'What the fuck?' The producer said that we needed to do it again. My face was red and by then I'd started to get a headache.

'No,' I said, 'I'm not going to do it again.'

'Please,' said the producer.

'Okay,' said Michael, 'I promise I won't hit you again, I promise.'

I had heard it all before and my numb face knew otherwise.

We all stood around – I really was not in the mood for comedy sketches, especially ones that involved him, but I gave in. 'Let's do it again.'

So, third time lucky – me and Justin arrived at the hotel desk. Again he popped up – 'Have you heard ze joke about ze Gestapo?'

'No.'

'LIAR!' He went to whack me across the face, but anticipating the smack, I ducked. He then shoved me on the floor. 'Have you heard ze joke about ze Gestapo? Have you? Have you?' Well, he started kicking me. 'Have you? Have you?' It was so weird, cowering on the floor, looking up through my now wonky Nancy Dell'Olio wig (it had crawled over my face after the second slap), seeing a demented Michael Barrymore dressed as Hitler kicking me – it's a memory that will always stay with me, it has been burnt on to my retinas. He was a man possessed. It seemed to go on for ever. Throughout the ordeal I kept thinking that he had never done this on *Strike It Lucky*.

Eventually he was pulled off me and the producer said we should all take a break. I retired to one side of the studio, well away from him. He went to the other side, out of breath after his 'performance'. I didn't trust him any more. We then got another mood, this time insular, and he became so withdrawn that we couldn't get any performance out of him – the day was truly turning out to be a roller-coaster ride on every level. We decided to adapt the show to make it more Barrymore-friendly. Due to the mysterious death five years earlier of Stuart

Lubbock in Michael Barrymore's swimming pool, the popular item 'Ask Me Anything' where the audience had free rein to literally ask the guest host anything, had to be renamed 'Ask Me "Almost" Anything' – we couldn't take any chances and the audience were asked to censor the questions a little bit for sensitive reasons. I dreaded to think what he would do if an audience member upset him; he tried to kill me and all I did was dress up as Nancy Dell'Olio.

To be fair, he was great on the show – he loved being the guest host and it must have been nice for him to be the centre of attention again, lapping up the applause and bathing in the genuine warmth people had for him. He had got his sparkle back and it was lovely to see. I, however, was on a knife edge – I couldn't really relax. We got to part four and I thought, thank God, we are out of the woods – where's the bar? Part four always had a game show vibe going on where a lucky member of the audience could win a big cash prize. As homage to Barrymore we had recreated the *Strike It Lucky* set – but instead of a 'Hot Spot' ('What's a hot spot not? A good spot.' Apologies to anyone under thirty who will have no idea what I'm wittering on about!), one of the Cheeky Girls would pop her head through. (We ended up working with Monica and Gabriela Cheeky loads – whenever *The Friday Night Project* needed a celebrity and fast, we would give the Cheeky Girls a call and they would do it for fifty quid and a hot meal. Sorted.) So, to recap, when the contestant got a question wrong, the Cheeky Girl would pop her head through with a cry of 'Cheeky, cheeky!' So far, so good. Anyhow, the contestant was upbeat and we were close to getting them a large sum of money to go home with – the crowd was buzzing and no one had been attacked or assaulted. Everything was going swimmingly – until Michael had one of his funny turns. The contestant got the question wrong and one of the Cheeky Girls stuck her head through the hole in the wall and cried, on cue, 'Cheeky, cheeky' – well, Michael just glazed over, walked up to her, put his hands round her head and tried to pull her through the hole! Proper yanking!! She was croaking 'Help!' and he yanked harder. I was screaming, 'Help, help – he's trying to murder a Cheeky Girl!' The Cheeky Girls are tiny, but even they couldn't fit through a hole the size of a cat flap. Thankfully, the floor manager came over and subtly took Michael away by the elbow; I think poor Monica got an extra fiver for her trouble.

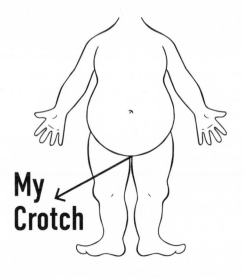

My Crotch

Love. Oh, love. Whilst living in Manchester, I had actually given up on finding love and bizarrely I'd been looking forward to my single future. I had it all planned. When *The Friday Night Project* came to an end I would up sticks and travel the world doing my main job, stand-up comedy, living the single life, doing what I wanted to do, being one of those confident people you see sitting alone in the window of restaurants, on their laptop or reading a travel guide, shamelessly content in their solitude. That would be me. Maybe I'd grow some dreads, who knows, but I would travel the world defiantly alone.

Love had evaded me. I'd been mistakenly told that fame is an aphrodisiac and that people, albeit shallow ones, would basically throw themselves at you and sleep with you just to say that they had slept with someone off the telly – I couldn't wait. Well, I had to wait, and wait and wait. I'd had my moments – look, I'd been living in Manchester, a twenty-minute stagger from Canal Street, and even the Elephant Man could get a quick shag on Canal Street – but there comes a time when you want something more. I was bored of doing the walk of shame, all those mornings trying to find my way out of the students' hall of residence, pushing open endless fire doors, a curling 'shag tag' dangling off my tit. I'd even started having an on-off relationship (mainly 'off') with a bloke in the army, a rear gunner no less (I know, I know). I tried to make it work but you know when you're forcing something so badly it just doesn't click and then you start changing yourself, which never bodes well. Looking back, I could kick myself for compromising myself so badly. I was such a doormat I might as well have had WELCOME branded on my forehead.

I wondered whether London would bring me love and, as it happened, it did. I had been at Antony Cotton's birthday party on Canal Street and had made friends with the actor Scott Neal and his partner Philip. We'd hit it off and soon became and still are firm friends. Well, now it was Scott's birthday and he was throwing a party at a private members' bar, Century. I nearly didn't go, I was in such a foul mood. Scott and Phil always look the business, so well-groomed, whereas me, I'm happy mooching around in a slanket and a headscarf, and if I can finish off this little ensemble with a carrier bag then BOOM! I am ready to rock and roll. But in preparation for the party I treated myself – got some suitably overpriced slacks, loafers and a dark blue Prada V-neck and shirt – and when I looked in the mirror I couldn't help thinking that I looked presentable, yeah, just presentable. I saw I had a couple of minutes for a cuppa so that's what I did, I made myself a refreshing brew, but then – disaster – I spilt it right down my crotch. I screamed and ripped my trousers off and my underpants. My genitals were on fire! I ran to the bathroom and basically limbo-ed under the cold tap. Due to my scalding I was now late, so in a dash I put on some new trousers, replaced my soggy loafers and walked out of the door, scowling at the kettle. It was only when I was coming out of the Tube and caught my reflection in one of those giant mirrors they have on the stairs – you know, the ones that look like a Cyclops' contact lens – I saw that my complete outfit was the exact same as a Tesco uniform. It was the spitting image – the blue V-neck, the shirt, even the slate trousers I'd thrown on, right down to my sensible black pumps. All I needed was an 'Alan Carr – Here to Help' badge and I could have slipped into a Tesco Metro and masqueraded as an employee without anyone blinking an eye. Why Tesco? At least if it had been Sainsbury's I would have had a bit of orange, which would have been ideal – warmer hues were in that summer of 2009.

Anyway, I digress. I was naturally disheartened and felt like going home, but I resisted turning round and carried on to the party instead. And I'm glad I did, it was a great party only slightly spoilt by someone asking me if I could give them a hand packing, but nevertheless a good time was had by all.

The party got even better when I saw this tall, dark and handsome man walk in. For me it was love at first sight, and I've never had that feeling before. There was a twinge in my pants, but then again it might have been the PG Tips still smarting. Scott introduced him to me. His name was Paul and he was dressed in the strangest of attire but then I suppose I couldn't really start dishing out fashion advice when I looked like I worked in a supermarket. I'm used to Paul's fashion sense now but at the beginning it was a huge eye-opener. How can I put this nicely? He would give Su Pollard a run for her money but strangely it works – I think because of his height and good looks he can sort of carry it off, whereas if I start wearing garish clothes, glitter, tassels and heavy prints I look like a three-piece suite.

Anyway, I left the party with a spring in my step and I couldn't stop thinking about him – I actually had butterflies. Normally 'self-loathing', my one and true constant friend, would rear its ugly head and mutter in my ear 'as if anyone is going to be interested in you' or start sucking its teeth with an 'oh pleeeeeaaassee'. But it didn't. It felt different and I know now, seven years down the line, that it *was* different.

I got Scott and Philip to organize a dinner and then to casually invite Paul along too. They went for the Wolseley, next door to the Ritz in Mayfair. Now this restaurant is old school and very, very classy; elderly ladies with trilbies on their heads and fox furs round their necks go there – you get the gist. It's also great for celeb spotting, but just the spotting; try to shove a selfie stick up Sir Michael Caine's trouser leg and you'll be out. We had a delicious meal, conversation was sparkling and the wine just right – so how the hell did we end up in Vauxhall's Fire nightclub at three in the morning?

In case you're not familiar with Fire, let me fill you in. If you were to drive through Vauxhall on a Monday morning you could be forgiven for thinking they were filming a remake of *The Plague of the Zombies* – they're not, that's just chucking-out time at Fire. I had to drive in early one Monday to do a sketch for my New Year's *Specstacular* at London Studios and I kid you not, as I drove through Vauxhall I put the security lock on my car because there were so many people stumbling and mumbling and falling over. Some were in a K hole, others were in a sinkhole. I genuinely thought it was a Zombie Apocalypse.

Fire is Sodom and Gomorrah with a disco ball, and it's a lot of fun. It's a huge mega club, with nooks and crannies everywhere. It's very cruisey, and I don't mean people are playing quoits, if you see what I mean. In most nightclubs if you lose your friends you cast your eye over the dance floor; in Fire you're peeping through glory holes – 'Morris, are you in there? Coo-ee, Morris.' (Names have been changed to protect the innocent.)

I can't tell you what happened in the club the night I went with Paul, not because it's too debauched or racy and I don't want to spoil my family entertainer persona, it's just that I can't remember. I couldn't have made too much of a tit of myself because we are still together, but what a place to end up after such a sophisticated start to an evening. I had been there before – 'Oh, here we go,' you cry, 'one minute you're gasping about how cruisey it

71

is and now you admit you've got a loyalty card! Ha!' No, I'd been there once before with my nymphomaniac friend from up north who comes down every six months to see me – hang on, who am I trying to kid, he comes down to shag fresh meat, and maybe see me for a cuppa and then disappear up north again. He'd rung me up and said he wanted to go on a night out but as I don't go out I was flummoxed – where did gays go out these days? I approached some of the homosexuals in the office, picking their brains on where to go. I helpfully suggested Heaven but they looked at me as if I had suggested Nigel Farage's house.

'Oh no, honey, all the gays go to Vauxhall.' They actually pronounced it VOHO – great, I'm so out of touch I don't even know how to say words any more. So I told my mate the plan and we went to Vauxhall, and after a right old laugh and few bevvies in the Vauxhall Tavern we went to Fire. The laughter soon stopped when I was barred from entering.

'It's Scally Night,' I got told by the doorman. 'Scallylads' – I'd heard of 'scally' on the streets of Stretford when I lived up there and its definition was definitely a grey area; you would be given very mixed messages about what it actually meant – one minute you'd be told it meant cheeky chappy, like 'scallywag', and the next it was a derogatory name for a homosexual. I couldn't keep up. Anyway, that night in Vauxhall it meant a homosexual scallywag.

'Why aren't I allowed in?' I protested. I had some lovely brogues on and a nice Diesel shirt, and this blazer weren't cheap either.

'It's council house chic tonight – only scallies allowed,' said the doorman as a skinhead with a facial tattoo in a white shell suit got whisked past me like Angelina Jolie at the UN. My friend looked crestfallen but thankfully someone in the cloakroom recognized me and we were begrudgingly allowed to enter. I tried to fit in and harness my inner scally, so like Madonna I reinvented myself. I ditched the blazer in the cloakroom, dirtied up my brogues and accessorized with an Aldi bag – voila! One scally to order. Once in I noticed to my dismay that the bar prices certainly weren't council house prices – fifteen quid for a gin and tonic! How much?! I baulked so much my rollie nearly fell out of my mouth. I felt like shouting at the barman, 'Where's your council house – Monte Carlo?!!' but I didn't. I bit my tongue and we grabbed our drinks and headed to the dance floor, which was so full of people in Kappa shell suits that you could hardly hear the music over the rustle. What can I say, it's council house chic, darlings!

Anyway, enough of the ins and outs of Vauxhall gay hot spots and back to the ins and outs of my heart. Aww bless, the initial date had been a success and I was hoping and praying that 'date' would become 'dates'. Thankfully, I didn't have to wait too long. The Wolseley was a treat and an excuse to get dressed up and be a bit frivolous, but for the second date it was back to normal – a Thai meal on the Harrow Road and a bottle of cheap booze, then a stagger home, you know, what life would REALLY be like if we did get together. What I found a bit of a struggle was the fact that he wanted to stay in the morning – actually wanted to stay. I had always rolled my eyes at those rom-coms where the morning after the night before the lovesick heroine has rolled over to find the other side of the bed empty and the shag from the night before making eggs in the kitchen, kettle brewing – 'Did you sleep well, honey?' Well, that romantic bullshit was Hollywood, while I was in the very real Holloway and that kind of thing did not happen to me. More often than not I'd be woken up by my date from the night before yelling at a taxi company, 'Can't you get here any quicker?!' or, worse, they'd be in the bathroom jet-washing their crotch. Paul, on the other hand, wanted to stay – he even suggested going to a pub for a Sunday lunch. I tried not to look shocked. Yeah, that would be nice. Look at me having a normal life, doing what normal people do.

However, the normality of dating didn't last long, oh no. On our third date we went to Vegas, baby. Look, I know it sounds decadent and fabulous (and yes it was!), but let me explain. Me and Justin Lee Collins always used to go on holiday together – always. As soon as a series of *The Friday Night Project* was finished, the very next morning, often still drinking from the previous night's wrap party (I know, naughty boys), we would go off on holiday. We tentatively started with a cheeky weekend break in Blackpool, thinking that just because we got along on-screen didn't mean that chemistry would overlap into our free time, and my free time is precious. So we decided to test out our showbiz friendship within the British Isles, thank you very much. As it happens we had nothing to worry about, we got on just as well riding the Big One together as sitting on the sofa. With complete relief we left our TV cares behind us and took in all the sights.

My personal Blackpool highlight was seeing a magic show at the Winter Gardens where an escapologist was slowly being lowered towards a water tank. We watched with bated breath as he was lowered down, hands and feet tied together with rope. At first I thought the struggling was part of the act, but when I saw a stain like the outline of Turkey appear on his crotch and the trickle of urine down his leg I realized that actually it was going wrong. My suspicions were confirmed when the lights came up and a smattering of stagehands came to his assistance. With an embarrassed look on his face and a swish of his cape he shuffled off – only in Blackpool could you see an escapologist piss themselves live on stage.

After our holiday trial period, our breaks away became more far-flung and soon Justin and I were flying together to New York and Miami and, for a complete change, a tiny island off Italy called Ischia. Ischia is authentically Italian – tavernas, churches, old humpbacked women dressed in black and repeat. That's basically the beauty of Ischia, so as you might expect its outlook borders on the conservative. I tried to tone down my demeanour, tamed my mincing leg and brought my voice down an octave or two – well, until I saw a lizard, but hey, I tried. Justin, however, is the most tactile person you could ever meet, and his touching is not gender specific either; he will pinch my arse, hold my hand, get me in a headlock – I was actually worried at one point that he was going to be gay-bashed.

Anyhow, eager to organize our next holiday together, we had settled on Vegas. The tickets had been booked, the dollars were waiting at the bureau de change, and the inflight magazine was ready for us to paw as the plane took off. But, alas, it wasn't to be Viva Las Vegas for poor old Justin, who as well as doing *The Friday Night Project* was also taking part in Channel 4's TV show *The Games*.

The Games was a sports reality game show where down-on-their-luck celebrities participated in a series of sporting tasks like weightlifting, diving and shit – just picture the Priory having a sports day. Sorry if I'm vague but I don't watch any sport-themed shows on telly; in fact to sit through one I'd have to be the one taking the performance-enhancing drugs. Anyway, that's what Justin was doing. God knows how he got roped into it because he's hardly the sportiest person himself, but anyway, that's between him and his agent. Justin ended up puncturing his ear drum after diving off a diving board into the pool, which still perplexes me because he was hosting the bloody show not participating in it! At first, it just seemed like an unfortunate accident but we soon realized that he wouldn't be able to fly. A punctured ear drum is painful enough but a sudden change of cabin pressure on an aircraft could make it unbearable. Poor sod, he was gutted. I felt really bad for him. We'd really looked forward to getting away and because of this it looked as if I would be heading to Las Vegas by myself, like a complete saddo.

I was determined I wasn't going to go there alone, so I umm-ed and ahh-ed about whether or not to ask Paul. Would it look weird? Would it look like I was trying too hard? We weren't actually together, together – we'd only had two dates. Well, after a deep breath I asked him and he accepted in a flash (of course, knowing Paul as I do now, there is no way he would turn down a free holiday – even if Hannibal Lecter had invited him along; if it was free, he'd go). So, this might sound harsh but while Justin lost his hearing, I gained a boyfriend (okay, I admit that does sound harsh).

Holidays are funny things – although they are meant to be relaxing they always start in the most stressful place known to man, the airport. I usually end up taking off the wrong item of clothing; sometimes you have to take your shoes off, sometimes your belt, sometimes your trousers – *what?* I thought that border control officer fancied me. And why, oh why, do I always bleep? Fuck knows why! There are people going through in suits of armour and not a peep, but when I step through you'd think I was a slave to intimate piercings. I just hate airports. I read an article in the paper about how 80 per cent of Brits head straight to the pub once they get through security – too fucking right, your nerves are shot, you've gone grey, your luggage has been interfered with – I know it's only 5.30 a.m. but I'm having a gin and tonic.

Paul, however, is oblivious to this kind of stress; with him, such agitation does not even touch the sides. I found out on the way to Las Vegas that we act completely differently in airports. As soon as that little message on the screen says 'Go To Gate' I am tugging at my wheelie and heading in my Birkenstocks to that gate; no, not Paul, oh no, he will amble and meander, I swear just to piss me off. 'I might just have one more browse around Sunglass Hut,' he'll mutter, shuffling off nonchalantly as if the ground under his feet is one long travelator for him to glide along, casting his eye over the shops like some Roman emperor. He won't even break into a sweat when it goes red and starts flashing ominously 'FINAL CALL'. It drives me insane – he hasn't had a good holiday till his name gets a mention over the tannoy. He doesn't realize that the change from 'Go To Gate' to 'Final Call' can be sneaky. One minute you're enjoying an egg and cress sandwich from WH Smith, the next you've had to sling it like a grenade in blind panic and leg it to the boarding gate, barging women and children out of the way. Once, on a mini-break to Italy, it changed in the blink of an eye – I remember doing a double-take at the information screen, seeing red and legging it to the boarding gate, noticing out of the corner of my eye that I was being overtaken by a woman in cork wedges. On closer inspection I realized it was Jane McDonald pelting along at – I was about to write seventy miles an hour but with Jane's nautical past on the *The Cruise*, which made her the star she is, I feel like I should put it in knots. She can't half run, and I was in trainers. If Justin had been there egging us on it would have been just like a scene from *The Games*.

Although at first glance heading off on holiday for your third date sounds flamboyant, spending nearly twenty-four hours a day with a person over a week means you've pretty much got the measure of that person in double-quick time – and, look, I wanted this to work. I don't want and quite frankly don't have the time to spend six months finding out if someone's a twat. I have come back from a holiday detesting the person who just seven days ago was my bezzie, so it's a good test. At Heathrow, though, I was nervous: say we argued, say we hated each other? For once these questions took precedence over

'Did I pack my passport?' (despite the fact I'd been patting myself down at two-minute intervals since I left the house). A few fans also holidaying in the City of Sin came over to the gate and asked for selfies or an autograph. An older man queueing behind us after the fans had left said:

'Who are you?'

'I'm Alan,' I replied.

'What do you do?' he persisted accusatively.

'He does porn,' interjected Paul, annoyed with his tone.

'Well, I haven't seen him in anything,' came the old man's reply.

Well, we were in bits and I knew then, in a weird way, that it would work out between us – does that make sense?

Needless to say, we hit it off, we had a great time. No arguments – well one, when he felt he needed to check if he had the best ringtone on his mobile phone and started sampling them all whilst I was getting to a really juicy bit in my Agatha Christie. The last time I'd heard such persistent telephone ringing was when I worked in the call centre – I had a flashback and told him in no uncertain terms that soon his phone would be going into a tunnel, and I weren't talking about the Blackwall if you catch my drift.

Our holiday in Vegas rolled on and our romance was like the weather: sunny and bright with no chance of rain. It was becoming evident that we were falling for one another and, scary as it was, it was worryingly clear that there would soon be a time when we would have to embark on the pilgrimage to Sunderland and Northampton to meet the parents. This thought actually made me feel nauseous. I had never ever introduced any potential partners to my mum and dad before, basically because I'd never had any I wanted to shout about, but I was so loved up now that a bit of me didn't care – if they threw me out on the streets and told me never to darken their door again, so what? I was in love, plus there's something quite showbizzy about having estranged parents, isn't there? You always see them in the papers looking forlorn in their sitting room, fingering a photo album and telling embarrassing family secrets about how their showbiz offspring don't talk to them any more – 'I don't know why.' Because you keep selling embarrassing family secrets to a newspaper! Have a word! Sort it out!

Well, the great day finally came and I invited my mum down to Holloway. I would introduce her first. I told Paul to be on his best behaviour – no outlandish clothes, no naughty anecdotes – 'and if you could please just for today be the personification of a perfect gentleman then we can all have an easy ride'. Me and mum were anxiously waiting in the lounge as Paul came in, all sweetness and light, a bouquet of flowers in one hand and a little gift bag in the other. Oh good, he's on the charm offensive, I told myself. My mum, who to be fair was probably as nervous as me, opened the bag as Paul chirped, 'Sexy and patriotic – perfect for you, Chris' – it was a Union Jack thong, one of the cheap (is there any other kind?) synthetic ones that you find on the market next to Kevin Kline pants and Fred Baker T-shirts. Thankfully my mum has a sense of humour so we all laughed and once I'd defused the situation with a bottle of white wine we all had a good time. My mum was naturally charmed by Paul and it wasn't long before she was modelling the thong – that's a joke, it went in the bin, and I only put that in because I know my mum will be reading this.

Next, it was time to introduce him to my dad. I had really worked this one up in my head. Stupid things, pointless things came into the equation: Paul's from Sunderland and my dad's from Newcastle and I was worried they might start having a fight because one's a Mackam and one's a Geordie. I had images of them brawling in the living room, my dad being thrown on the coffee table, Paul hitting my dad over the head with a vase, my mum just standing there in a Union Jack thong – okay, enough with the thong now, Alan. This didn't actually happen, of course it didn't – nothing like this happened because not everyone is insane and I have an overactive imagination when it comes to conjuring up unlikely scenarios.

We travelled up the M1 to Northampton and I had taken the trouble of booking a lovely restaurant just outside the town. When we arrived at the house everyone politely introduced themselves to each other. Paul was wearing his usual shorts, green socks and Crocs combo. Sometimes he can look so nice and handsome but other times he looks like Timmy Mallett. I could see my mum's face darken as she ran her eyes up and down Paul's garish outfit. Diplomatically, she said, 'The restaurant's quite nice, Paul, maybe you should go and change, put a nice shirt on or some trousers – Alan's still got some clothes upstairs.' Paul disappeared upstairs and I chatted to my dad as usual about what roads I'd taken to get up here, traffic, flyovers, A-roads, you get the gist. Then we hear,

'What about this, Christine?' We look up and see Paul wearing my mum's blouse and denim skirt, holding her handbag. My brand-new boyfriend is standing in front of my father wearing his wife's clothes – this is NOT how I envisaged their first meeting. All of a sudden that fight in the living room would have been an improvement. He seemed to be standing at the top of the stairs for ages – my dad was now shaking his head like the Churchill dog, 'No, no no.' But then everyone erupted into laughter and praise the Lord for that.

Do you know what, in a really perverse way it was the best thing that could have happened because my Paul is a character and he does things like that – my toes have curled over so many times in so many social situations that I've been left with a hoof. I'm immune to it now. The time he came out of the plane toilet wrapped head to toe in toilet paper like a mummy? Water off a duck's back. Meeting me at the airport, naked with just a mac on and an Afro wig? Not bothered. The list is endless but there's not a lot he can do to embarrass me – and believe me, he keeps on coming up with new and exciting ways. Only recently I had to endure this when Paul had some dis-comfort downstairs – no, not down the front but round the back. You get the gist. With me not being a proctolo-gist I didn't have a clue what it was – it looked like a lump. I asked him whether he wanted me to book him an appointment and did my usual partner-trying-to-give-a-shit spiel: 'You should get it checked, darling' – I threw in a 'darling' for good measure because I could see he was worried about it. He said he would see what happened and give it a few more days. Well, I never heard anything more from him and it was only when I was chopping up some baby beets for a salad that I remembered his embarrassing ailment.

'Oh, how's your lump? Are you still in pain?'

'It's fine,' came the reply, 'it's just a boil – nothing serious. They're quite common.'

I laughed. 'Oh, are you a doctor now, in your spare time?' I said as I carried on chopping.

'No, Dr Christian said.'

I stopped chopping. 'What? How does he know?'

'I sent him a photo.'

'You sent Dr Christian a photo of your anus?'

'Yeah.'

He had taken the number off my phone and taken a photo of his bum boil – God knows how, he hasn't got the longest of arms, but anyway – and then sent it to Dr Christian.

I was horrified – poor old Dr Christian Jesson, already forced to see some of THE most embarrassing bodies in his professional life and now having to endure them while he's having his tea.

Paul is good for me, and although we are very alike in many ways, he is pragmatic, while I am completely impractical; he's a doer, while I'm a dreamer; he does while I just talk about it. He's just a great sorter-outerer. He has cupboards of stuff, just stuff, for any eventuality. In one of our early meals together my dental bridge became dislodged and fell out mid-curry. I looked down – my bhuna was smiling at me. Oh, fantastic! I thought. It's

Saturday night, the dentist is going to be shut tomorrow, so I guess I'm just going to have to spend Sunday in a little bit of pain, drinking soup all bloody day. But this was before I knew about Paul and his cabinet of wonders. Lo and behold, he delves inside the cabinet and pulls out some dental paste to apply to bridges; this stuff is professional, you can't just get it in Superdrug, it has to come from a dentist. How the hell he had got hold of it I did not know, but I didn't care anyway – I just wanted my smile back. He pulled out some surgical gloves (always prepared) and pestle and mortar from his cabinet and started mixing up some dental paste for my bridge. Once he'd got the right consistency he started applying it like he'd been a dentist for years. Well, knock me down with a feather – it worked and it stuck and I am wearing that very bridge now as I write this. Spices, sanitary towels, high-vis jackets, visas – you name it, he has it in that cabinet. I never see him buy the stuff and I never pry in there because I don't want to spoil the magic – I know sadly one day I'll ask for something and it won't be there but until then I will keep on marvelling at his amazing cupboard of curiosities.

Don't get me wrong, we have our arguments and fights like all couples and his OCD can be infuriating. We had a row just the other day about a wonky National Trust car sticker. I had just slapped it to the windscreen willy-nilly so he had to pull over and, as if performing keyhole surgery, squinting, placed it exactly two inches above the tax disc – yes, because we wouldn't want the car park attendant at a stately home to start slagging us off would we?! Plus, alcohol, once the fossil fuel that spurred us on at parties, was in fact spoiling the parties and more often than not we would end up arguing and on some occasions fighting. It was damaging our relationship and we didn't even know it; worse still, it was affecting our health. The party really needed to stop but could we stop it?

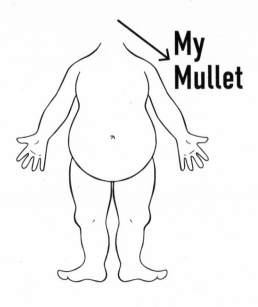

My Mullet

There aren't many streets in London I can travel down where I don't get a gentle nudge from Nostalgia. Photo shoots, parties, outside broadcasts and sketches have taken place all over the capital and as these memories filter slowly back into the foreground I am left (sometimes) with a smile on my face. Many of them took place in studios but others were in rather more impressive venues. Walking along the South Bank one day as I passed the London Aquarium, Nostalgia didn't so much give me a gentle nudge but more of a Chinese burn, for it was here that we had done some filming with David Hasselhoff.

It was our first day of meeting him and the team had had the great idea of us spending time with David at one of London's top tourist attractions – the London Aquarium. I foolishly thought that the water in the aquarium would be like a hot tub. There were tropical fish in there, so why wouldn't the water be warm, clear and tropical? I genuinely thought I would be breast-stroking in my own little puddle of Seychelles, slap-bang in the middle of London. I was wrong, so wrong. Once I'd decanted my body fat into the waiting wetsuit – I looked like a hot-water bottle that needed to be winded – we met the Hoff, a really nice guy, upbeat and one of those people you couldn't help liking. We went on to the side of the water and instantly the stench of fish and salt hit me – this wasn't the Maldives, this was Billingsgate Fish Market! The attendant at the aquarium asked if I had brought contact lenses – I hadn't, so I removed my glasses and popped on the goggles. Then, basically blind, I waded gingerly into the water, foolishly thinking, look, if anything happens we've got the Hoff. He is a hero in every sense of the word. He played a lifeguard on telly for God knows how many years, he single-handedly brought down the Berlin Wall – we are in such good hands.

The water was surprisingly freezing. I thought, these are tropical fish, aren't they supposed to love warmer climes? Isn't that why you never see a swordfish in a balaclava? Even through the wetsuit I could feel the waters swirling around my nether regions. I've never been a comfortable swimmer but you cannot believe how unnerving it is to see fish, some huge, whizzing past your face. I couldn't tell you what they were as I didn't have my glasses on but the shadows of bigger fish would pass over my face eerily and each time I let out a feeble yelp my

1. Mariah Carey bringing us to our knees

2. Gatwick please, Carol

3. Bubbles get everywhere

4. Taking in the sights of Hanoi

5. Cute! And the puppy's not bad either

6. No one EVER looks good in a helmet

7. Alan as Jeremy

8. Don't cluck with me, fellas

9. Lowe limbering up for a *Friday Night Project* sketch

10. Kim Carrcrashion

11. Bloody minotaurs!

12. JLC and Kanye with me dressed up as a toffee penny

13. AC and JLC

14. Shamone

15. Get your hands Hoff me

mouth would become filled with brine. Basically, I wasn't having a great time, and when I heard a West Country scream and saw wild flailing I knew I wasn't the only one. Even with my myopia I could see that Justin was in trouble. As I doggy-paddled over to assist him, I could not believe my goggled eyes – a stingray had got caught in his hair.

'Get it out, get it out,' he screamed. How was I supposed to 'get it out'?! I'd never manhandled a stingray before – I'd opened a tin of tuna, but never this. I said, 'Come here, come here,' making that sort of *puss puss puss* noise you make to try and coax a stray cat off a fence. Of course, if this had been one of David's television programmes he would have swum over, probably in slow motion, ripped the stingray out of Justin's hair, scooped us both out of the water and saved us from the evil predator fish and an early grave, but sadly, David did not come to the rescue. In fact he didn't even notice, he was too busy doing somersaults and goofing about for a host of Japanese tourists who were peeking through one of the portholes, clicking their cameras and waving, ecstatic that they had caught David Hasselhoff in captivity. The stingray eventually loosened its grip on Justin, as I had on life itself, and we exited the aquarium on all fours like two flatfish that had been given an evolutionary kick up the arse and turned into newts – we crawled out, relieved and distraught all in one.

David was more use in the studio, really game for a laugh and ready to take the piss out of himself at a moment's notice. He loved incorporating a sentence with his nickname the Hoff – he was always popping Hoff here and nipping Hoff there. He told us straight-faced that he was bringing out a book of photos from his illustrious career, a Hoffie-table book. *Please.* However, there was one bone of contention on the day – we did a sketch and the premise was that Justin loved David Hasselhoff but the love was unrequited because David didn't even notice Justin because he was so in love with me – d'you get it? Good – eh? We would do a pastiche of all the greatest love scenes from rom-coms, quick little comedy snippets hopefully with a high gag rate. The first one was *Dirty Dancing*, where Jennifer Grey is held aloft in the swimming pool by Patrick Swayze. I come into the studio Jennifer-Greyed up to the max (I was the woman – of course) and what was I greeted with?

'Whoa, whoa – I can't lift THAT!' David pointed. 'C'mon, guys, c'mon, I've got a bad back here. No, no, no!' He mimed lifting me up, pulling a face. All right, all right, I got it. Well, in television you don't have bullying in the workplace so I took myself off the studio floor and ran back to the dressing room where I broke down in tears and ate a whole box of Celebrations – of course I didn't! I took it on the chin. Or chins, if you're looking through David Hasselhoff's eyes.

Then we moved on to the *Lady and the Tramp* scene where I had to share a bowl of spaghetti with the Hoff – we were each to take the end of the same piece of spaghetti and slowly we would chew along, culminating in a kiss. I'm sure you have seen it, it's classic Disney. I come round the corner all lady-ed up again and then I hear it.

'Whoa, whoa! No, man, I'm not kissing that. C'mon, I

have over a billion fans, what if they see me kissing a guy on YouTube? C'mon.'

I was beginning to see a pattern here. And you wonder why I have self-esteem issues?! Of course, I totally understood – why would a heterosexual red-blooded man want to kiss a camp homosexual? But to be fair to me, I wasn't that happy about kissing him either, to be honest. What about my rights?

The rest of the show went well and for me that was a real stand-out episode. David was a lot of fun and he had some great anecdotes about *Knight Rider* and *Baywatch* – he was a legend, no doubt about it, but when it came to my body confidence he can fuck right Hoff.

You certainly get to meet a lot of people in this business. Some of them are stars that you've grown up watching on the telly and you hope and pray that when you do actually meet them they will be as nice and lovely and everything as you want them to be. When we heard that we had Joanna Lumley hosting *The Friday Night Project*, it was one of those moments – obviously like the whole of the nation I adored her as Patsy, as Purdey in *The New Avengers* and, hell knows, even that Mellow Birds advert. Basically, I loved her. Talented, beautiful and oozing class, in some ways she reminds me of a younger me. We were to film a sixties-themed photo shoot as our bonding day in Fournier Street, in a beautifully preserved eighteenth-century house tucked down the side of Spitalfields Market in the East End. I was so nervous to meet her – say she wasn't nice, say she strode in, scowled and said, 'Who's this specky poof?' Well, life wouldn't be worth living. My faith in humans would be over and I would move to a monastery.

She glided through the door like she was on coasters, numerous scarves flowing, and instantly threw herself on the floor in a blaze of chiffon. Look, I know *The Friday Night Project* is good but please, there is no need to worship us like idols, Joanna. 'Oh, darling,' she exhaled in that velvety-breath voice that at times borders on emphysema, 'your shoelace is undone, darling, please let me do it up, you'll fall over and hurt yourself, darling.' And there she was, a National Treasure on all fours doing up MY shoelace and we hadn't even exchanged a word. As you'd expect, she continued to charm and work her magic as only she could. It's so nice to meet someone off the telly and they are actually as you WANT them to be. Believe me, the amount of times I have met so-called National Treasures or family favourites and they have been complete arseholes. Seriously, you think, how hasn't this filtered down to the general public? Why don't people know that this person is a real nasty piece of work? But then again I suppose that is a skill in itself – being able to disguise your nastier side is just as much a talent as keeping a theatre mesmerized with a monologue or tearing the roof off the O2, but really, it must be exhausting for them.

Sometimes the fun times we've had during the recordings overflows into our personal lives too and we get to experience some really wonderful things. Jamie Oliver took us to dinner at his flagship restaurant 15 and before we knew it we were at his house having a barbecue – I know, get me. Mel C did *The Friday Night Project* in the winter of 2007 and she was a dream guest, didn't mind dressing up, took the piss out of herself and the Spice Girls, she just got it. What made it even better was that it was a *Friday Night Project* first: we actually went abroad to film, seriously abroad, like with a passport and everything. We went to Magaluf to meet Sporty, and I ended up singing the Bryan Adams duet 'When You're Gone' with actual Melanie Chisolm. We were in the Eastenders Bar in Palma Nova and being a huge Spice Girls fan I found the moment very surreal; being watched from the walls by framed photos of Fat Pat and Wellard made it even more surreal but it was definitely a story for the grandkids.

Not only could I cross that off my bucket list, but the day after the show went out the Spice Girls announced they were going to reunite! Frustratingly, naughty Melanie had denied it on the show, but any bad feeling about this swiftly evaporated when Melanie got me front-row seats at their comeback gig at the O2. Tickets for the gigs were like gold dust and for me to sit there in the front row (the kids call it FROW) next to Posh Spice's mum blew me away. I was so close to all the action that when Posh Spice minced down the catwalk and pointed she nearly took my eye out, and during 'Spice Up Your Life' who did Mel pass the mic to when she needed the audience callback? Yes, you guessed it, little old me.

I didn't think we could top flying to Magaluf, but we did later on in the series when we had Mark Ronson as the guest host. What a lovely guy! He is one of the nicest people you ever want to meet. Luckily for us, we got to spend more time with Mark than we usually did with our guest hosts. *The Friday Night Project* producers must have cashed in some bonds or found some money down the back of the sofa because before we knew it we were flying to the Big Apple to spend a weekend with him – how cool is that. The bonding film we did with Mark was a tourist's wet dream: the Statue of Liberty, Central Park, the Empire State Building. We did them all – even playing a tune on the Walking Piano at FAO Schwarz on Fifth Avenue, made famous by Tom Hanks in *Big*. Mark was so accommodating – we went to his house and he took us to lovely restaurants. You can't beat local knowledge for finding the cool places to go. Back then I wouldn't have known what was cool in NYC – I'd probably have ended up having a Whopper in Times Square – so to get a guided tour from a bona fide New Yoiker (sic) was a real bonus.

One thing we hadn't taken into account, however, was that our visit to New York City was on the exact same day as the National Puerto Rican Day parade. And, believe me, Puerto Ricans know how to party! Colourful, flamboyant, jubilant and loud, very, very loud. A swirl of rainbow colours rounded off with a Latino beat are the perfect ingredients for a party but the last thing you need when you are doing a link to camera and only have two minutes to do it. In the end we couldn't use any of the audio in the record because, frustratingly, every link was peppered with honks and whistles: 'All right HONK, let's go and see if Mark WHISTLE wants to HONK WHISTLE HONK with us when we go HONK WHISTLE.' I was literally hoarse with shouting but what could I do?

I couldn't piss off a whole country, I couldn't say 'Look, Puerto Rico, can you please pipe down, I'm trying to make award-winning television here?'

A few months later Mark was kind enough to invite us to his birthday party back in the UK – and what a night that was. I had been to a few showbiz parties before but they usually consisted of a handful of Z-listers hovering around a half-open box of Celebrations. This, however, was actually a cool party. I hadn't ever been invited to a cool party before, a party where cool, 'in' people would be. The party was in Buckinghamshire in this massive stately home. Manicured lawns lapped the huge driveway, topiary punctuated the landscape and a throng of paparazzi were at the gates holding their cameras expectantly – so why oh why did I go dressed as Madonna? Not even fun, lacy gloves, 'BOY TOY', *Like a Virgin* eighties Madonna – no, *Confessions on a Dance Floor* era Madonna, the ginger Farrah Fawcett flicked, sequined, disco diva Madonna, the era that had her toned, sinewy body squeezed into an unforgiving purple leotard. The reason for this was there written in gold under the address of the party: 'Come as your favourite album cover.' I had loved Madge's *Confessions* album, a real return to form, and I thought what a wonderful homage it would be for me to go as that very album cover to a fabulous party, so that was the look I tried to carry off . . . and, yes, I was right, leotards are pretty unforgiving but I ploughed on. Thankfully, the tightness of the leg holes chafing my legs took away from the excruciating pain my glittery pink tranny wedges were causing me.

The agony did not dim my enthusiasm and I decided

to suffer for my art, crossing everything as we got into the taxi that my outfit would turn heads and hopefully not stomachs. There's nothing like a traffic jam to put the dampener on a night out – in the house we had been giddy, listening to Madonna, sipping Prosecco and slut-dropping, laughing at how ridiculous I looked, but in the slow lane of the North Circular, bumper to bumper, it wasn't so fun. The laughs became shorter, the smiles became weaker and the alcohol measures got smaller. This was boring. Plus I badly needed a wee. I looked enviously at Paul, who had decided, quite sensibly, to go as Adam Ant. After what seemed like ages, we finally got off the motorway and I pointed (I was so desperate I couldn't talk) to a lay-by – the taxi pulled over and I ran to relieve myself behind a wheelie bin. The relief of actually finding a place to finally wee was overtaken by the sudden realization that I didn't have flies. I scratched frantically at the gusset like I had crabs, finally pulling the elasticated gusset to one side – ahh, the relief . . . oh no, I'm wearing tights – shit! Stop, stop! Well, it was like telling Niagara to go back, I just couldn't stop. I tried miserably to tear through my tights but they weren't ripping and the urine gushed through my fishnets. It must have been an awful sight to behold, a ginger she-man gymnastic publicly urinating in a lay-by, clinging awkwardly for support to a wheelie bin, but I won't deny that the relief was so nice. I don't know whether it was my empty bladder or that the rush hour had passed but we seemed to make much quicker progress after that.

Once we got there and passed through the migraine-inducing bulb fest that was the paps, I was thankful to see that no one else had decided to choose *Confessions on a Dance Floor* as their favourite album so there were no embarrassing clashes and, to be fair, the wee stain on the gusset of my leotard just looked like I had a sweaty vagina and I'm sure Madonna has one of those the amount of dancing she does on stage so it truly was win-win. It was a really fun night, and luckily no one mistook me for the real Madonna so I didn't have to fall back on my old cheeky wink, lifting up my glasses schtick – 'It's me, Alan.'

Nick Grimshaw cross-dressed himself as Lily Allen, though in fact his ensemble of a spotty dress and hairband was factually wrong – Lily has never worn that on a CD cover so by rights he should have been evicted from the party but I bit my tongue and decided not to bring this to the attention of Mr Ronson. I wished I had when Grimmy turned to me and said, 'Who've you come as – Cilla?' Cheeky bastard – ha! I put it down to jealousy and slut-dropped off.

Some of the celebrity appearances on *The Friday Night Project* coincided with the promotion of a new single, a film or even an underwear range as for gorgeous supermodel Elle 'The Body' Macpherson, but sometimes people were flogging something that defied description such as David Gest. (Yet another person who has sadly passed away this year.) He had written *Liza Minnelli: The Musical,* which was due to open in a theatre in North Finchley. Knowing that he wasn't exactly bezzie mates with his ex-wife Liza Minnelli, me and Justin were intrigued to see what he had in store. We were excited to meet him too – he had come across as so eccentrically funny on *I'm a Celebrity . . . Get Me Out of Here!* that we wanted to experience this quirkiness in the flesh.

We arrived in North Finchley and the theatre was abuzz with rehearsals, David was all excited and was literally chomping at the bit to get a West End transfer as soon as possible.

'Do you want to see some of my show?' he asked excitedly.

'Oh yes!' Justin and I cried in unison. We sat down in the stalls – all that was missing was popcorn and a little tub of over-priced ice cream. The person playing Liza was a drag queen and as he/she came on to the stage not only was she dressed as Liza as 'Sally Bowles' but she was holding a bottle of vodka, slurring and wearing a suicide vest of empty vodka bottles. She was singing 'I'm Losing My Mind' whilst staggering across the stage, pissed as a fart. It was highly offensive – forget 'Liza with a Z', it'll be 'Liza with your balls on a spike' if she ever sees this, I thought. Then three women came on walking sideways wearing Oriental dresses.

'Who are these?' I whispered to David.

'They're Liza's crabs.'

'Oh!' I replied, hiding my shock. I'd seen Elaine Paige play a tabby on stage in *Cats* but I'd never seen anyone play an STD before. Then for some unknown reason they were joined by some 'little people' singing. I forget who they were meant to represent in Liza's world but I thought it best not to ask. Finally it ended.

'Well, guys, what do you think?' David asked.

'Very entertaining,' we enthused, and it was, I had been

98

mesmerized by what I had just seen. Good or bad, I couldn't take my eyes off the stage. I did wonder how it would go down with a theatre-going audience and also with Liza's lawyers.

In the studio, the madness continued when me and Justin were both handed Tiffany boxes. 'I got you guys a present,' David explained. In the boxes were two crystal candlestick holders, one each, which sort of undermined the effect but who cared, no one had ever brought us presents before. I held mine up to the light and admired the crystal – I had never had anything before or since from Tiffany, and was so chuffed. The receipt was still in the bag and I could see it was off a list, but not just any old list – after further snooping and a quick call to the shop it turned out to be from a wedding list. And not just any old list but the wedding list of Liza Minnelli and David Gest. I had a piece of showbiz history in my very own home – who would have thought it?

David was a real charmer on set and had us all in stitches with his name-dropping and showbiz anecdotes; he seemed to have everyone on speed dial. I spoke to soul singer Candi Staton on his phone one night and at one point went to ring Hollywood legend Jane Russell to say 'hello' but she didn't pick up. Look, I don't know if it was her, who's to say, but he believed it was. I performed some sketches with David down at the studio, some ridiculous nonsense where I was Michael Jackson and he was 'Bub-bles'. David then went for lunch and after he came back he said he had rung Michael and told him about the sketch and 'he had laughed, laughed, laughed'. Now again, I don't know if this actually happened – David was a bit like his hair in that you didn't know what was real and what's been made up – but hey, as I'm doing my housework and buffing my Tiffany candlestick, a part of me likes to think that the King of Pop over there in Neverland did hear about our little *Friday Night Project* sketch and did laugh and laugh and laugh – wouldn't that just be the insanest thing ever!

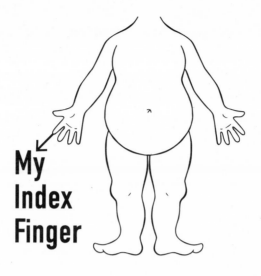

My Index Finger

We've all sat in front of our televisions, switched on and gone, 'Oh God, not them again,' at the sight of a new talent that seems to be on everything. You'd bet your last penny that they'd been cloned, how can they be on everything – multiple channels, panel shows, chat shows, cookery shows, you name it, there they are. I always have to bite my tongue before calling up *Points of View* because that was once me. When you get on television and you sort of become a 'name', you're soon inundated with invites to do other shows, shows that you yourself watch and enjoy, and at first you do accept them all. You're like a kid in a televisual candy store. 'Yes, yes, yes,' I would shout to my agent, 'I'll do it.' You are blissfully unaware of the word 'overkill' and naively have no idea that your perpetual appearance on television could impel the viewer to lob a brick at the screen or perform hara-kiri on themselves. And let's not forget that these days you've got incessant repeats and all the plus-one channels on your Skybox – people can get pissed off at seeing you AGAIN an hour later as you pop up like the last rotisserie chicken in Sainsbury's. I accepted everything, and I mean everything, from *8 Out of 10 Cats* to *Countdown*, *Gok's Fashion Fix* to Gordon Ramsay's *Hell's Kitchen* – oh, and if it had 'Celebrity' in the title you couldn't hold me back. My acceptance of virtually any job offer that came into my agent's inbox was getting too much, plus my judgement about what direction my career should be going in was worryingly suspect. I turned down *Top Gear* yet said yes to hosting the National Porn Awards. I know, I know. The National Porn Awards sounded right up my street, a bit low rent, cheeky and probably a lot of adult saucy fun, but when my agent got the script and saw that the categories were 'Best Blow Job', 'Best Use of a Dildo' and 'Best Newcummer', pun intended, he declined on my behalf.

My agent suggested I look at appearing on *Top Gear* again. 'Have a little think about it,' he said. I didn't fancy it. You just knew the studio would smell like a boy's bedroom. I thought I'd sleep on it. It was my friends that made me say yes. When I said I'd turned *Top Gear* down they looked at me like I'd stuck a winning lottery ticket into a shredder. They were incredulous.

'What? But you've got to go on *Top Gear*,' they insisted. 'It's an institution, are you crazy?'

'Oh, okay, I'll do it,' I relented. Their incredulity then

turned to envy as I headed off out of London to Duns-fold Aerodrome in Surrey on a balmy June afternoon to film 'Star in a Reasonably Priced Car' with Jeremy Clarkson, James May and the Hamster. I was dreading being asked about cars or anything automobile-related – it just doesn't interest me. I once had an argument with the lady at the congestion charge office because I didn't know the make of my own car.

'You don't know the make of your own car, sir?' she said, and even though it was over the phone I could hear her eyebrow arching.

'No, I don't.'

I daren't tell her I called it Des.

I knew about fan belts and tights but that was from lazy Sundays watching black and white romantic movies in a slanket rather than slipping into an oily jumpsuit and sliding under a car bonnet.

Although my knowledge of the motoring world was minimal, I had heard a little bit about *Top Gear*, especially the Stig, who filled me with intrigue – the mysterious co-host slash man of mystery whose identity was unknown due to him never removing his helmet. At first I thought this was just television folklore to drum up a bit of mystery, but no, his helmet stayed on. The whole time I never saw his face once – even at the end of the record he stood there nodding and making polite chit-chat, still with the damned helmet on. I am proud to say that I beat Justin Lee Collins's lap: his was 1:51.8 minutes, mine was 1:51.2 minutes – yeah, take that, JLC! It's odd because I would never class myself as a speed demon, I avoid speed or danger at any cost. Even my exercise bike at the gym has a basket on the front (I once got mistaken for Miranda from *Call the Midwife* in the middle of a spin class). But the more I hurtled round that track, the more I wanted to do it again and again, faster and faster. It's fair to say that adrenaline got hold of me – I was buzzing, I needed my fix, and considering that I had been dreading going on the show I thoroughly enjoyed myself. The atmosphere was surprisingly 'gay friendly'; I even saw a woman working on the show – yes, can you believe it, an actual woman – and it didn't smell like a boy's bedroom at all. I had got it into my head that when I turned up to the studio the crew would be like 'ooh, hello, sailor' and 'backs against the walls, lads, here he comes', but it wasn't like that at all.

Out of all the shows I have done, that fleeting moment on *Top Gear* has had the most impact on me abroad, which is testament to what a global phenomenon it actually is. South America, the isles of Greece, Cuba – you name it, people come up to me saying 'Top Gear'. At first you think, ay up, they're selling me drugs, and it's only when they start making a steering-wheel gesture that the penny drops. Ahh! That balmy evening at Dunsfold Aerodrome where I zoomed round a track in a Nissan Sunny.

As with my experience on *Top Gear*, peeking behind the scenes can often enhance the magic and endear you to a show even more; sometimes, however, the stardust you see lighting up the screen on closer inspection can turn out to be asbestos. One such show was *Celebrity Apprentice*. This came under the umbrella of Comic Relief – they take over a well-known show and put a celebrity twist to it and they usually drip-feed it to the viewing public over the night of the fundraiser. It's such an amazing charity, as you know, and I'm sure you've all donated too, so obviously when you get the call from Emma Freud or Richard Curtis asking for you to get involved, it's a no-brainer – it's an Almighty YES! I have done numerous things with Comic Relief, some of them really cool. I was once in a Jennifer Saunders sketch spoof of *Mamma Mia*. After being brought up on *French and Saunders*, this was a big deal for me and when I got asked by Jennifer to be one of the prospective dads to Sienna Miller, again it was an Almighty YES!

More recently I was part of a spoof Take That for their Comic Relief charity single. We spent the whole day in a freezing warehouse on the outskirts of Ealing dressed up as Take That, taking the piss out of Take That to their faces. James Corden was Gary Barlow, Catherine Tate was Jason Orange, David Walliams was Robbie Williams and John Bishop was Howard Donald. I was Mark Owen, which was the worst casting ever – no, Catherine as Jason probably pipped me to that accolade – but poor Mark, he was about the size of my leg. I tell you, I will never tut and roll my eyes at a boy band dance routine again, they are hard, and I was just lip-synching. I had a stitch before the first chorus. The poor make-up girl kept having to come over and mop me down, I was so unfit. Respect, boys, respect.

Anyway, obviously when Emma rang up out of the blue and asked me to do *Celebrity Apprentice* it was an Almighty – oh, okay, you get the gist.

I was an avid watcher of the show and jumped at the chance to be on it. Looking back, I think that was the problem – I loved the show too much. The penny should have dropped when I saw Margaret Mountford, who on screen was a severe matronly type, no nonsense, a force to be reckoned with, laughing loudly with Nick Hewer over a pastry wearing a pair of Reebok Classics. What? Where's her clipboard? Why ain't she scowling? Then when we were told that we'd be going to see Lord Sugar in his office, instead of turning right to the throbbing metropolis of Canary Wharf we headed left towards Acton and pulled up on an industrial wasteland next to a DFS. What, Lord Sugar has a Saturday job in a settee shop? It messed with my head.

One thing I'll never forget was when we were filming the bridge scene. Anyone who has ever seen *The Apprentice* will know the bridge scene, where all the apprentices strut determinedly across the Millennium Bridge, eyes bright with ambition and with a look on their faces like 'Who's farted?' We went to get the filming done early in the morning but the person who had organized it had not realized it was Lord Mayor's Day and security was paramount, so we had to get out at Holborn and walk to the bridge. What? But I'm a celebrity, I don't walk. The irony wasn't lost on me as I lugged my carry-on case down the street and I couldn't help thinking that if this was a task the person who had organized it would probably be fired – just saying!

Well, the biggest slap in the face was still to come and on the last day of filming I was fired – yeah, fired. Fuck you, Sugar! Okay, not wanting to sound like one of those disgruntled employees who goes to an independent tribunal for justice, but fuck you, Sugar! *Alan, stop it, stop it, he's not worth it.* I'm not very good at rejection as you can see, reader. I was stitched up. Stitched up, I tell you. Watching the edited programme was like watching another show altogether: footage of the rest of the team zipping around London talking into their phones held horizontally as they always do in *The Apprentice* was spliced with me sitting sipping a tea, looking aimlessly into the distance; Jack Dee and Jonathan Ross haggling frantically with the owner of a toy shop, cut to me, shuffling around a warehouse – and not only was I shuffling but they had put some plodding music over the top to accentuate the fact, just in case the viewers couldn't make their minds up. 'Is he plodding? Yes, I think he's plodding.'

To be fair, I wasn't the most dynamic of the team – my motto is 'When the going gets tough, the tough get going, and I get a bin bag and do a bit of light tidying-up.' It's interesting seeing those shows as a human experiment, seeing where you fit in as part of a team. Jonathan Ross and Gok Wan are very much alpha males and as soon as they were given the task they leapt into action, ideas, action plans, strategies flooding their heads – I did what I always did and retired to the kitchen to make a cuppa. I was quite proud that by the end I knew everyone's tea preferences, who had two sugars, who had Canderel, who had it black and who liked a little bicky on the side . . . Reading this back, maybe I did deserve to be fired and hey, I'm not stupid, I know there has to be a fall guy in the show to give it a narrative, and it was for Comic Relief so I can't complain too much, and it's not about how I come across, ultimately it's about raising money – it's just that I wanted to impress Lord Sugar.

We'd only met once before and that was on Jonathan Ross's chat show earlier in the year. Lord Sugar was a guest and Jonathan asked me as a favour to wear a blonde wig and sit at a desk like the receptionist in *The Apprentice* and introduce the guests one by one via a telephone, all filmed from behind so that no one would see it was me. It was going really well, getting laughs off the audience, until a drunken Johnny Vegas took a shine to me, grabbed my head between his hands and tried to make me faux fellate him in front of a shocked Lady Sugar. I always wonder whether Johnny thought I was a genuine woman.

Anyway, I'm going to put the whole *Apprentice* ordeal to bed now. It made me a stronger person and, let's face it, it wasn't the last time that I would be edited down for better or worse – but fuck you, Sugar!

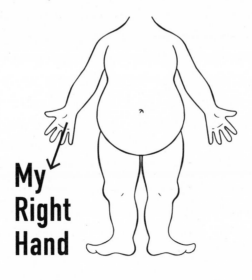

My Right Hand

One of the most rewarding television shows I've done is *Who Do You Think You Are?* Being the nosey person that I am I've always been drawn to going through other people's dirty laundry – sorry, finding out about different people's lives – and as my own family tree is less of a tree and more of a Japanese knotweed my interest deepened further. I jumped at the chance to do it for a couple of reasons: firstly, it would be nice for the British public to see me in a more subdued light, not gurning, squawking or dressed as a woman but being me and, dare I say it, doing something with gravitas; secondly, there was an anomaly in my family tree on my mother's side – my great-grandad had changed his name and no one knew why. Anyone who had been able to remember his real name had died and the trail had gone cold, basically leaving the present generation with a genealogical sinkhole.

The *Who Do You Think You Are?* team were absolutely great. The research they put in to searching every nook and cranny of my family tree was astounding and I am for ever thankful to them for that. We spent a week on my dad's family tree and then a week on my mother's family tree. For my dad's, we spent a wonderful time in the North East in the beautiful county of Northumberland – I love going back there as it always reminds me of my grandparents who lived in West Moor, Whitley Bay, and of searching for cockles near St Mary's lighthouse. The Carrs being a generation upon generation mining family meant my journey took me to Burradon, where there had been a devastating pit explosion in 1860 that had killed my great-great-grandad and, unknown to me (they revealed this in the local pub to me on camera later that day), it had also unbelievably killed my great-great-grandad on the other side – my dad's mother's side. Not only that, they had been found holding each other in a gruesome embrace, both burnt to death – one had gone back to help the other instead of fleeing the explosion. Tragic, totally tragic, and properly spooky that two lines of a family tree would be brought together generations later through this awful tragedy. It was a real moment for me and writing it down now it still gives me chills. I genuinely thought it would be a dead cert for the show but apparently Kate Humble had had a mining disaster in the last series so they decided not to include it – such is television.

My mum's ancestral story took me to Dartford and Woolwich. Didn't any of my ancestors fancy going anywhere exotic? Didn't any of them flick through a Thomas Cook brochure and think 'Ooh, Trinidad and Tobago – wonder what that's like?' Apparently not, I realized as I drove through the Blackwall Tunnel for the fifteenth time. One thing I hadn't known about the show was the huge amount of filming that would be involved. I'd been doing my own shows for a few years so I knew it could drag, but really, the amount of filming was excruciating: driving over bridges, driving under bridges, driving on motorways, driving on B-roads – doing three-point turns on B-roads when you missed the turning for the A-road. Believe it or not, it wasn't the hours and hours of driving footage that got to me the most, it was the sentimental shots, the ones where they film you wandering in front of somewhere dramatic or geographically important, looking whimsical and full of thought. Oh God, I found them so eggy, plus they were difficult. More often than not I would get the giggles and then when I started doing the universal mime for thinking, stroking my chin, I would get a 'Cut!' from a disgruntled director – you just couldn't win. The most excruciating moment I had to do was sitting in a roadside cafe, fingering through a couple of photo albums, staring thoughtfully at the A1 over a Belgian bun – I mean, please. They also wanted me to do long shots, where I'd walk across a bridge or up a cobbled street and the camera would film me from afar – I had to wander up and down one bridge so many times, looking so contemplative, that people I passed kept giving me anxious looks, thinking I was going to chuck myself off.

But for all the filming and repetitiveness it was lovely to do and the experts were so generous with their time and knowledge. It also filled that niggling gap on my mother's side about why my great-grandad had changed his name. I was taken to an old weapons artillery shed in Woolwich and was told by the expert that Henry had gone to war. He signed up in Peckham to fight WWI with his mates, and that particular battalion had fought in the Battle of the Somme and then the Battle of Ypres. 'And . . .' dramatic pause from the expert, 'Henry had survived both.' I looked to the heavens, what lucky star was I born under. 'He survived,' the expert continued, 'because he wasn't there. He'd deserted – twice.' Shit. Oh shit. The number of *Who Do You Think You Are?* episodes I'd watched where they had found out that the long-lost relatives had been an admiral or an inventor or, in Brooke Shields's case, a couple of popes and a saint (which I think is just plain old showing-off!). Why a deserter? Why? All caught on camera too! Admittedly, it was embarrassing, but at least we had found the reason for his name change and the subsequent confusion it had caused. You never know, if he hadn't deserted and had carried on to fight at the Somme or Ypres he might not have come back and then there would have been no me – which is a bad thing – yes? Yes – a bad thing.

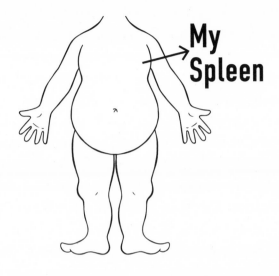

My Spleen

When you become a 'TV personality', that godawful misnomer (do you know the amount of people I meet who work on television that have no personality?!), things change. You don't, but things around you change. The only way I can describe it is it's like you're having an out-of-body experience – you sort of drift off, leaving yourself down here while the perceived 'you' floats up into the sky, gets stuck in a tree and everyone treats it like a piñata. Yeah, grab a stick – get bashing – enjoy yourself – knock yourself out. For the most part I have had a wonderful charmed life mainly thanks to you and your support over the years and, believe me, my arms are purple with the amount of times I pinch myself at how it's all turned out. I have become a 'celebrity', whatever that means, and inherited all the responsibility that comes with it. It's a right royal mess being a celebrity because it means so many things to so many people. I struggle to grasp what I'm supposed to be half the time. Celebrity! Let's face it, there aren't many words in the English language that can mean 'icon' and 'twat' at the same time, depending on that person's point of view. If you slip into a pub and sit and read quietly in the corner, you're aloof; if you walk into the same pub and say hello to everyone, it's 'Who does HE think he is?' You can't win. If I ran into a burning orphanage and saved every last child from a fire there's always going to be someone who says 'Looks like someone's drumming up a bit of publicity for their DVD', or worse, 'Someone's got fat ankles.' The best thing to do is just roll with it. Like beauty, fame is in the eye of the beholder – and depending on their interpretation of 'celebrity' you could be talented, you could have a gift, you could even be an inspiration, a role model perhaps to thousands, or conversely you could be shallow, vain and narcissistic. Just recently 'tax dodger' has been added to the list of suspicions you have to put up with. 'Are your tax affairs in order?' a journalist quizzed me on the red carpet; a valid question, yes, but a bit insulting, don't you think? Fair enough, if you meet me and I don't take my eyes off a compact mirror, preening myself whilst you chat to me, yeah, call me vain; or if you see me in the Cayman Islands making a 'deposit' then you go for it, call me dodgy – judge away, boo and hiss behind your computer – but don't pile all this prejudice on my doorstep just because I clock into a television studio now and not a call centre.

I try to do my bit because I have awful guilt about the amazing opportunities that have come my way, but a lot of the time it feels like you're swimming upstream. Once when I was on the red carpet at the Pride of Britain Awards an autograph hunter squashed behind the barrier pointed at some nurses and carers on their way in to collect well-deserved awards and said, 'It's them that are heroes, not you overpaid stars. Real people, people who don't get any recognition.' I wholeheartedly agreed with him: soldiers, nurses and teachers are all real heroes who need to get more recognition and respect, but you're the one who's waited here since one o'clock, screaming and shouting, to get a photo of yourself with someone from *Emmerdale* – instead of lecturing me, maybe you need to have this conversation with yourself.

Those responsibilities I mentioned aren't just supporting charities, or donating money, or retweeting fun runs, etcetera, sometimes they are closer to home – sometimes the responsibility is to stop yourself becoming a dick. Because you've become famous you have to act like you're famous – right? Wrong. That is a one-way ticket to Twatland. I remember once in the early days sitting in my garden and seeing a flash. 'God, I've been papped – please, please, please, all I want is to be left alone, can't the press just get that into their heads?' I pleaded, grabbing my stuff and stalking to the safety of my lounge. The paparazzi, it seemed, was God as it hadn't been a camera but a flash of lightning. Oh. Even more embarrassing was the day I was driving back to my house and I thought people were recognizing me from being on the telly the night before. They were waving and waving as I drove along. It turned out I was driving in front of a bus, blocking its way. Cringey or what? I was comfortable enough with myself to give myself a good talking-to: 'Just because you are on the telly Friday nights for an hour, Alan, does not make you Madonna! You are not the centre of the universe, you are not even the centre of Holloway – get over yourself!'

I remember tweeting about a contestant on *Deal Or No Deal* who had sadly missed out on the big money. 'If you really cared, you'd give him one of your MILLIONS,' came the quite frankly bonkers reply, the malevolence bubbling just under the surface for all to see. I went to my keyboard and began to type, 'If I had all those millions I wouldn't be sitting here watching *Deal Or No Deal* on a rainy Monday afternoon, I'd be in St Tropez on a yacht being pummelled by a house boy, you miserable . . .' but I bit my tweet. Alan, it's petty, leave it. Considering that it was probably one of the least vile things I have had said to me on Twitter, it still irked. It's not just confined to social media either – family members muscle in too with their half-baked assumptions of what I am like. Paul and I went to Vietnam and, no offence, Vietnam, but we didn't like it. Don't get me wrong, I loved the charming old town of Hoi An with its cute little lanes and trees adorned with coloured lanterns, and Halong Bay was breathtaking, but we found the cities depressingly polluted with not much to do. I remember when we arrived in Ho Chi Minh how we laughed at all the people going about their business wearing these protective face masks – we spent the first hour pretending to moonwalk up the street, doing our high-pitched Michael Jackson 'hee hee' and 'shamone' to anyone who would listen. After an hour, when I'd got a chemical headache and bogies as black as coal were being picked from my nose, we gave in and got a protective face mask each. On telling our families we didn't like Vietnam, a cousin who had obviously had a different experience to us asked, 'Did you even step out of your limo and see the real Vietnam?' What? Why would I be driving around a Third World country in a limousine, you wouldn't get to see anything would you? Then it dawned on me: Oh, I know why, because I'm on the telly and that means I'm rich and stupid – okay, I get it now.

People say to my mum, 'Has he changed?' by which they mean have I become more precious or queenie. But change can be a positive thing too and, do you know what, I hope I have changed. Looking back, I hope I have embraced it, gone with it, run with the ball that Fate has thankfully thrown my way. Inevitably you pick up friends and are put in situations a million miles away from your humble position but that's okay, as long as you aren't a dick about it. I once stayed in a hotel that had an honesty bar – an honesty bar, seriously. I said to the hotel manager, 'So, you help yourself to the drinks and then you put in this box here the money you owe for all your drinks – right?'

'Yes, sir,' he replied.

I had never heard of such things, I thought it was a wind-up.

'Come off it, where's the secret camera?'

But it was true, apparently in some posh hotels you can help yourself to the drinks and pay what you owe without scrutiny – who knew? I had a vision of me at 4.00 a.m. in the morning, slumped in a chair covered in sick, with red-wine lips, muttering to the night manager, 'I only had a Ribena.'

You end up rubbing shoulders with people you would never ever have met on the industrial estates of Northampton. I once had a lunch appointment who cancelled, saying, 'I can't make lunch, darling, my friend's just been assassinated.' How the hell did I get a friend who knew someone powerful enough to be assassinated! Pre-celebrity lunch cancellations were rooted mainly in the 'ooh I've got a hangover' camp, or 'my bus hasn't turned up'.

I remain a rock – I'm just good old Alan From The Block – but occasionally it's important that my friends do realize I've changed. I remember meeting up with my nymphomaniac friend, who was making a flying visit to London. Having lunch with him is hilarious but there are three people in our relationship – me, him and Grindr. There it is on the table face up next to his napkin; if you didn't know him you'd think he had a lazy eye because he will be looking at you with one eye while the other will be checking intermittently to see if there are any potential suitors in the area. God help you if there is – because mid-starter he will be off. Off! He will and does get sex anywhere. I've left him from an afternoon of drinks and he'll ring me up later and say, 'You won't believe what happened. I was waiting at the bus stop and then a man in a convertible pulled up and winked at me and I got in

the car and we ended up making love. I've just this min-ute arrived back from his penthouse. Fabulous, darling.'
Now that never happens to me – the only time I've ever been propositioned is when a tramp grabbed me from behind, pinched my cheek in Manchester's Piccadilly Gardens and said, 'Cheer up, Queenie – might never happen.'

As I was saying, me and my nympho friend were in Balans having a boozy lunch, swigging mojitos and catching up on six months of gossip, when his eye arced down to the screen of his smartphone. His face lit up. 'Look, there's a man just off Oxford Street looking for a threesome – oh my God – we've got nothing to do after lunch – let's go for it,' he said, wolfing down his salad niçoise so fast that I ordered Rennies as an amuse-bouche.

'No,' I said loudly, 'I can't just meet up with strangers and have bloody threesomes – I'm on the telly.'

He looked at me with genuine pity on his face. 'Oh.' And carried on chowing down on his tuna. Oh, and besides, I have a boyfriend, I remembered through the haze of the mojito – I couldn't possibly.

Most of the time being famous is a lot of fun – although some of the myths about being famous that I believed when I was growing up have sadly turned out to be just that, myths. Of course, maybe that's because I'm not famous enough or the wrong type of famous. You don't get any fashion designers fighting to dress up a chubby homosexual. Yes, I get freebies, but it's nothing you would actually want and often the 'gifts' border on the offensive – teeth whitening, hair plugs, male Spanx, enough! I remember after I had made my television debut my dentist saying to me, 'Now what are we going to do about these teeth of yours?' Charming, I thought, what are we going to do about your Crocs and halitosis? But I kept my cakehole shut. My refusal of a free dental make-over may sound ungrateful but I quite like being a work in progress. Not that I'm averse to a freebie, so if you want to send me something free I do have a lovely size 10 foot that would fit in a complimentary Gucci loafer just splendidly, but I won't hold my breath.

Mind you, there are several times in the year when I do get freebies which always put a smile on my face. These sporadic gifts often come out of the blue, or should I say *into the blue* (a little clue there to the sender) and turn up at my house. They are from no other than Aussie poppet and singing-sensation Kylie Minogue. Over the years I have had signed CDs, duvet covers, candles, pillows, T-shirts, posters, calendars and DVDs from the very generous Ms Minogue. I remember the production manager at *Chatty Man* ringing me up, sounding bemused.

'You've had a box of socks arrive.'

'Socks? Who from?'

There was a rummage and then a 'Min?'

'Oh, that's Kylie.'

'Why is Kylie sending you socks?'

'She's Kylie Minogue, she can do what she wants!'

Some people have Argos for all their gift ideas – I have Kylie.

The only time I can think of when I've been treated like a superstar is when I was in a gift shop in Aberdeen and the shop owner spotted me and said to just give her the nod if I wanted the shop closed so I could browse in peace, which I thought was really sweet, but when you've only popped in to buy a tin of shortbread for your nan, a comedy sporran and a Highland fridge magnet it seemed a lot of faff to deny other shoppers the chance to buy tat. In a way I think I've avoided a lot of hassle with the press and stuff by just getting on with it; keeping my head down and not jumping on any bandwagons has saved me a lot of grief. You'll never find me telling you who to vote for, or march for, it's none of my business – you do whatever you've got to do, my loves, as long as you're not hurting anyone. I am fully aware that having a television show does not make you the oracle.

Thinking about it, there was one time when I inadvertently strayed into the harsh media spotlight and actually got myself into a bit of trouble and that was when I dedicated my British Comedy Award to Karen Matthews. Who's Karen Matthews, you ask, boy, she must be a really special lady for you to honour her with an award dedication on national television. Well, actually Karen Matthews faked her own daughter's kidnapping, stuck her under her bed and sparked a nationwide search for her in the hope that the general public would donate money to her in pity and give her free shit. It was all very camp and I became a bit obsessed with her; even her toothless 'Come home, princess' that she ended her television plea with worked its way into my vernacular. A friend on a rubbish holiday, a family member at work with a hangover, anyone having an awful day, would be greeted with a toothless 'Come home, princess' when they rang me up.

So, I find out that I've been nominated for Best Comedy Performance for *The Sunday Night Project* at the Comedy Awards. This is all very exciting and as it's televised I go out and treat myself to some nice new clothes to wear. Why I bother getting a nice outfit for the Comedy Awards I will never know. I never learn – every time I go there I end up looking a state, mainly due to the never-ending flow of Pinot; I don't when I leave the house, I look lovely as I step over my doormat, but it doesn't last long.

Everyone gets a bit sniffy about the Comedy Awards as they are so raucous; something outrageous always happens and the next day everyone's up in arms about the debauched goings-on. They have become the *enfant terrible* of the award shows and some say rightfully so. No one sets out to be edgy or controversial, it's just that someone needs to tell the organizers that three bottles of Blue Nun and a family pack of Haribo on each table do not a sit-down dinner make. Waiting for the show to start, you are herded to your table and left to your own devices. There is nothing to do but drink and that's what everyone normally does.

Anyhow, I'm sitting there, Alec Baldwin comes out and opens the envelope and what do you know – he reads out 'Alan Carr'. Well, I am in shock. I really did not believe I would ever win a Comedy Award and of course I didn't have a speech prepared. I mumbled something drunkenly, can't really remember what it was and Alec kindly guided me off the stage.

Believe it or not, that's not the worst speech I've ever done – check out the National Television Awards 2015.

Oh boy, that is a humdinger and it's not even as if I can blame the alcohol – I was sober as a judge. I genuinely thought Graham Norton or Jonathan Ross would win, but when Mel B opened the envelope it was my name she read out. Again, I had no speech prepared and as I walked up the stairs I couldn't think of anything, nothing at all. *Chatty Man* was speechless. All I had in my head was that Mark Ronson 'Uptown Funk' tune, going round and round. At the podium, lost for words, I pointed at Dermot and heard the anticipation as the O2 waited for at least one witticism or reference to the night's proceedings, but nothing came out. In complete fear I performed an excerpt from 'Uptown Funk', but it wasn't 'Uptown Funk' at all – it had morphed into the advertising jingle for FunkyPigeon.com. What the hell was I thinking?! It was so embarrassing and I shuffled off.

Anyway, I'm getting ahead of myself – that was 2015, let's get back to 2008. So I come off stage and then because I am a winner I have to do press. 'Doing press' is when you get led into a room full of journalists who ask you a whole load of questions about the night. One journalist says to me, 'Alan, that speech was a bit rubbish. It's the Comedy Awards, you're meant to say something controversial!'

'Oh no, I'm so not controversial.'

'Say something – go on.'

Hmm! What could I say? 'Come home, princess' swam through the Sauvignon Blanc and my eyes lit up. 'I dedicate my award to Karen Matthews, she's my inspiration. I would love to meet her one day. Karen, this award is for you.' Everyone laughed – it was ridiculous, stupid, who in their right mind would dedicate their award to someone like that? I carried on working the room and answered all the questions as best I could and then staggered home, totally oblivious to the storm that was a-brewing.

The next day I went to meet Justin in Camden and there waiting for me was a scrum of journalists. Now how did they know I would be there? It's only after recent events involving Justin that this question has raised its ugly head. No one knew I was going to be there, at that place at that time except for me and Justin, but they were waiting for me – strange, wouldn't you say? Anyway, this didn't even cross my mind at the time, I just thought that after my win the previous night my star had risen so sharply that from now on I would have a constant swarm of paparazzi every step of the way.

'Do you have anything to say?' asked one journalist, thrusting a tape recorder into my face.

'About what?' I asked innocently.

'About your dedication to Karen Matthews?'

'Oh, it was a joke,' I said. But they kept probing so I dashed into the toilet for some peace and it was only then that I checked my phone and saw numerous missed calls from my agent. He was furious.

'Did you just dedicate your award to a woman who stuck her kid under a bed?'

'Yes, but it's not what you think . . .' Still, he wasn't impressed.

It all escalated very quickly – I was mentioned on BBC news and I even got a mention on that red stripy thing that travels across the bottom of the screen giving you the most-up-to-date stories. (I don't know about you but

I never seem to catch it at the beginning on those looping news reports – I always get the arse end of the sentence so I'm like 'Who's died at the age of 102?' 'Who's resigned for taking part in a sex tape?' and then I have to wait what seems like for ever for it to snake itself round again.)

An apology was issued by someone, somewhere – it definitely wasn't from me, as far as I was concerned I was innocent – but it all calmed down. Apparently an apology makes it all better. The apology even got on the news, I couldn't believe it. I'd never been the centre of attention like that before, it was all too exhilarating – but as always with news, people naturally moved on to other stories and before you knew it I was chip paper. Still, that was enough for me, I'd had my fill. It was quite a change for me to be seen as edgy or a bit of a loose cannon – it wasn't really me though, I like the quiet life. One positive that did come from it – and I suppose I must really thank the journalist who caused all the furore – was that the sales of my DVD and book, *Look Who It Is*, available at all good car boot sales, went through the roof. I guess that old adage is true: 'All publicity is good publicity.' I can see now why people like Madonna and Lady Gaga like to create this media storm – the benefits are endless. So there you have it, and if you see me in the coming months at an awards show dedicating an award to Rose West then you'll know that the sales of this book haven't been as impressive as one would have liked and someone's look- ing for a cheeky boost.

Being in the limelight, you can see why so many famous people are messed up, or to be more polite 'have issues'.

You spend a worrying amount of time in front of a mirror, in my case a dressing-room mirror. I swear over the years I have seen every wrinkle creep across my face – there are so many now that my face has started to resemble a jigsaw. When you're not sitting there scrutinizing your reflection, you're dressed up as someone else, and for someone who has body-image issues and who really – and I mean really – doesn't like the way they look, the dressing up and being someone else can actually be a blessed relief. But sitting in front of a mirror, whether it's before *Chatty Man* or a stand-up show, is an absolute hell for me. I've watched myself age before my very eyes and it hasn't been pretty. So to sit in that make-up chair and become someone else is a real treat and, sad as it seems, I actually get excited about it, especially if they've thought about it and there's a budget. Of course, sometimes there are photo shoots with no budget – I recall one in particular for *New* magazine where I was dressed as Tippi Hedren and then whipped repeatedly with crows on sticks for a whole afternoon in a *Birds* pastiche. Don't ask me why, I have forgotten/blanked it out.

Heat magazine do great photo shoots and even when my schedule is busy I always make time for them. They are a nice magazine with a heart. There's none of the malice with them that you get with other magazines – they always put what you say and they don't twist or manipulate things. They are fully aware that I say enough shit and have enough drunken rants on Twitter to get myself into trouble, thank you very much, without them having to make stuff up. *Heat* have always been really supportive of me, even when some of the shows I've done haven't started so great; they knew I would get it right and gave me a chance and for that I am thankful. I started dressing up for them – God, I sound like a high-class hooker – with *The Friday Night Project* and since then I have been everyone; well, it feels like it anyway. I always make time for their Christmas edition where we recreate an iconic celebrity photo and over the years I have been Madonna, Anna Wintour, Paris Hilton, Lady Gaga, Kim Kardashian and let's not forget Lauren Goodger – do you see that, NO men, and you wonder why I have body issues. Last Christmas I had to recreate Madonna's fall at the Brits, where I'm sure you can recall she was yanked off the stage by her own heavy-handed minotaur. I spent the whole afternoon dressed as a matador being pulled down some stairs – unlike Madge I had a very comfy crash mat to land on, but still, what a way to spend an afternoon. *Heat* are so pernickety with the shot being an exact replica that every detail is painstakingly checked.

'Oh, darling, I think her right ankle was just a smidge to the left – could we do it again?'

'Of course,' I mumbled as I slowly ascended the stairs to await being pulled off (thank you, thank you, get your mind out of the gutter).

The Kim Kardashian photo shoot was a hoot. We were recreating the selfie of her (I know, that narrows it down), the one where she is wearing a very unforgiving white swimsuit showcasing her truly truly scrumptious derrière. This all seems so tame now because since then we have seen every part of Kim, tits, fanny and a very oily arse, but anyway, kids, I didn't have a time machine so bear with. Anyway, there I was in my *Chatty Man* dressing room in this tiny swimsuit with a gusset like barbed wire going right up and splitting my difference. As you'd imagine, I felt very exposed and it didn't help that the dressing-room door had to be held ajar due to the mass of equipment being used. Anyone walking down the corridor could see me and comment – and they did. 'Disgusting. I've seen some sights in my time but that takes the biscuit,' said Paul O'Grady, mock horrified, with the parting shot, 'And I've worked in a brothel in Manila.'

I was cross-dressing for *Heat* even as early as 2006, when they had suggested that me and Justin recreate Abba's *Greatest Hits* album cover, the one where they are sitting on the bench, all autumnal, one couple looking pissed off and the others necking like two love-sick teenagers. Justin would be both Agnetha and Bjorn, and I would be Frida and Benny (of course) and we would re-create the scene. It was a lot of fun and after a few goes we found that we had achieved the perfect re-creation, it was spot on. We changed back into our ordinary clothes but just as we were about to step into our waiting taxi we heard the photographer calling us back: 'Alan, Justin – wait!' Something had slipped through the net; well, not the net as such, but the knickers. It seems Frida had opened her legs a bit too wide and her/my testicles had come out. Everyone hovered around the computer, giggling and pointing. I don't know how they could have been seen – on the album cover she has her legs closed tightly and she's wearing a long skirt, but maybe they do hang low. Anyway, it was all very embarrassing – we were in our own clothes now, our make-up had been taken off and we had another important engagement to go to – the pub probably – and we couldn't possibly get re-dressed as Abba, so I had the humiliating fate of having my bollocks Photoshopped – don't worry, reader, it's not as painful as it sounds. That could have been my first and only full-frontal magazine spread – thank God for the eagle-eyed photographer.

My dressing-up became so frequent that I started recognizing the actual wigs on telly. I'd be watching *Where the Heart Is* and all of a sudden I'd go, 'Wait a minute, I wore that wig as Rula Lenska.' Sometimes the dressing-up wasn't even culturally correct – when we went to the Notting Hill Carnival with Cilla Black for *The Friday Night Project* my outfit not only got the wrong country, it was the wrong continent. When you think of British West Indian culture you don't normally conjure up an image of a man dressed in a glittery slit-to-the-waist dress with high heels and a bowl of fruit on his head. I got so many frosty looks I was lucky I didn't get a cap in my arse or at least bits of fruit shot off my headpiece. They had promised us our own *Friday Night Project* float but this never materialized and in the end we were balanced on a wooden palette on top of an ice-cream van. Poor Cilla Black, no spring chicken herself, had to be fireman-lifted on top of the ice-cream van and then simply clung on for dear life as we went around a housing estate in west London – we didn't know if her legs were quivering from the mode of transport or the bottle of Moët she'd necked before the filming. One thing I learnt from that episode of *The Friday Night Project* was that Cilla drank a lorra lorra champagne – and good for her. Sadly, most of the footage was unusable; infuriatingly, any dialogue recorded atop the ice-cream van was either drowned out by various PA systems – 'Here me now, here me now' – or the music of steel pans. It was one of those ideas that had probably sounded brilliant around the table in *The Friday Night Project* office but once put into practice was a health and safety nightmare and not as much fun as it should have been.

Whenever I dress up I always like to keep a 'trophy' – a little memento of the day and who I've been – so as you can imagine I have quite a substantial dressing-up box which gets wheeled out whenever we have a party. I've often come downstairs the morning after, hungover, to find a high heel or a nun's outfit hanging from a light fitting. On one occasion, unbeknownst to us, a Cilla Black wig went AWOL – well, when I say AWOL, my red setter Bev had eaten it during the night, but I didn't know this. It was only once we were over the park and she was having her morning poo that I saw these ginger matted fur balls coming out from between her legs. I did a double-take and screamed, 'Shit – she's having puppies!' It was only on closer inspection that I noticed one of the 'puppies' had a 'Do not boil' wash label attached to it and I realized her litter was actually my Cilla wig. Thank God for that! Ironically, her having puppies made me have puppies.

As I'm writing this now in a hotel room in Buxton, Cilla is back in vogue but for the saddest reason possible – she died of a stroke last week and her funeral is on every front page whilst her *Greatest Hits* CD is back at the top of the charts. One of the blessings of doing my job is that you get to meet these legends before they go, you get to see first-hand why they have made such an impact on our lives, why they were so loved. I'm instantly reminded of when Robin Williams graced the *Chatty Man* sofa. What a lovely man; he was everything you wanted him to be and more, so nice to everyone backstage – and I mean everyone – with charm by the bucket-loads. I think of Amy Winehouse too. Me and Justin had taken the piss out of her on numerous occasions on *The Friday Night Project*, plonking on a massive beehive and screeching 'BLLAAAAKKKE' at every opportunity, so when she died, I did feel a pang of guilt. We hadn't known she was that tormented and ill, and if we had maybe we would have treated it all differently, I don't know. I guess we'd sort of bought into that 'panto drunk' persona that the media had painted of her, with endless photos of her looking the worse for wear and then photos of those bloody ballet pumps disappearing through a cat flap in Camden when she'd lost her house keys. She actually did keep losing her keys – I had dinner with her once in Balans and she suddenly patted herself down, said, 'Oh no, I've lost my keys,' and phoned up a Camden locksmith. It was almost like they were expecting her call – she didn't even have to say her name.

Of course, sometimes you meet celebrities that – how can I put this nicely, hmm – that you never want to meet again. Now we all have off days and I know what it's like sometimes in this business, you can't just switch it on, you can't. Believe it or not there are days when I just want to mince around the house in a poncho and jeggings, eating a family pack of Monster Munch. But Avril

Lavigne refused to even come out of her dressing room to perform – she refused. Point. Blank. She would not come out. The door had to be smashed down and she was forced by her management to perform. She stomped on stage, scowling. Do you remember in *Corrie* when Tracey Barlow would say 'I'm going upstairs to play me tapes' and stamp upstairs – just like that she was. 'It's Avril Lavigne, everyone!' we announced, full of our usual joie de vivre. Well, the look. Shade ain't in it!! You'd think I'd done a shit and wiped my arse with her album's sleeve notes. Like I said – maybe she'd just had a bad day. Mind you, even when Rihanna had her leg in a brace after a recent fall, then toppled over and got stuck in the ITV lift for fifteen minutes because no one could get her out, she was still all smiles and full of fun when she hobbled on to *The Friday Night Project* performance stage. She even made a foot brace look sexy.

One person who didn't like me and, I'm not going to lie, I didn't like him, was Hollywood action film star Steven Segal. He was the host on *The Friday Night Project* in early February 2007 and Justin was excited – I mean so excited. We first met him in High Wycombe, I kid you not. He wasn't in a TK Maxx or anything, he was performing at the Swan Theatre with his blues band and, to be fair, he was really good. Justin was a huge fan of his film *Under Siege*. Well, I'd never heard of it, and when I saw Steven in the flesh the only thing 'under siege' was his belt from his gut. The producers had met him beforehand and they had gone into his dressing room and found him reclining in his chair with a Japanese woman on her knees sucking his fingers wet and then slipping his rings on them. In the flesh the man is very imposing: he is huge, broad-shouldered, over six foot tall and very well-endowed – I know this fact because he kept telling everyone.

The Friday Night Project would always say to the guest hosts that if they had any ideas, whether it be pranks, days out that could be filmed or characters they would like to dress up as, please come forth with the information and we will do our utmost to incorporate the idea into the show because you are the host, don't you know. He had a great idea. Someone in the audience would stand up mid-show and say, 'Steven, I love you, please go out with me.' Steven would say, 'Sorry, I'm like Alan, I'm gay.' Then without any irony he continued, 'All the women say "no way" and start crying. I see them crying and say "only joking". All the women in the audience cheer and start taking their clothes off and dancing in their bras and panties.' Well, there was a stunned silence in the production office – 'Riiiiiight . . . hmm!' we all said. Believe it or not we didn't go for that idea because, well, we weren't in the 1970s.

He sort of got his wish though, because for the section called 'Ask Me Anything' (basically a question-and-answer session from the audience) he only wanted beautiful women to ask him the questions. We had to endure a weird casting of suitable ladies – all big-busted with dark hair. So if you're watching it on Dave or some other satellite channel and you're thinking 'Phwoar, that's a good-looking audience,' you have Steven to thank. He was adamant that we show a (long) clip of the first *Under Siege* – why, I will never know. The lean, muscular, chiselled Steven

Segal action hero kicking terrorists' asses on a ship was in stark contrast to the chunky, jowly man sitting in the studio with spray-on hair.

Although he wasn't particularly nice to me, his stories had me mesmerized. His life had been saved in Japan, he told us earnestly. His house was on fire and he hadn't realized – then a stray dog came into his house off the street and told him, 'Your house is on fire' (yes!) and he ran out. He leant in closer: 'And you know what, I never saw that dog again.' *No, because it was dead – you left it in the burning house!* I screamed on the inside. He also told us that he was reincarnated from a Native American chief (I've noticed that these people who are reincarnated never worked in a caff in the past, did they? Or as a rag and bone man?). He was always accompanied by a man who carried a bag. I later found out that the bag contained the 'magic' bones of a Native American chief and if they ever touched the ground they would lose their power. Well, I didn't have the heart to tell him that while he was filming I caught the man with the bag having a sneaky Marlboro Light in a doorway with the bag of magic bones at his feet – yes, on the floor!

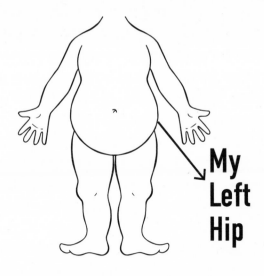

My Left Hip

Like Shakira, my hips don't lie. They ache, creek, bend and buckle. On stage I semi-affectionately call it my mincer's leg and like most comedy there has to be a grain of truth in it to work. And there's more than a grain. Some people will roll their eyes and go 'Yeah, yeah, mincer's leg,' but seriously, years of mincing has put so much pressure on my left hip that the pain has become excruciating at times and I've had to have physiotherapy. Ridiculous, isn't it? There was me growing up gay, terrified of contracting AIDs or of weekly visits to the Gay Men's Health clinic because we all lead such promiscuous lives, obviously – who knew it would be my mincing hip that would be the silent killer? I had been in pain for a while with it and, typical man, I had just soldiered on in ignorance until one day, walking up the hill in Crouch End, it went! My leg just went! Not into a shop or a Costa Coffee, I mean it suddenly went from under me. I fell down and my shopping bags dropped to the floor. I started rolling back down the hill but thankfully my back fat got wedged under a paving slab and I remained beached. It was so embarrassing and painful. Using my baguette as a staff I managed to grab hold of the nearby fence and pull myself up, then leaning on the fence as a makeshift bannister I hobbled back down the hill.

I should have got help ages ago when I first felt the twinges but now I really did need to get help. My over-active imagination was conjuring up images of amputation, so it was a relief to finally get to see the physiotherapist. He said that if I hadn't sought help then I would have ended up with a stick or a wheelchair. What?! I was in my mid-thirties! How much mincing had I done? You never really think you'll end up like that – maybe it's the naivety of youth but you assume people get old for a bet or a laugh, that they get up one morning saying 'Do you know what – today I'm going to shuffle. Yeah, shuffle! I'm sick of walking upright so I'm going to acquire a hump.'

The whole process of having your hips realigned is bloody painful, lying there in your pants as the physio pulls and pummels. I'd assumed he was going to massage through my jogging bottoms, but no, I had to take them off. Typically, I had the worst pants on – they were clean but a bit grey and baggy round the leg. It's the story of my life. Nice pants – my trousers never come off; crap pants – life will in some way create an ingenious ploy for you to lose your trousers.

I remember once, we were filming a promo for *The Friday Night Project*, and it was a huge affair. It was back when there were budgets to advertise TV shows; nowadays you just get a clunky montage but back then the adverts were made on film sets. For this one we had a Winnebago, catering, costumes, dancing girls, dancing guys, and the backdrop to it was a stately home. Well, to cut a long story short, the final scene of the day was Justin running through the grounds, Rocky-style, firing a machine gun with explosions behind him whilst I flew down on a wire dressed as a cheerleader. Confused? Good, because I was. It was all going to plan until Justin actually shot me with the machine gun – he fucking shot me! I screamed in pain, looked down and saw blood oozing out of my leg – at which point I panicked even more. As I was writhing on the floor, thinking 'I'm a celebrity – get this bullet out of me!' a hunky nurse on set ran straight over. Very easy on the eye, he was, which eased my pain slightly. Without a second thought he knelt down, ripped off my tights, stuck his hand up my skirt to stem the bleeding and gingerly removed the bullet from my milky thigh. 'Thank you,' I whispered, whilst surreptitiously filing the whole episode into my wank bank. As it turned out, it wasn't a bullet, it was a shell, but hey, I wasn't to know – something black and hard came out of the end of the gun and to me that's a bullet! With ragged tights and a bruised knee I had to remove the bloody cheerleader's skirt in front of everyone and, yes, you guessed it – awful pants.

Now I come to think about it, I don't have much luck with promos. We were filming the New Year's Eve *Specs-tacular* and I fell off the two-metre-high stage when I stepped back without looking where I was going. I fell on to concrete – the thud was so loud. The whole sound studio went silent and then everyone ran over. I couldn't get up as I'd landed on my bad hip. People buzzed around me asking if I was all right, someone brought water, someone laughably brought a crash mat – bit late, mate, bit late. I didn't cry in front of everyone but waited till I was in my dressing room and then I burst into tears and cried and cried and cried. I was so winded that I went into shock and the nurse on set gave me oxygen – in a can to suck on?! 'Beyoncé has the same thing when she comes off stage during costume changes, dear,' said the nurse warmly, rubbing my back as I vomited into the toilet.

You know all those television adverts, bumper stickers, radio announcements, posters, etc. saying 'A Dog is for Life Not Just for Christmas' that have basically never been out of our sight the whole time we've been growing up, yes? Well, my Paul must be the only person who has never ever come across these wise words as for our first anniversary that Christmas he got me a dog as a present and then the following June another dog – as a present. Two dogs, two years into a relationship, what was he thinking? I'd never wanted a dog. Don't get me wrong, I love them, it's just that I'd noticed it was always dog walkers who found dead bodies – have you noticed that too? Always on the news, someone walking their dog on some waste ground early one morning coming across a dead body. You never get that with cats, do you?

Of course, now I can't remember a time when I wasn't being dragged around the park at all hours, shouting 'Down' as they jump up to lick a child's Magnum, but back then I was dumbstruck when he said 'Surprise!' and held out a handful of red setter in my lounge. It had genuinely been a surprise because I hadn't even mentioned I wanted a dog – wait there, I hadn't even mentioned the word *dog* – and now after just ONE year of being together – you've got us a DOG!! For fuck's sake! Bye-bye freedom, bye-bye expensive holidays, hello dog-shit bags and hello dog-friendly B & Bs, ugh, I could taste the fur ball in the back of my mouth just thinking about it.

Red setters or Irish setters, whatever you want to call them, have an undeniable charm but are sadly not as popular as they were in the seventies. They've sort of been overshadowed by labradoodles, cockerpoos and jackadoos, or – as I like to call them – mongrels. Red setters *will* win you over whether you like it or not, they will, they are possibly *the* best dogs in the world – admittedly they are not the sharpest knife in the drawer but they have absolutely bucketloads of personality and an appetite that knows no bounds. The amount of arguments, confrontations and bare-knuckle fights I have got into because of those dogs you would never believe and more often than not food is the source of the tension. When it's a sunny day and it seems the whole of London has decided to picnic in Hyde Park, you will often find me apologizing profusely to a horrified family, handing them a fiver to get more sandwiches with one hand whilst scooping a Scotch egg out of my dog's mouth with the other.

I don't have a PA or an entourage, something Paul failed to realize before he bought me the dogs, and a word of warning if you are thinking of getting a setter: they need a lot of exercise and I mean a lot, in all kinds of weather. You will often see me walking my dogs with a scowl on my face, a bit like Pauline Quirke with her black Lab in *Broadchurch*. They are so hyper, even my parents make excuses now when I want them to look after them when I go on holiday. The first time we went abroad, my parents said, 'You go, go on, we'll look after the dogs.' I remember pulling up on their drive when we got back and seeing my mother's exhausted face appear at the window, then Bev jumped up, pushed her on to the floor and just stood there licking the window – my poor mother.

So with me and the dogs being social pariahs I often have to bring them with me as I can't bear to leave them alone in the house for hours on end, it's just not fair on them. I was doing a photo shoot in Wapping once and nature called for the dogs so I decided to take them out to the local park. On cue, unbelievably, Graham Norton comes into the park with his two dogs and all hell is let loose – our dogs hate each other. My two, normally so ditzy and carefree, were baring their teeth and salivating, and Graham's dogs, hackles up, were barking angrily. I often think it would have made a great pap photo – or an advert for a new Channel 5 programme, *Celebrity Gay Dog*

Fights. We both apologized for our dogs' behaviour and kept our distance in the park.

The dogs come down to the studio a lot when *Chatty Man* is on and with no unsuspecting picnickers to terrorize, Bev turns on my peers in her desperate search for food. She once ran into the *Loose Women* dressing rooms and nicked a plate of croissants. She doesn't care which channel either – on the *One Show* a good few years back when it was hosted by Adrian Chiles and Christine Bleakley it had been Christine's birthday and the BBC surprised her with a birthday cake. We all started with a chorus of 'Happy Birthday to you, Happy Birthday . . .' But we never got to finish it because just as the cake was plonked on the table there was a ginger flash, a gasp from the production crew and there she was on her hind legs tucking into the cake like Patisserie Valerie had made it Pedigree Chum flavour.

Mind you, the randomness of watching a dog on its hind legs wolfing down a birthday cake sort of fitted in with the randomness of the *One Show* itself. The talking points of that show are so disparate: the subject matter can veer from elephantitis to exercise bikes in the blink of an eye and the research chats before you go on the show are always entertaining. In one of these chats I was asked whether I had ever handled a bird of prey, visited Chile or fallen down a sinkhole. No, no and no. I felt like I was being ever so unhelpful but I hadn't done any of them – a pigeon had landed on me in Trafalgar Square once but it was totally unsolicited, I promise you.

It's not just birthday cake with Bev either – when our

lovely friends Sally Lindsay and Steve White were getting married down in Greenwich, Bev managed to get out of a locked car, run into the pub, belt up the stairs and take a bite out of the wedding cake before Sally had even had a chance to slice the bloody thing. Do you know how hard it is to yank a marzipan mini bride and groom out of a dog's mouth?

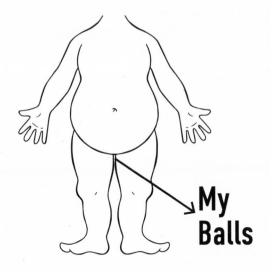

My Balls

I've done a lot that I'm proud of – my stand-up comedy tours, *The Friday Night Project* and *Chatty Man* – but there are definitely some shows that I would choose to forget. One of those is *Celebrity Ding Dong*. As *The Friday Night Project* was increasing in popularity, Channel 4 decided to give me my own show – a panel show, a game show, it could be anything we wanted. We all agreed that it should be Celebrities versus Civilians. Liz Hurley had recently in a magazine called people who weren't famous 'civilians' – I thought it was ridiculously stupid but could be a good hook for a game show, exploiting the perceived stereotypes between celebrities and civilians: that celebrities are self-serving, vain and sneery while civilians are uncouth, unworthy of even breathing the same air as Carol Vorderman or Lorraine Kelly and who left unsupervised would be nicking things out of your dressing room. My role as panel-show judge was to be a bit snide and contemptuous to everyone – a role which, looking back, wasn't really me. I felt a bit uncomfortable slagging off members of the public and being rude to celebs who I'd met outside of television and who were actually really nice.

I would see the laugh-out-loud *Celebrity Juice* on ITV2 with its anarchic games and feel that we had missed a trick. It was everything that *Ding Dong* wasn't – fresh, innovative and fun. I was in a grey suit and I'd put on tons of weight – it hurt when I walked because of my hip so I'd stopped doing any exercise, plus I was depressed about the leg and the show so I was drinking a bit more than I should. It just wasn't one of my finest moments and, hey, we all make mistakes. Maybe I'm being too harsh; in retrospect, there were some funny moments. There was a TV show on MTV at the time that was all the rage called *MTV Cribs* – it was basically a trendy *Through the Keyhole* set to a hip-hop beat. The viewer got an intimate look inside the homes of some of America's most successful and famous multimillionaire rappers and basketballers and got to be horrified at the huge amount of vulgar shite they had spent their many millions on. I watch that show with my mouth open, not in awe at the wealth but the actual revoltingness of the decor. Not only can money not buy you happiness, but also curtains that match and a front room that doesn't look like a bunker.

In one episode we found out that Missy Elliott had an actual car sawn in half for a bed – for God's sake, that's just wrong, and I've woken up in a car park a few times. Well, in homage to *MTV Cribs* we decided to do, wait for it, *MTV Crypts* – where just like *Through the Keyhole* we would subtly reveal clues to a celebrity, in our version a dead celebrity in an actual crypt, and the panellists would have to guess who it was.

The day of filming was a beautiful sunny day although I wouldn't get to enjoy the rays as I was six feet under in a crypt in a cemetery in Kensal Green, north-west London. I wasn't alone, however, I had a camera crew with me and Scouse spirit medium Derek Acorah and his spirit guide, Sam. Derek Acorah would go into a trance and through props and little hints would slowly reveal clues about a celebrity that had 'passed over'. The game was silly and I probably would have forgotten all about it by now if Derek hadn't had one of his turns. Mid-filming, Derek looked abruptly to the side and started a conversation with person or persons unknown, hidden in the shadows. At first I thought he was talking to a runner who'd inadvertently walked into shot but there was no one there. Whether you believe in that stuff or not, standing in a pitch-black tomb smelling of damp, with Gothic Victoriana greeting you at every turn and then hearing, 'It's all right, love, we won't hurt you,' to a 'presence' that you can't see would fill even the most steely-hearted cynic with fear.

'Who are you talking to?' I said.

'A woman over there.' He gesticulated to no one over

there. 'She wants to know what we are doing here.' He turned back to the 'presence'. 'It's okay, love. We're just filming a show called *Alan Carr's Celebrity Ding Dong.*'

There was a pause.

'She just walked off,' said Derek.

'Charming! Even the dead don't want to be on my *Ding Dong.*'

Throughout the shoot Derek got more and more dead people coming through, as if they were waiting at some spiritual turnstile, and of course when you think about it we were in Kensal Green Cemetery, which houses over 65,000 graves. In Derek's head it must have been a bit like a haunted version of Westfield on a Saturday, hordes of people in purgatory, shuffling trance-like in a daze, dead behind the eyes – no wait, just like Westfield on a Saturday.

Who is this now? I was thinking, slightly miffed, as Derek engaged in yet another conversation with a dead person. Normally it's a car horn or an overzealous member of the public that disrupts a shoot, not a visitor from the spirit world. After a while even I started seeing and hearing things; more than once I thought I heard the swish of a Victorian wench's petticoat behind me only to find it was Derek Acorah's mac catching in the breeze. Strange as it was, I started feeling less and less nervous. My eyes were becoming more adjusted to the dark and, besides, if it ever got too dark Derek's dazzling white veneers would twinkle at the end of the passage like a makeshift beacon, giving him the appearance of the Cheshire Cat in *Alice in Wonderland* just before he disappears.

Once Derek had spoken to all of Kensal Green's undead we eventually concluded the filming, mentally and spiritually knackered. We emerged from the tomb like some extras in the Michael Jackson *Thriller* video into the Kensal Green sunshine. It had been a lot of fun, and once it was edited and played on the actual show it proved to be one of the (rare) highlights. I often think *MTV Crypts* would have made a good spin-off for me; who knows, when I'm not so busy, maybe me and Derek could reprise our roles. Our chemistry worked well and he totally understood the ridiculousness of the show. Plus I'd never made so many friends on a shoot before – admittedly they were all dead, but still, friends are friends.

I was halfway through my *Ding Dong* series when Katie Price pulled out at the last minute (lucky cow – I wish I could have pulled out of it), so with an hour till filming we were a guest down. We were filming in the iconic BBC building, the doughnut one that is now sadly being turned into flats, and I had heard that Paul O'Grady was in the building. Well, when I say I heard Paul was in the building, I actually did hear him. I know I can talk but his voice is loud, it penetrates every wall and corridor – seriously, he's got a voice you could go fracking with! It was always hysterical when we were filming *Chatty Man* the same day as *The Paul O'Grady Show* as we would have adjoining dressing rooms and I could hear him having 'guest chats' with his producers, his dulcet Scouse tones pummelling the walls – 'And you can tell her to fuck herself if she thinks I'm promoting that shite.' That's the great thing about Paul, he doesn't hold back, and it was nice to know that chat show drama just before a recording wasn't exclusive to *Chatty Man*. Sometimes we would meet up afterwards. He'd pop over to the offie and come back with some booze and we'd drink, collecting unsuspecting passers-by, and rave or slag off our guests depending on how our shows had gone. So anyway, I asked Paul if he would come on *Ding Dong* and seeing that I was up shit creek without a paddle, and being the absolute superstar that he is, he stepped in at the last minute.

As I mentioned before, *Ding Dong* wasn't the best and sadly that show in particular was pretty dire. I felt bad because I was always made to feel so welcome on Paul's show and I loved going on it. I'd really wanted to repay the favour and give Paul a good time, but I could see he wasn't happy. As Oscar Wilde said, 'No good turn goes unpunished.'

I called up a friend and said, 'That show is doing my head in – do you fancy getting away? Mini-break?' Before you could say 'bureau de change', there we were in Heathrow at 'bag drop' preparing to spend a last-minute weekend mini-break in Vienna, Austria. Licking my wounds about the show and still embarrassed at the thought of how pissed off Paul must have been, I suddenly hear, 'Now how do you work this fucking thing?' slicing through Zone B like a chainsaw. I'd have recognized that Scouse drawl anywhere – yes, there was Paul in a trilby and mac, jabbing and scowling at one of those self-check-in machines, muttering profanities unsuccessfully under his breath.

To be fair to Paul, I hate those machines too – they're a hindrance more than a help, they're awful. I'm sure you've had the same annoying experience: first you put your booking reference in, then slide your passport (face down, mind) in the slot and then type in your flight number, only for UNABLE TO ASSIST GO TO CHECK-IN to appear on the screen. You want to headbutt the bloody thing. Mind you, if you did, given how temperamental they are, it would probably say ALL CHECKED IN, MR CARR, PLEASE PROCEED TO YOUR GATE. Anyway, Paul was visibly struggling. I went over to him, didn't mention, you know, the *D D* thing, and found out he was going to Vienna on the same flight as me for the same amount of time as me. Shit, he must have hated me for dragging him on the show and now we were going to have this awkward bumping into each other on the Ringstrasse. But do you know what, it's the best thing that could have happened because we met up and even went on the lash.

I went to visit him at his hotel, hoping and praying that his room just had a door knocker or a buzzer – I couldn't face a 'ding dong' announcing my arrival, let's not spoil a lovely evening by mentioning the panel show that dare not speak its name. If you've read his brilliant autobiographies you will know that with Paul there is always a drama. I found him standing on a chair having a drag on a ciggie out of the window, complaining about the hotel giving him 'Hitler's fucking bedroom' – it did look quite 'Third Reichy' with its austere and sombre decor and you wouldn't have been surprised if the eyes of the huge oil paintings that hung on the wall above his bed started to move and follow you around the room. It was a very entertaining weekend, but don't worry, I did give him some space. I wasn't one of those people you meet on holiday who cling to you like a tapeworm – 'So I've booked a sightseeing trip at ten a.m., then a museum at twelve, wine-tasting at two p.m.' etc. You end up leaving a pile of clothes and a note by a canal, faking your own death so you can have an afternoon to yourself. I'm so pleased we got to hang out as I'm a huge fan both of him and Lily Savage and I hope it went some way to repairing his feelings about his appearance on you know what.

There was one occasion when I actually got cautioned by the police on a *Ding Dong* shoot – no, not because it was shit, but because of an item we were doing in a local park. Let me explain. Do you ever look back on something and think how did it ever get to that? Wasn't there at least one person who was thinking maybe this is a bit wrong? Well, apparently not that day in the *Ding Dong* office. One of the games we played was 'Guess the Celebrity'. Dear reader, could you recognize a celebrity if he or she was flashed to you for a matter of seconds when you least expected it? Maybe, maybe not, who's to know. But would you recognize the celebrity if their face was stuck over my cock and I jumped out of a bush and flashed you by opening my mac? Hmm, maybe you're not so sure, but at least you can see where the police caution comes in. I kid you not, that was the game: me in a park, naked except for a mac, jumping out at people and flashing them and then asking the shocked member of the public to describe who they had seen on the end of my knob. Can you believe no part of that made alarm bells ring? None.

So like a lamb to the slaughter I headed off to Battersea Park. Took all my clothes off in some disgusting public toilets, and slipped on my beige mac while the poor runner, armed with some string and a glue gun, attached Arnold Schwarzenegger to my penis. There was an added frisson to the whole game as, unbeknownst to me, it was the school holidays and the park was teeming with children, so if I was going to jump out and flash someone, I would have to pick my moment carefully. I must admit, after filming this game I had a bit more respect for professional flashers, it's harder than it looks (which in itself sounds a bit wrong). I was told to wait in the bushes for someone 'unsuspecting' to walk by. Isn't anyone who is about to be flashed at by a complete stranger 'unsuspecting'?! Anyway, I saw my victim, a young woman walking through the park, and I chose my moment as she passed by – I jumped from the undergrowth and opened my mac. Did she guess who the celebrity was? Did she giggle? No, she called the police.

Thankfully, one of the policemen had seen *The Friday Night Project* so they recognized me, and knew that I wasn't a proper wrong'un. Once we pointed out the hidden cameras behind the hedge and up the tree, and the director emerging from a bush, the police were somewhat reassured – nevertheless, we were cautioned and told to pack up all our belongings and make ourselves scarce (inside I was relieved to stop – it had all been very humiliating).

Once an episode was recorded, it went into post-production, where they added all the bells and whistles, and one of those bells and whistles was the sound the buzzers made when a punter got the question correct. We had a little brainstorm about what noise the buzzers should make (yes, reader, when you create your own game show do remember that all these stupid little piffly bits need to be sorted and you have to make the decisions). Such days are infuriatingly long; firstly, it's boring, over-analysing the minutiae of a game show. What colour should the 'Ding' go if the answer's right? What about the 'Dong?' Black? Too sombre. Yellow? Too sickly. Green? Bogies! Sitting round that table you would think we were discussing how to create peace in the Middle East. But they really matter, all those little details like fonts, clothes and lighting, because they add an ambience that is so important to an audience – it can make or break a show. One thing we were sure of was that when an answer was right and the 'Ding' or the 'Dong' lit up we wanted comedy legend Leslie Phillips to say them. I remembered seeing him on a *Carry On* film once where a woman petrol pump attendant had stuck the nozzle of the petrol pump suggestively into his tank, he'd turned round in his open-top Jaguar and with a raised eyebrow said lasciviously in that wonderful plummy accent, 'Ding Dong!' It was perfect! Just perfect! I loved him and was a huge fan so I was double delighted when he said he would come to a studio, watch the show and sprinkle his Ding Dong over my Ding Dong. He sat down and watched the opening credits – I came out, did a wave and said,

'Welcome to Alan Carr's *Celebrity Ding Dong*.' Leslie looked at the screen with a scowl, then said, 'What the hell is this shit?' Well, like I say, you can go off people.

Looking back, though, maybe I should have taken his outburst as a premonition. Maybe it just didn't look good and maybe someone like himself who has graced our screens for decades can tell straight away if something isn't right or ever going to be right. The show plodded along for another series and then we put it out of its misery.

One show that did deserve another series was *Singer Takes It All*. It got slagged off a treat but I loved it. I loved it and I don't care. Now this is where I turn into one of those pushy mums who hangs around the school gates and will not have a word said against their kids. It was a show where members of the public sang live on a conveyor belt whilst people at home voted via an app on their mobile – if they liked them they moved forward on the conveyor belt, and if they went back too far they eventually disappeared through a smoky flap. That show was so much fun – it was live and I could ad-lib, something that I was doing every night with my stand-up comedy and which I relished – but people just hated it. The *Guardian* sneered, 'Is this the worst game show ever made?' and you know if the *Guardian* hate it you're doing something right!

But things went against us from the outset. If a game show is controlled solely by an app and that app goes down in the first minute then, yes, it is going to be a tough record, especially with an unchanged autocue on which every other sentence is 'and don't forget to vote using the app that you downloaded' . . . 'Er, oh yes, it's not working. Thank God this isn't going out live. Oh, it is – shit!'

It's a cheesy cliché but it's true – you never get a second chance to make a first impression. People just got it into their heads that the app didn't work so the show didn't work. Social media was in its element: with malicious glee everyone was loving the fact that it was failing – live! Interestingly, I spoke to a young writer who had penned a sitcom and he said how depressing it was to see that before the opening credits and theme tune had even ended, 'This is shit' and 'This is awful – I'm switching over' were appearing on social media.

Obviously I know I'm in a very lucky position being able to be part of a TV show, and I totally get that if you put yourself out there to big audiences then not everyone is going to love you or what you do, and that's fine. I just think it's sometimes a pity how quickly the negative comments come through on social media. I love getting feedback from audiences but I do think some things are slow burners, some shows evolve, and some things are worth being given a chance. *Chatty Man* was slagged off in the beginning (and still is in some quarters) but I have never won so many awards for a show in my life – it's up to sixteen series now, shown all over the world, and as I write this has been recommissioned for another two years.

The reviews for *The Friday Night Project* were so appalling that I went back to doing warm-up for the *Jonathan*

Ross Show, genuinely thinking, well, I had a go at this TV lark – I guess it's not for me. Jonathan Ross saw me by the side of the stage and said, 'What are you doing here? You're on the telly – you don't have to do this.' I was only pre-empting my eventual sacking which was surely just around the corner. The sacking didn't come and the show was recommissioned. It not only went on to garner two BAFTA nominations and a Rose d'Or but lasted a very dignified eight series.

I'm not saying 'Do not criticize me', please do – but be fair. Yes, *Singer Takes It All* was flawed but it was live and it was interactive, with the outcome controlled by the general public via an app – of course it's going to be flawed, it had never been done before. Ironically, if I'd trotted out yet another panel show with the same old faces it would probably still be running. Anyway, it's only telly at the end of the day – I took a chance and it failed, hey, it happens. It's the level of malevolence at my failure that was quiet disturbing.

I don't really know what's going to happen to Twitter. I wouldn't have got involved in it if I'd known there were people who would dish out rape threats and death threats to those who dared to disagree with them, and the perpetually offended who care more about a missing apostrophe than a missing child. I came off of it last year as it was affecting my mood and I was starting to lose faith in the general public – I'd switched on my phone and read 'I wish you would die of AIDS' at 7.30 in the morning. Listen, I'm not exactly a morning person either, but at least I wait until after my Coco Pops to send death threats. Right, that's it, I thought, I'm coming off.

Anyway, I was busy working on my Yap Yap Yap tour. It was the tour that reinstated my love for people, gave me back a bit of perspective, a bit of that old-fashioned human interaction that we've relied on as a species for thousands of years. There is a reason why when teenagers are coping with anxiety and depression they are told to get off social media – to get out there and interact with proper humans. We have lots more in common than we are told to think.

I look forward with interest to see what becomes of the government's 'Reclaim the Internet' campaign, because something obviously needs to be done. The anonymity of Twitter can turn the public into 'the mob'. I was the victim of bullying at school but at least when I left the playground it stopped; sadly, due to social media, the bullying now follows young people back to their bedrooms and home life. It must be the worst and I really feel for them.

Of course, not everyone on it is awful. I have had some wonderful conversations and laughs with a lot of people on there, and sometimes if you're a bit lonely and stuck in all by yourself you can strike up a conversation with a complete stranger just to pass the time and have a right old giggle. And as there are no IQ tests to set up a Twitter account the level of stupidity on there can sometimes make you smile. I think my favourite rant was when the *Chatty Man* set got a makeover. There it was, bold as brass on my timeline: 'You disgust me. How could you? I thought you liked animals. Using elephant's legs to hold up your coffee table – how low can you go?!' the angry tweet screamed. What? I rewatched *Chatty Man*, disgusted that this could have happened on *my* show — and burst out laughing. They weren't elephant legs, of course (do I even have to say this?), but freshly sawn tree trunks holding up the table top. Unbelievable! Let's hope we reclaim that internet sooner rather than later, eh?

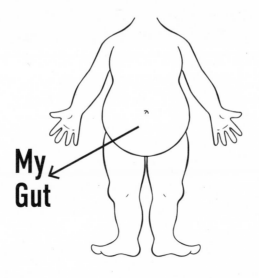

My
Gut

So what next? What next for little old me after *Ding Dong*? A few game show offers had trickled in but I didn't really want to go there again. *Ding Dong* had soured my experience of doing a game show. Besides, for me the best one had already been invented, the *Generation Game* – and, okay, maybe *Tipping Point*. Coming up with a new and exciting game show was like reinventing the wheel, and a lot of the time not so much reinventing as recycling. Who was it who said, 'Game shows aren't like lasagna; they don't get any better reheated'? Oh, it was me!

So a lot of people came to see me and pitched me some ideas whilst I sat in a revolving chair with my back to them, stroking a cat. There was a lot of shit, as you can imagine. Some were wrong for me, some were not my cup of tea, some were just insulting and some, it seemed, had only been thought up on the basis of a pun. 'TV funny-man Alan Carr jets around the world speaking to influential and famous homosexuals in foreign countries – we present to you *Around the World in Eighty Gays*.'

I actually did one pilot which I thought had legs, despite the fact that it relied on a pun. It was called *Hire Carr*, do you get it? I would do odd jobs for people who didn't have enough time or experience to do them themselves and of course it would be filmed with 'hilarious consequences' – we all hoped. Although I filmed a few things, they never saw the light of day. This family in south London didn't have time to take their children to swimming lessons as they had important meetings that day so would I be able to take their two boys to the swimming baths somewhere near Victoria?

I turned up at the house to collect them, full of the joys of spring, swinging my brand-new kit bag, excited for my new job and hopefully, fingers crossed, for my new series. So all three of us, plus camera crew, headed to the Queen Mother Sports Centre in Victoria. (Because when you think of naming a sports centre you instinctively think of the Queen Mum, don't you? 'Linford Christie? Sally Gunnell? Kriss Akabusi – no, I know, the Queen Mother. Boy, did she love a crosstrainer!') All was well as we filtered through the turnstile and headed to the changing rooms, it was only when I removed my top that these mild-mannered children turned into the spawn of Satan. 'Why have you got breasts?' said the littlest one, the question cutting through the chlorine-soaked air and rebounding off every tiled wall. Whilst I hissed for the boy to be quiet, the other one started whipping my bum with a towel – it was like being back in the school changing room.

My next job was to take a lady to antenatal classes as her husband was away on business. I don't know if this genuinely happens at antenatal class or whether it was set up for telly but I had to wear a very realistic bump and a truss to replicate the feeling of pregnancy. We sat in a semicircle on a rug and they placed a doll up inside the truss between my legs and I had to breathe whilst the wife comforted me with pats on the back. Then with deep breaths I had to try to force the doll out through the hole in my truss. It was very embarrassing, especially doing it in front of a group of genuinely pregnant and visibly unimpressed women. I heaved and grunted as best I could but, alas, it was a waste of time as it never got shown – the sight of the baby's head coming out midgrunt from between my legs was apparently too 'graphic' and 'upsetting'!

It's about getting the right vehicle and also about seeing if you can work with a particular bunch of people. Sometimes you will just have a feeling that it's not going to work but then sometimes you'll get on swimmingly and it will be something totally out of your hands that scuppers the whole pitch.

I went to one meeting about a sketch show that would obviously involve a lot of dressing up. They all seemed very enthusiastic and the meeting was going very well until my eyes caught something written on one chap's notepad: 'Check if he's still fat?' Well, that went down like a cup of cold sick. Jabbing the notebook, I said to him, 'Yes I am,' and wobbled out – finishing my pain au chocolat first, you understand, I'm not an idiot.

You also have to keep your wits about you because these sneaky production companies always try to sell an idea with a dream cast – 'Victoria Beckham, Gordon Ramsay and Prince Harry driving across America's Route 66, doing tasks picked by the public' is to me TV heaven, but obviously Alexander Meercat and that woman who put a cat in a wheelie bin going up the M6 . . . all of a sudden not so enticing.

I think I was badly miscast when they asked me to host the Q Awards, it so wasn't me. For a start, I had no idea who any of the bands were and when I did smile at them or wave I either got a scowl back or was completely blanked. Muse were nice and that's the only friendly conversation I remember. I've got no idea why I agreed to host the bloody thing, I'm hardly rock 'n' roll, am I – chubby calves that have never seen a skinny jean and a head too fat for a trilby. It must have been the money and, boy, did I earn it.

Weirdly, I'd had a good time on the previous occasion I'd gone when Kylie Minogue had asked me and Justin to present the 'Icon' award to her at the Q Awards. We got very merry, and my personal highlight was Sir Paul McCartney knowing who I was and giving me the old Macca thumbs up – to me, little old me. 'He Loves Me – yeah yeah yeah' I thought. As the awards finally started winding down, I went to the loo and what did I see there sitting on the floor next to the toilet bowl but a Q Award.

Well I never, I thought. I picked it up and it had 'Amy Winehouse' on it. I finished my business and went to show Justin – 'Look what I found' – and in that befuddled grey area that lies between drunk and sober, right and wrong, innocence and guilt where that askew logic comes to the front of your mind and says 'Stand back everyone I'll take care of this situation,' I decided to keep it. I've never owned a Q Award before and with it being Amy Winehouse's I thought it would be a collector's item. As I left, all the paps outside started clicking. Triumphantly, I waved the trophy aloft, shouting, 'Look, I've got a Q Award!' and me and Justin went off to a pub as we always did. Then we got the phone call from the organizers – had I stolen Amy's Q Award? Apparently I was the last person to be seen with it.

'Er, er, pardon?' I said, playing for time as I scanned the pub for a vat of acid to destroy the evidence. 'Well, I wouldn't say *steal* as such . . .' Then I caved in and gave it back. Yes, I was the proud owner of a Q Best Album Award for forty-five minutes until it was cruelly taken back and given to its rightful owner.

We had Amy Winehouse on *The Friday Night Project* and she was so much fun, such a laugh, ready to throw herself into anything. We had to re-enact some sex scenes as part of the panel show item. I did the 'Wheelbarrow' with Amy whilst Justin did the 'Reverse Italian Chandelier' with George Galloway. Justin's position didn't go well and he slipped and ended up grabbing George's cock and balls – George walked off set disgusted at being manhandled. Me and Amy won by default and can I say we gave wonderful wheelbarrow. To think that my nose was at one point resting on the top of that now iconic beehive makes me burst with pride.

Well, hosting the Q Awards was a whole different kettle of fish. Meatloaf came on and being a big lad myself I ignored his profuse sweating – it was hot up there under the lights and there was no air. Then he started swaying to and fro and suddenly toppled forward. I ran from the podium, grabbed the fringing on the arm of his leather jacket and yanked him back. As I have said many a time in my life, thank God for fringing. If he had dressed conservatively he would have been dead and so would the guests at the table at the front. I assumed he was pissed and made a quip about it. I was then taken to one side during a Duffy VT and told it was medication and jet lag, *not* alcohol, so I felt bad. The whole thing was a horrible experience and not only did I not get asked back, I didn't even get a Pride of Britain Award for saving Meatloaf's life. Charming.

Another ill-fated pilot I did that I in no way regret and would do again in a heartbeat was *The End of The Pier Show* for Channel 4. It was a game show filmed in Blackpool, you guessed it, on the end of the pier. It was rubbish and the only saving grace was my co-host Lionel Blair. Sorry, Justin, but I have never worked with anyone before or since who has made me laugh so much. And don't be fooled by his image – underneath that perfectly coiffed hair is a mind jam-packed with saucy anecdotes and rude jokes that would make even Roy 'Chubby' Brown blush. We filmed one sketch where Lionel and I had booked into a B & B, the joke being that we were both oblivious to the fact that the B and B stood for Bisexual Brothel. The scene opens with us both sitting down for a full English breakfast and as the waiter turns round we see that in fact his trousers are bumless. So far, so camp. All Lionel had to do was stick a fork in the Cumberland sausage, unzip the mouth of my gimp mask and shove it through. Don't ask why I was wearing a gimp mask, but anyway, this sausage-shoving took thirty-six takes – thirty-six! I didn't even have any lines, I just kept convulsing with giggles – a sketch that shouldn't have taken more than twenty minutes took over two hours because I was shaking with laughter. There were actual tears coming out of the eye holes (probably not for the first time). I'm even chuckling as I write this and I'm thinking that I must try to find that clip – maybe I'll put it in as an extra on one of my stand-up DVDs.

The End of the Pier Show was going to be the first television show filmed at the end of a pier and I was to travel the length and breadth of Great Britain to different piers (with Lionel Blair, of course), entertaining excited holidaymakers – well, that was the plan. Whereas on *The Friday Night Project* we had a studio and all the technology that comes with a studio to hand, for *The End of the Pier Show* pilot everything had to be imported to Blackpool, and as we didn't have the luxury of multiple stages, the poor audience sitting on deckchairs had to wait for the stage to be set up. It was soon beginning to dawn on me that there was a reason why this kind of show had never been done before!

After one very long day of filming and sketching, me and Lionel were enjoying a drink at the end of the pier

when a man rushed in. 'I need help, quick, quick, someone is hanging off the end of the pier – he's trying to kill
himself!' Well, the man's eyes scanned the bar and for
some reason stopped on me and Lionel. Really? We were
hardly Batman and Robin. Am I really the best person to
go and talk someone down from a pier? I've hardly the
most soothing voice, have I? Anyway, we both ran to the
end of the pier and there was a man hanging off the end,
shouting, 'I want to die, I want to die!' Thinking back, it
all happened so fast, but the one thing that does stick in
my head is that his clothes had been neatly placed in a
pile next to his shoes, which were paired up. We spoke to
him calmly, my body not once betraying the adrenaline
that was bubbling up and down like a SodaStream. Slowly
the man came round and he thankfully decided not to
end it all. We reached out, grabbed his hand and pulled
him over the railings to safety. The police were called and
he was taken away without even the mention of a Pride of
Britain Award for me and Lionel. Charming! We were
inundated with calls from the local press, wanting our
take on the prevented suicide – we even got asked to go
on *BBC North West Tonight* to give our side of the story.
I'd never been a hero before (or since!).

Well anyway, as you can imagine, *The End of the Pier
Show* soon ended up 'The Bottom of the Bin Show'. It
never saw the light of day, and although I hadn't given the
audience the gift of laughter at least I gave a stranger the
gift of life and if that means you decide to nominate me
for a Good Samaritan-style award, so be it. I also made a
friend in Lionel and the year after we kept in touch – he
came to one of my shows and I went to see him do his

wonderful ballroom-dancing show at the Birmingham Hippodrome. We went out around some bars afterwards and ended up at the Nightingale nightclub. The music was so loud in there that Lionel found himself gesticulating for a drink — I couldn't help thinking that if he couldn't get himself a large gin and tonic from miming after umpteen years doing *Give Us A Clue*, then there was no hope for me.

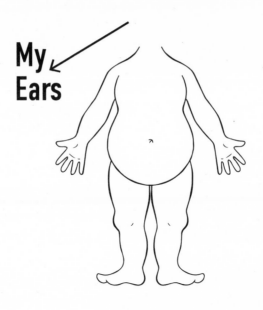

My Ears

Although *The End of the Pier Show* didn't work out, it wasn't long before I found myself back up in the Vegas of the North for my radio show. Radio 2 had decided for a weekend in September to up sticks from London and travel the 250-mile journey to Blackpool. It felt like a real Radio 2 family affair; lots of shows were being recorded live from there including the Chris Evans show from the Tower Ballroom and there were concerts with people like Paloma Faith, JLS and Pixie Lott; but more importantly, I had been asked to turn on the Blackpool lights, which was a real honour for me. As a teenager I had come up to see the Illuminations with my family as a treat and if anyone has bothered to read my previous autobiography they will know that this was a real reversal of fortune; I had lived above a launderette on the seafront up there and an illumination of Father Christmas had filled our bay window for months, so to be able to follow in the footsteps of such greats as Dale Winton, Julie Goodyear and Frank Bruno and switch on those very lights, well, who was I to decline?

It was blustery and raining heavily on the evening I did it – I know, who'd have thought it – but it didn't dampen the huge Blackpool crowd that had come to see me do the all-important 'turning on'. I'd known it was rainy and windy before I even left my hotel room thanks to the lack of insulation around the window frame; the fringes on my table lamp were swinging violently and every so often my face would be sand-blasted by a gust from the Golden Mile. It was a relief to get outside on to the seafront away from the breeze in my bedroom.

Blackpool definitely knows how to party and I dare anyone not to have a good time up there. I ended up, naturally, at the Flying Handbag, Blackpool's most famous/ notorious/iconic/scariest (depending on your own viewpoint) pub, which was a bit naughty as I was doing my radio show *Going Out with Alan Carr* the next day with my original co-host Emma Forbes.

Lovely Emma had never been to Blackpool before and I don't think she realized what had hit her. When I lived in Manchester we'd often headed to Blackpool for a night out, swigging tinnies on the train and lubing ourselves up for the anarchy that would ensue, so at least I knew what to expect. Emma and I weren't doing the radio show in a studio, oh no, we were going to do it on a tram – around Blackpool. We sat in a car by the tram tracks waiting for our transport to arrive and ferry us along the newly illuminated illuminations. As we waited, a pissed-up hen party staggered towards us holding a bottle of wine – well, it was half four in the afternoon. Spotting Emma in the back of the car, the bride-to-be lifted up her tutu (yes, you read that right – tutu), pulled down her knickers and squashed her arse cheeks against the rear window. 'Emma, welcome to Blackpool!' I cried. What an introduction! Not a minute too soon the tram finally arrived and we leapt on board. It had turned out rather nice – the tempest that had pebble-dashed my face the previous night had subsided and the evening, dare I say it, seemed quite pleasant. It was very strange to think that I would be communicating to the whole of Radio 2 whilst on a tram hurtling around Blackpool. People lined the tram tracks and waved and halfway along we picked up Mika, who sang us an acoustic rendition of his hit 'Love Today'. As if the whole day wasn't surreal enough, I was dressed as Olive from *On The Buses* and Emma was Blakey – there had never been a spin-off called *On The Trams*, hence the homage to another mode of transport. It was a lot of fun and after being cooped up in the studio most weekends it made a nice change to be getting some fresh air down the iconic Golden Mile. Mind you, we couldn't relax too much due to the sudden blasts of static from the tram that occurred sporadically above our heads, showering us with sparks like acid rain.

I definitely earned my broadcasting stripes that day, replacing 'shit!' for 'shoot!' and 'fuck' for 'flipping hell' at a moment's notice as I patted the burning sparks down on my porcelain skin.

Once back from Blackpool we had a change at Radio 2 – we had to lose Emma Forbes, which was a shame, and she was eventually replaced by Melanie Sykes. Like with Justin before, there is always that slight worry about whether or not you are going to get on with your on-air partner – is that chemistry going to materialize there and then, creating entertainment gold? You meet up with potential co-presenters usually for a spot of lunch or a cup of tea at the production company's office in full gaze of the bosses and producers who are scrutinizing you, a bit like zoologists do with pandas on a mating exercise. Well, what can I say, we not only mated, we multiple-orgasmed together. She was great. If you've ever heard the show you will know that we are both down to earth and turned out to have the same sense of humour – double entendres, single entendres, we would be in bits. After a rather unsuccessful juice diet I once pronounced live on air that 'I was just gagging for something solid in my mouth'; this was enough to propel Mel into a fit of uncontrollable giggles, while I realized how rude it sounded and gesticulated wildly to the producer to put a bloody song on pretty bloody quickly before we got taken off the air by Ofcom. It was strange to think that I had made my first ever TV appearance with Melanie on *Des and Mel* on ITV years ago. She had seen how nervous I was and made me feel so welcome and I will always be grateful to her for that. So although 'Alan and Mel' did feel a bit weird, it also felt right.

Working with a partner evens the workload – no, scrap that, working with a GOOD partner evens the workload, it gives you companionship and a shared experience. It's not for nothing that people equate good conversation with a game of tennis – with a good partner you always get the ball back. When you're on the radio by yourself it can be like a really hard game of Swingball. I did a Radio 2 Christmas show single-handedly a few years before and can I just say I have so much respect for those radio DJs who do their shows alone, especially the ones on the night shift. It is so difficult to just talk, to let the words fall out of your mouth and disappear into the ether hoping that some of them will make a connection with a listener. I hated doing it by myself. Everyone goes, 'Oh, Alan, you're so chatty, you can talk to anyone you can,' but they should have heard that Christmas special. 'Yes, it's Alan Carr and you're listening to my Christmas Day Radio 2 special. How are you doing?' No reply – obvs (to be fair, if I'd had a reply that would have been schizophrenia and that would have been worrying). Wishing I'd got an imaginary friend to talk to, I started flailing; seeing my ashen face, the quick-thinking producer thankfully popped on Mariah's 'All I Want for Christmas is You'.

I blundered through what was essentially a two-hour monologue, saying anything that came into my head, and I mean anything, anything to kill the dead air. I was pleading with the producer not only to keep cramming the airways with Christmas songs but to pop on the twelve-inch versions, anything so I didn't have to talk. Finally the two hours came to an end and I had survived – just. I had talked about everything; every minute detail of my life had been revealed at length. The only thing I hadn't revealed was my PIN number, I think, although there had been that awkward link before 'Rudolf the Red-nosed Reindeer' . . . anyway, like a lonely precursor to Twitter, I had an opinion on everything and didn't hold back. As I left, the sound engineer said to me he'd never heard Myra Hindley mentioned in a Christmas broadcast before; I got my coat.

So to share the studio with Melanie was a godsend and a real treat, and although our shift was 6 to 8.00 p.m. on Saturday evenings, what we lost in social life we more than made up for in giggles and friendship. I think the reason it worked was our attitude and honesty. Unlike other partnerships on radio, we weren't always 'up' and effervescent, we would often tell the listeners what we were going through and how we felt; if we were in a bad mood, hungover or quite simply didn't want to be there we didn't hide it. It was always inclusive, it was never snide, and the 'banter' (God, I hate that word) I hope never felt forced. We often got criticized for giggling but in our defence it was genuine giggling – we did get along and enjoy each other's company, and besides, that was the Radio 2 remit: a fun, upbeat, humorous show, crammed with ABBA and other disco faves that people would listen to as they got ready to go out clubbing. That was the idea, though in reality it was listened to by people like myself, sitting at home, uncorking a bottle of red, wearing a slanket, waiting for the cottage pie to cook. Hailing a cab and getting off their heads in some club was probably the last thing on their mind.

As always, it's the regular listeners who make the show. Reoccurring themes kept popping up, the listeners kept us informed about what they were up to, and it felt like one big family. Me and Mel seriously had a ball and on the odd occasion we would go out afterwards for a drink, the giggles would continue. One morning I remember waking up with a sore head and seeing Melanie's moon boots at the end of the bed (it was that winter when London finally got snow). I thought, oh no, I haven't – have I? I was so relieved to find out that the lump under the covers next to me was my red setter Bev and not Ms Sykes. She was asleep in my spare room. Sometimes we didn't wait until the show finished to have a drink. There was one evening when – for some unknown reason – Radio 2 had decided to plop the BBC New Comedy Awards nominations slap bang in the middle of our show, so we had to vacate the studio from 7 to 8.00 p.m. and return to the studio at 8.00 to continue our last hour and announce the winner of the New Comedian of the Year. Well, most professional broadcasters would relax for an hour and go through the script, prepare various talking points and potential music choices – oh no, not us, we went across the road to a taverna for a bite to eat and a carafe of wine. Why does carafe sound so much posher than a bottle? Whatever receptacle you drink it from, you're still going to get pissed. We were fine and dandy in the tavern, necking our wine and chowing down on our calamari and meatballs, it was only when the cold air hit me that I turned into Oliver Reed on *After Dark* – I couldn't speak properly and I'd acquired a limp. This could only mean one thing: someone had spiked my calamari. It was a nightmare, it would have been better if me and Mel had just come clean and said that we were tiddly; it's when you try to hide your drunkenness that you start acting weird, your speech gets slower and you over-enunciate everything in a valiant attempt to show everyone that you are so sober you can pronounce everything amazingly. My ears were deceiving me though, I was slurring, and in my panic to appear sober had gone blind and could not even pronounce the name of the winner of the BBC New Comedian of the Year.

I must apologize to the winner, it was unbelievably unprofessional and I wish you all the best – you deserved better that day. If it's any consolation, I won the BBC New Comedian of the Year in 2001 and look at me – just think, in fourteen years' time you too could be on the radio, pissing on some other young comedian's dreams, forgetting their name and drowning out their finest hour with slurred speech and drunken waffle.

Amazingly, we didn't get fired and our show carried on; they still gave us things to do and unbelievably trusted us. One show we had to go to live was the *Last Night of the Proms* where Dame Kiri Te Kanawa was performing in London's Hyde Park. I was to introduce her over the tannoy to thousands of her fans who were waiting for the wonderful dame to grace the stage. Even though we had been doing the radio show for a year by this point, I was so nervous – it was the thought of talking to such an elitist crowd in such a public place. When the producer pointed at me to start the introduction I could actually hear the hubbub of the Hyde Park crowd in my headphones. I took a big gulp of air. 'Now, ladies and gentlemen, it's the *Last Night of the Proms*, please welcome to the stage Dame Kiri Teknackerwacker.' What? Shit! Teknackerwhacker? Oh no, no, no, no! Stop, stop! Block, block! Everyone's going to think I'm a moron. Maybe I was, after that display, maybe I was. I was told later, thank God, that due to a few minutes delay they had shaved off my Dame Kiri Teknackerwacker and had just left it as 'Now, ladies and gentlemen, it's the *Last Night of the Proms*.' I don't know if that's true or not, I daren't listen to it again. Hopefully, she didn't hear about it.

I could kick myself sometimes. It's not the 'live' thing that bothers me – I do stand-up comedy most nights – it's the 'Live – NOW!!!!' thing that freaks me out. I remember I was the guest announcer on *Ant & Dec's Saturday Night Takeaway* a few years back and I swear I nearly fainted in terror, what with my legs shaking and the ringing in my ears, and all I had to say then was 'It's Ant and Dec.' I can go on stage and do stand-up for two hours at a time, no problem, but as I said, it's the 'Live – NOW' scenario which ups the ante to unbearable levels.

Doing radio has in recent years been spoilt by the totally unnecessary addition of webcams to the studio. I believe that radio is aural and should remain aural. What is this fascination with watching every going-on, every sip of tea, every shrug, in my opinion the drab nuts and bolts of making a radio broadcast? To me the joy of radio is to join the dots with your imagination, to conjure up your own scenarios. I love doing Grimmy's breakfast show, and his predecessor Chris Moyles's, but those web-cams take no prisoners, especially when your call time is 6.30 a.m. The great thing about radio is not giving a monkey's fashion-wise, turning up in your trackie bs and Uggs – now, thanks to the all-seeing eye, you end up getting called out like it's *Fashion Police*. On Radio 2 we had a webcam installed and for the whole two years Mel and I could not get our heads round the idea that we were being watched – all the time. On one occasion Mel had come in, sat down and said, 'What do you think of my new bra?' lifting her top up triumphantly.

'Mel!' I screamed, pointing at the webcam. With a squeal, she yanked her top down – yes, it was a lovely bra but this wasn't the time or the place. Listeners would phone in to the show and on one occasion the caller had gone on for far too long and we needed to play some music pronto; I drew my finger across my throat to the producer indicating that the call should end soon and it bloody frightened the life out of me when the caller said, 'I saw that!' Damn you, webcam!

I loved doing the radio show but eventually I had to admit that I had taken on too much, as I always do. I found that having to sacrifice every Saturday was a bridge too far, all work and no play and all that. I was missing out on so many things, and I don't care what you say, everything important happens on a Saturday: birthdays, weddings, christenings, you name it. My friends would ring up, trying to organize a cheeky little weekend city break, and before they'd even finished 'Barcelo—' I'd interrupt with 'NO! I'm working.' Also, my parents are getting older now and I don't want to be skyping them at their birthday parties because I'm too busy working – again, there is more to life than work, right?

I even had to shoehorn my brother's stag do around the radio show – now that was a weird day. Being a good brother, it was my job to organize his stag do and as most of his mates lived in Northampton and rarely came down to London I thought I'd give them the whole London experience: open-top bus around London, beers on the bus, see all the sights, big old boozy lunch in a London pub, a whizz round the London Eye, panoramic photos of London, bish bash bop. I would then do my two-hour radio show, and join them afterwards for a slap-up dinner followed by a nightclub, boom, day complete, everyone has fun, I'm the best brother in the world.

I met them all at their Holiday Inn, and even though it was only midday I could tell they were already pissed. Nevertheless, they all piled on to the open-top double-decker, me responsibly counting everyone on like I was a supply teacher on a school trip. The chanting started as soon as the bus set off; every turn of the bus warranted a manly roar and every traffic light stop got a 'BOO!' Although they were told specifically not to bring alcohol on to the bus they had somehow smuggled it on and they would swig it when I wasn't looking – it seemed I had taken on the role of humourless, law-abiding team leader. The more they drank, the rowdier they became. We made our way through Notting Hill, stopping for a drink (or three) at the Cock and Bottle (I had water, thank you very much), then we went up through Bayswater, along Hyde Park and past Buckingham Palace (which got a big cheer – who knew all my brother's friends were such huge royalists?). It was only when we approached Big Ben and Parliament Square that things started to get really vocal and, dare I say it, political. Protestors have always chosen to camp on Parliament Square due to its proximity to the Houses of Parliament and the chance to flex their democratic muscles in full view of the MPs and, with any luck, the prime minister. Well, once the busload clocked the tents and the white people with dreadlocks, their hessian clothes, sandals and dogs on strings, a chorus of 'have a wash, have a wash, have a wash' was suddenly struck up. I hit the floor quicker than Madonna at the Brits. The protestors must have shouted something back because one of the lads on the bus replied, 'Yeah, you! You soap-dodging twat.' I crawled along the bus floor, trying to get my brother's attention, yanking the hem of his trouser leg violently: 'You have to stop this – I'm on the telly.'

The traffic is always shite near Parliament Square so we had to spend an excruciating fifteen minutes in a traffic jam as the protestors and my brother's friends exchanged insults, the protestors a few minutes ago so angry about the Middle East, now so angry about a stag do from Northampton. Thankfully, we left the world of politics behind as we crossed Westminster Bridge, and we were all set to go on the London Eye. It was a confined glass box that rotated on a giant axle so the chance for mayhem or confrontation was surely limited. I looked at my watch – it was approaching 2.30 p.m. My radio show was on at 6.00 p.m. and I liked to get there for 5.30 at the latest to prepare with Mel what we were going to talk about, the music we were going to play and have a good old gossip before we went on air.

So we had three hours to go round the London Eye, that was more than enough time, easy-peasy. We could have thrown in a matinee performance of *Cats* to boot and still had oodles of time, plus I'd already bought the tickets so no annoying waiting at the box office for us, oh no – when big brother Al sorts out a stag do, it's queue-jump tickets all the way, baby!!

The double-decker pulled over once we got to the South Bank, we all disembarked and the bus driver probably took some tranquillizers and wondered why he hadn't taken the day off. We headed straight to the London Eye. With one eye on the clock, I was relieved to see that the queue wasn't too big, and before long we were tantalizingly close to the turnstile where we would board our pod. As you can imagine, security at the London Eye is paramount what with it being such an obvious landmark and as we were queuing I was aware of a smattering of security guards keeping a watchful eye on the proceedings. Just as we were about to step into our pod, a security guard spotted one of the lad's bags.

'What have you got in the bag there?'

'A bomb,' came the reply.

As me and all my brother's friends were yanked out of the queue and walked to a holding pen by two security guards, I couldn't help thinking how easy my life would have been if I'd been an only child. After forty-five minutes in the pen persuading the security guards that we weren't from Islamic State but were in fact from Northampton, Rose of the Shires, they let us back in the queue. Time was seeping away due to the detention, but as long as the pod didn't break down I could still make it.

By the time we eventually got into our pod, the mood in the group had moved from tipsy rowdiness through to hysteria and confrontation, culminating now in lethargy and an urgent need to use the loo. As the pod door closed and we started our ascent, one of the lads said, 'Is there a toilet on here?' Unbelievable! What do you fucking think? I thought, looking around at the pod – unless that seat is a commode, then no, I'm afraid there is no toilet on here. The boys, now desperate for a wee – thank God it was only a wee – started relieving themselves in some paper cups they had found on the floor. May I remind you all that the pods on the London Eye are completely see-through – I could see tourists in other pods pointing and taking photos. I didn't just want the ground to open up and swallow me, I wanted the pod to snap off, plummet into the Thames and get washed away to somewhere, anywhere, away from here.

The pod finally completed its laborious rotation and I couldn't wait to get out – not because I was horrifically late for my radio show (which I was) but because the constant weeing had caused the pod to smell like a public toilet. I ran out, said I would see everyone later and hurtled across London to the studio. I made it – just! I raced through the door, leapt on to the swivel chair and, with a cue from my producer, started the show:

'I'm Alan Carr.'

'I'm Melanie Sykes,' said Mel and we were off.

Usually on a Saturday as I sit in that studio hearing about everyone's plans for the evening I get serious FOMO (fear of missing out) but that night, sitting safe within the confines of the show, cradling my polystyrene cup of tea, I embraced the two hours of calm and let my batteries recharge because I knew that at 8.00 I would have to head out again to finish off what had already been a hell of a day. I met up with them somewhere near Leicester Square in a sports bar and, as is always the way with daytime drinking, it wasn't long before a feeling of ennui took over and the evening turned into a more subdued affair. Thankfully, we ended up having a drama-free night. As it happened, the nightclub I had chosen as the climax of the day was having a lingerie fashion show to accompany the music – yes, it was one of THOSE nightclubs – which of course went down very well with the gang of lads whose eyes were now on stalks. They ordered some shots and I slipped out after an hour and let boys be boys. Of course, trying to catch a taxi from Leicester Square on a Saturday night was a ball ache – countless buses passed me but I felt that tonight I would rather get a taxi. Let's just say I'd had my fair share of being on a double-decker bus for one day.

My brother's wedding to Carly was a far classier affair. They got married in one of the most beautiful places in the world – Santorini, a tiny little island in the Aegean Sea. The ceremony was held overlooking the beautiful town of Oia, so beautiful in fact that the town has been recognized by UNESCO as a world heritage site. The village could pass a Daz doorstep challenge any day: every building is a crisp bright white, and the only relief from the whiteness is the blue roofs and cupolas that dot the cove, complementing the blue of the sea. It's so pristine and classically Greek that it is often the inspiration for mouthwash and yoghurt adverts.

We spent a really lovely week there, exploring the island on quad bikes, overdosing on feta and drinking ouzo. Every pamphlet and Santorini guidebook raves about its warm thermal baths and the accompanying health benefits, so it was at the top of my family's to-do list. Who doesn't want to feel replenished for the big day? Who doesn't want healthy glowing skin for the wedding photos? Who doesn't want to have huge open pores the size of manhole covers once the wedding photographer points his camera and says 'Feta'? Or 'cheese' if we were in England. (I am not apologizing for that joke.)

To get to the thermal baths meant a short ferry ride to a surprisingly still-active volcano that after nearly two million years of activity has left a flat black hump protruding out of the water which from certain angles makes it look like the Aegean has a bald spot. We took the ferry to the volcano and, popping on our swimming trunks, gingerly shuffled down the side of the craggy path to dip into the thermal baths. I get it, I know the rancid smell comes from the sulphur, I remember that from my science lessons at school, but it hardly fills you with confidence when you see a mountain goat turn round on a ledge above, lift its tail up and do a shit, and said shit pinballs down the side of the mountain, finishing with a plop next to me and my family. I soon realized we were swimming in a goats' toilet. And as for 'thermal', I think someone on Santorini needs to turn the thermostat up. After five minutes I was begging for the goats to have a piss in it just to warm it up.

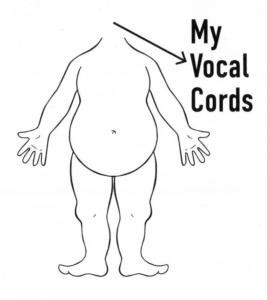

My Vocal Cords

One day my manager threw in a curveball – he suggested a chat show. Now, a chat show had never really crossed my mind. Doing *The Friday Night Project* I'd found I'd drifted off listening to some of the guests tell their anecdotes and thankfully a quick shout from my producer in my ear brought me back into the studio just in time to do a polite chuckle or a 'What are you like, eh?' Hmm, would I suit a chat show?

In the early stages of developing the chat show we toyed with ideas of how we get could get A-listers on the show whose tight schedules might not permit them to actually come to the studio but who would be willing to give us some of their time during the day. James Corden's hugely successful 'Carpool Karaoke' is a fantastic example of this. The A-listers can sing (and plug) their little hearts out without ever stepping foot in a studio; it is, no pun intended, the perfect vehicle for them. We hit upon the idea of having a flat-pack men's room that could be assembled in the blink of an eye wherever we wanted. I could leave my chat show in the studio saying, 'Ooh, I just need to use the loo,' go through the toilet door and, voila, come face to face with a (pre-recorded) George Clooney or Angelina Jolie washing their hands (I hope). I could have a little chat with them, plug their film, have a laugh and return through the toilet door back to the studio – an A-list interview in the bag, thank you very much. We liked the idea and thought we'd give it a go.

The problem was, we decided to do it with Marilyn Manson. Now, Marilyn Manson scares the shit out of me on a good day but a Marilyn Manson off his tits on absinthe and God knows what else doesn't bear thinking about. To say the interview was unusable is putting it kindly; not only was he slurring, staggering and sweating profusely, the interview was interrupted every few seconds with cries of 'coke time' followed by a knowing look to his manager. He was so twatted he couldn't focus, his one brown eye was so dilated and spinning that it looked like a Minstrel on a waltzer and, not only that, he mistook the pop-up men's room for an actual toilet and undid his trousers to take a piss. Look, I wanted the toilet to look as authentic as possible but the aroma I could do without. Marilyn then started telling a charmingly whimsical anecdote about his grandad's sexual proclivity for animal porn and we decided to call it a day. We canned the idea

in the end – who knows, it might have been a huge success if we hadn't tried to road-test it with Marilyn. It might
have been my 'Carpool Karaoke'. People might be having
water-cooler moments all across the country, saying 'Did
you see this week's *Chatty Man* when Alan bumped into
Barack Obama in the bogs – wasn't it just hysterical?!'
Well, you never know.

As I was leaving after the Marilyn interview, his PA
sheepishly approached me. 'I hear you have a Radio
2 show . . . I know this hasn't gone so well, but if I could
trouble you to maybe play Marilyn's new single or give it
a plug on your show, we'd really like that.'

I bit my tongue and said, 'Sure – what's it called?'

'"Arma-Goddamn-Motherfuckin-Geddon",' she said
with no hint of irony.

I thought, good luck with that one, love. We'd been
told the week previously that even Tina Turner's 'Steamy
Windows' was a bit risqué as it alluded to dogging. I wonder what Radio 2 would have said if I'd slipped 'Arma-
Goddamn-Motherfuckin-Geddon' on the old wheels of
steel – I dread to think! I said I'd do what I could to help,
took the CD from her and, once I was out of sight, slung
it in the bin. This helping each other out lark, it works
both ways, love, it works both ways.

These wacky added extras were all fine and dandy
but the fact of the matter was – could I even host a chat
show? Cut to me sitting in a draughty community hall,
my garden-centre chair slowly being carried around the
room from the reverberations of a Zumba class next
door. Surprisingly, the audience liked it and then after a
few more draughty run-throughs we progressed to a

pilot – thankfully, a non-transmittable one. Any budding TV chat show hosts out there, please always make sure your TV pilot is a non-transmittable one – it stops them putting it out on the telly and, believe me, you do not want that bobbing up on one of those *Before They Were Famous* programmes like an unflushed turd.

Guest-wise, the pilot was all right, as pilots go. We had the late great Ronnie Corbett and my old mucker Gok Wan. Gok was the perfect choice of guest, a friend who would support me, who was also warm, funny and nice, and who knew how much I needed this pilot to work. It was Ronnie Corbett I was worried about – this man was a legend, someone who I had grown up with and enjoyed watching all my life. Of course, with a chat show you are going to meet your heroes (hopefully) and you need to prepare yourself for that. I can't remember much of the pilot, it sort of went by in a blur and I daren't look back at it as I'm too scared to see how awful I was. I know that at the end of the Ronnie Corbett interview I said, 'Give a big thank you to Ronnie Barker – sorry, Corbett.'

'You did that deliberately,' Ronnie snapped.

'No, I didn't,' I responded truthfully. To be fair to me, we had previously been talking about comedy partnerships and I think my brain, seeing the end of the interview in sight, must have clocked off early. So if you *are* thinking of becoming a chat show host and want some advice, remember not to call the interviewee by their long-time dead comedy partner's name. Another bit of advice is don't forget to give your interviewee enough of your attention, which is easier said than done – you have to be looking at the next question on the autocue and at the same time keep listening and have an opinion on what that person is saying. It's an awkward balance to get right. There have been times when I've been so interested in the follow-up question that it looks like I've got a lazy eye, or worse, the producers have talked in my ear over the interviewee's answer – then you just have to do a nondescript smile and maybe throw in a nod. If the audience laugh then you laugh, but don't laugh in isolation – they might have said something really sad. 'Well, at that moment I knew I had to turn the life-support machine off.' Hysterical laughter. That's not the best combo.

The first show eventually came about and as usual I was a bag of nerves. Our first guests were Sir Bruce Forsyth, Heather Graham and Ross Kemp, with music from the Pet Shop Boys, and we already knew we had Katy Perry chatting and performing for the second show – not bad, eh? Of course, none of the anxieties that had kept me tossing and turning in my sweat-soaked bed sheets arose: no one died, the set didn't catch fire, none of my guests choked on a rogue glacé cherry poking out of their pina colada – of course not, why would they? As it happened, not only had my nights of anxiety been sleepless, they had been pointless because the show went swimmingly. The opening credits rolled and I just stood there, gained my composure, walked down the stairs and did what I had been doing all my life in call centres up and down the country – I chatted.

Interestingly, I have just got back from the 'Just For Laughs' Comedy Festival in Montreal, Canada, where I was doing my Yap Yap Yap tour and it turned out to be a very rewarding experience. It's an international festival and it attracts not only the biggest comedy names from all over the world but comedy lovers from all over the world too and sitting in the bar after my show hearing Canadians, Kiwis, Aussies and South Africans approaching me and saying how much they enjoy *Chatty Man* and retelling their favourite moments from the various series makes my heart fit to burst. Remembering those early days, 'I'm not good enough' ricocheting around my brain, the worries, the anxieties, and here I am thousands of miles away, years later, talking to someone from another country celebrating *Chatty Man*, well, it's a delight, and if anyone reading this is nursing an ambition to be a comedian or a presenter or otherwise needs any more reason to follow their dreams, then I tell you, *go for it* – because if I can do it – you can.

Anyway, seven years earlier, away from the comedy love-fest that was my 'Just For Laughs' experience, at Channel 4 we were trying to conjure up a successful chat show. Look, the first series of anything is always fraught with glitches and gremlins and of course you can have brainstorming sessions, flipcharts and focus groups till you're blue in the face but only when it has been put before an audience do you get any idea if you have done the right thing. So you have to iron out any problems in the full glare of everyone's eyes and once they see you changing things they get a whiff that things are wrong and you are lost.

The creative types at Channel 4 came up with a brilliant advertising campaign for the start of *Chatty Man*.

The campaign went under the banner 'Born to Chat' and featured a child that looked like me, styled in the fashions of the seventies and filmed in a retro living room that actually looked remarkably like our genuine living room at Lowick Court in Northampton. The child would chat incessantly, demonstrating that from an early age I was 'Born to Chat'. All we needed now was to find a child that looked like me and, hey, we were in business. My friend who works at Channel 4 casting went out to find the little Alan. Finding no child that looked like me down the usual casting routes (I must have one of those faces), she decided to throw her net wider and scour the Arndales and shopping centres of south London to find my young doppelgänger. It didn't go well – after she approached one woman with a bespectacled child, saying, 'Ooh, he looks just like Alan Carr,' the insulted mother gasped and told my friend to 'fuck off'. Everyone she approached to ask whether their offspring would do an advert for a new chat show because they resembled my good self either gave her abuse or walked off in a huff – the situation was hopeless and I had to be called in to a studio at the last minute and have my own face superimposed on to a child's face. I spent a whole day with adhesive spots on certain points of my face which directly correlated with certain points of the mystery child's face so they could be swapped with ease. Although at the time I was pissed off at the inconvenience, the finished advert is absolutely brilliant. It was cute and sinister in equal measure and got some lovely positive comments. It was even nominated for an award. With that whetting potential viewers' appetites, I did the usual slew of chat shows to publicize my own, then recorded the first show and just hoped for the best.

After the first episode came out, the ratings were great – at least people had tuned in to see whether they would like it or not. I think it's fair to say though that viewers didn't exactly fall in love with it and that depressed me. Here we go again, I thought, *Chatty Man* is going to go the same way as *Celebrity Ding Dong* – two flops on my hands in direct succession. I went up in the loft and brushed off my Barclaycard call centre headset, Ashford & Simpson's 'Reunited' playing in my head as I looked down at it sadly. I went up to see my parents in North-ampton to get out of London, have a bit of TLC from the folks back home. And then, out of the blue, I got a boost from an unexpected source, one voice of cheerfulness in a cacophony of boos. I was at Weston Favell Shopping Centre with my parents, helping them unload their trol-ley, when the phone went – I didn't recognize the number and thinking 'pissing PPI' I didn't pick up. It was only when I got home and sat down with a cuppa that I lis-tened to the message – it was Brucie!

'I just wanted to say how much I enjoyed being on your show and can I just say I think you have a hit on your hands.'

Well, it was just the tonic, what a lovely thoughtful gesture – totally unnecessary but so needed by me, and I will be for ever thankful to him for that message. Maybe it wasn't as bad as people were saying. Sir Bruce seemed to have had a good time and he's a TV legend, and do you know what, that was good enough for me.

He has been on the chat show several times since and

he is always such a good sport. I had the honour of sharing a dressing room with him at the Royal Albert Hall in 2012 for the Royal Variety Performance. Me, Brucie, Jimmy Tarbuck, Des O'Connor and Ronnie Corbett (who thankfully had forgotten Ronnie Barker-gate from the *Chatty Man* pilot) were all in one room. Sharing a dressing room with all these legends was very humbling for me, plus one of those very rare occasions where I was the youngest in the room. It was genuinely one of those 'How did this happen?' moments. I had grown up watching these men on the telly and to be standing here in their gang with them recounting showbiz anecdotes and memories of Royal Variety Performances past was of course surreal.

They wanted to watch the live feed from the television so they could see what was happening on the stage and they looked at me, being the youngest (did I mention I was the youngest in that room?), to tune in the television. I am a complete technophobe but I half-heartedly fiddled round the back and finally got hold of the right cable with one hand and with the other wiggled the aerial aloft. There must have been brief flashes of the performance on the screen because they all started oohing and ahhing, then groaning when I lost the signal. As I waved the aerial, no lie, Brucie was going, 'Higher! Higher! Lower! Lower!' I thought, is he taking the piss? If he says 'You get nothing for a pair, not in this game', I'll shove this aerial where the sun don't shine.

At one point they were all speaking about a certain celebrity who was, completely against his public persona, a complete pothead. Brucie turned to me and said, 'The trouble is, you young'uns think you're the only ones that do 'em.' I had to laugh; he was right. It's the naivety of (relative) youth. We always think we are going to be the generation that rips up the rule book and turns everything on its head but in fact these performers had seen it all, done it all and, in the case of this unnamed old-school celebrity, 'smoked it all' – THEY had lived.

I remember I had been smuggled into the back of the Royal Albert Hall earlier that night through the tradesman's entrance, not because I had a beef with Her Majesty but because I was a surprise performer in the night's proceedings. I had received a text from David Walliams months back out of the blue asking me for a favour. My curiosity was pricked, and I couldn't wait another minute, so I rang him. As it happened he was presenting not just any old Royal Variety Performance but the one-hundredth-anniversary show and he wanted to know whether I would do a comedy skit with him on the night. I absolutely love David and said yes immediately, but was naturally intrigued as to what he had up his sleeve. Ashleigh and Pudsey the dog had wowed the audience and the judges with their Flintstonesque performance earlier in the year on *Britain's Got Talent* and it turned out that David wanted to recreate that performance in front of the Queen. I took it all in – to be fair, there are some really impressive dog costumes and if I got it made in the right material I suppose it would be easy to move around in. 'I'm going to be Pudsey the dog,' David went on, 'and you're going to be Ashleigh.' Images pushed to the front of my memory of Ashleigh astride Pudsey wearing leopard-skin moon boots and a hip-skimming leopard-skin miniskirt – one false move and Her Majesty would see my bearded collie. I seriously wondered about employing a ball boy like they do at Wimbledon, so that every time my ball became visible below my miniskirt they could run across the stage, pop it back in my (probably leopard-skin) knickers and then run back to refresh themselves with a lovely glass of barley water. Ball boy or not, I really wanted to do it – it would be such an honour. 'When do we rehearse?' I said to David.

I do love the Royal Variety Performance. It's the adrenaline rush you get from rubbing shoulder pads with royalty and I think even the staunchest republican, given the chance to go backstage and feel the buzz, would be won over. It is ridiculously crazy. You have musical legends, stand-up comedians, opera stars, ballet dancers, magicians and animals all swirling backstage with one thing on their minds: *Don't mess this up – even if every other gig I do is an abject failure, please let me at least get one laugh!* I mean, seriously, if you did mess it up – God forbid – it's not like it's just confined to the theatre. You get a dirty look off Princess Anne, so what, who cares, but as you know, this show is televised. You could become a social undesirable and never work again – the stakes are high.

The last time I had performed on the show was in 2005 when I was an unknown, so really had nothing to lose. Thankfully, I had a good one and even got told by one of the Queen's entourage that Her Majesty had laughed at my Tesco Clubcard points joke. My first thought was, ooh, I wonder if I could put that on a poster? 'I LAUGHED' – THE QUEEN. My second thought was, how does she know about Tesco Clubcard points? Still, I thank you for the laugh, Ma'am.

I wasn't even listed in the programme for this performance so when I came on as a lacklustre Ashleigh and got such a lovely cheer it really did give me goose bumps – I've got so much skin showing, you can actually see them popping up. Anyway, it was a big success and we got lots of laughs. I packed up my stuff and went to go home.

'Alan, where are you going?' asked an officious young lady with a headset and clipboard.

'Oh, I've done my bit, I'm off home,' I said, unscrewing my ponytail and dumping it on the dressing table.

'Oh, I'm afraid not,' came the reply. 'It's protocol that everyone who performs on the Variety Show has to meet the Queen in the curtain call at the end.'

'But I've only got jeans and a jumper,' I confessed, pointing to my holdall.

'I'm afraid you're going to have to meet her like that.'

'What?!'

'Like that,' she said, pointing to me and turning on her heel.

If you look back at the curtain call for the Royal Variety Performance 2012, you can see me adorned in leopard-skin moon boots and leopard-skin miniskirt, with a ponytail now screwed back into my weave hanging loosely atop my head like a flaccid pipe cleaner. I'm standing in between the real Ashleigh and Pudsey and boy band supergroup One Direction. The Queen walked along the line-up of cast and crew, smiling that fixed grin she is so good at. She shook my hand and for a moment I thought she was going to say something, maybe, 'Oh, one did love that Tesco Clubcard joke – would one do it again?' but it never came and she glided off without a word, leaving Prince Philip to give me the most curious stare, which of course I don't blame him for – last time he'd seen so much leopard skin he would have pointed a gun at it and shot it.

One of the great things about standing in that curtain call is overhearing the conversations as Her Majesty goes down the row. 'And what is it *you* do? she asked Louis from One Direction. And then I felt complete relief – if she didn't know who Louis was, from THE biggest band in the world, after seeing them perform no less than an hour ago, then she would have forgotten about me a long time ago. Maybe I'd got away with it.

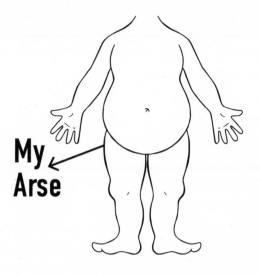

My Arse

You might be thinking we've already covered quite a lot of arse action – stop it – what with the rumpologist and my explosive Girls Aloud Christmas dinner. Well, this isn't about my bum – I'm sorry to disappoint – it's about an ever so slightly more infamous behind, one that can carry its own champagne and break the internet at the same time. Now you're with me . . .

I'd gone into the *Chatty Man* offices and heard that Kim Kardashian was coming on the show. Not only was she coming on the show but Kanye West had told her to come on the show, and not only had Kanye West told Kim to come on the show but he was going to be in the audience watching Kim actually be on the show. Well, my head nearly exploded as you can imagine. Kanye West in the audience – all that went through my mind was Kanye running on stage, grabbing the microphone out of my hand and shouting, 'Graham Norton should be hosting this show!'

I had first met Kanye on *The Friday Night Project* – in fact it was him choosing to do the show that really turned it around. All of a sudden people changed their attitude towards it, it became a cool show and celebrities started asking to come on. Obviously when you get a huge star like Kanye, you work around them, it's you who bends over backwards – so much so that we were walking around in the crab position. Normally we film a day with them but due to his unbelievably hectic schedule this proved to be difficult. His people came up with a suggestion: 'Why don't you and Justin fly in his private jet to Oslo to watch him perform the night before – would that be something that you would be interested in?' Errrr, let me have a think – now where did I put my diary? Hell yeah! A private jet, Kanye, probably Cristal, probably bitches, probably I'm going to have the best night of my life. Alan, you have made it! I rang up my agent and told him about my new and improved social life and that Monday I would be out of the country hanging with Kanye forshizzle.

'Monday. Monday you say?'

'Yep, Monday.'

'You've got that charity event in Soho for blind kids.'

'Excuse me?'

'Remember, it's a charity night, it's been in the diary for ages, mate.'

Damn! I panicked – 'Couldn't I just do an audio-tape recording of my act? They wouldn't know I wasn't there – they're blind.'

There was an unimpressed, judgemental pause. Then, 'The audience isn't blind – the money goes to a charity that helps the blind.'

I just said it. 'Fuck the charity, I'm out of here, get someone else to do it. I'm Alan Carr and I'm going on this goddamn private jet if it kills me.'

Of course I didn't say that – I honoured the charity commitment. Yes, that's right, if you are up there, God – I chose to do good, I put a charity first instead of myself – yes, next time you choose to make my mincer's leg flair up, remember that eh?

We always used to do sketches with our celebrity guests on *The Friday Night Project* and Kanye was no exception. We had written our own pastiche of one of his songs. We had the whole of Studio One and we blinged it up. I was wearing a gold lamé tracksuit with chains around my neck – I didn't look gangsta, I looked like a toffee penny – and we did our bits, rapping and generally mugging for the cameras, doing our rapper posturing, *brap brap brap*, etcetera, and then we waited and we waited for Mr West. Finally there was a buzz, he had turned up, and we could hear a commotion behind the set. Snippets of information trickled down to us. He would appear in the sketch but he would NOT allow his songs to be parodied – which was unfortunate to say the least as we had spent the whole morning performing 'Gold Dogger'. His song was called 'Gold Digger' – d'you get it? Clever, huh? Not only did we have to reveal to him that we were

actually doing a piss-take, ahem, homage to his international hit 'Gold Digger', we had to explain what 'dogging'
was! Do you want a side order of embarrassment with
your embarrassment, Mr Carr? His face was a picture.

The Friday Night Project team disappeared with Kanye
West's team and they had a discussion for about another
hour. I don't know what was said or what happened
but 'Gold Dogger' went ahead. He was bemused a lot of
the time – my voice when excitable can be a bit seagully
and the Americans didn't really understand Justin's
West Country twang so I don't think that actually helped
the situation, but the sketch was fun and everyone seemed
happy. I will always remember Kanye leaving the set
and overhearing him say to his manager, 'This show is
fake – I'm being *Punk'd*. I'm not falling for it – this guy
isn't real.'

Well, even after all that Kanye couldn't have been that
put off by me – maybe he still thought I couldn't be for
real – because he decided to come on *Chatty Man*, which
was such a thrill, and he didn't come alone, he brought
his protégé at the time, Mr Hudson, to perform their
new single 'Supernova'. Well, as you can imagine, we were
all so excited. The interview went really well although
maybe I had overdone my WKD measures because
Mr Hudson's voice had cracked and we had to take a little
break in the filming to warm his vocals up. Kanye was
using a vocoder so I couldn't tell what his voice sounded
like, but to be honest after a vat of WKD I actually sound
like I'm using a vocoder, or sometimes if I'm really pissed
I sound a bit like a shredder. Once Kanye had come off

stage my Paul cornered him in the green room and told him about our impending Californian holiday. They swapped emails and Kanye did say (and I have witnesses) that we must hook up. Of course, you mustn't forget, dear reader, this is the world of showbiz and people don't always mean what they say. It's why celebrities love air-kissing so much – *I want to kiss you, but not really, I'll just kiss the air around your face. Mwah mwah, darling.*

I was so excited about travelling to California. I'd been there before with my friend Catherine when I was skint – but youth hostelling it and sitting staring blankly at your washing finishing its spin cycle in the launderette is, I'm certain, not the kind of California Dreamin' the Mamas & the Papas sang about. It would be nice to go back there with a bit of brass in my pocket and maybe do something more exciting at night than watching my off-white smalls go round and round in a washer-dryer.

You'll be pleased to know the 'Sunshine State' did not disappoint and it proved to be one of our favourite holidays ever! We were advised to hire a convertible and drive up the 'PCH' – that's the Pacific Coast Highway to you – so that's what we did. What no one told us was that if we were having the top down we should apply copious amounts of sunscreen as even though it was thick cloud those harsh rays do filter through. No one had told me that my bald spot was coming into its own either so when we arrived seven hours later in San Francisco (seven hours – the PCH looked about an inch long on the map!) not only did I have the complexion of 'The English Patient', but my bald spot was so red and protruding that my head resembled one of the buzzers on *Britain's Got Talent*. Unbeknownst to me, we hadn't been driving a convertible but a George Foreman Grill with wheels.

San Francisco was everything I wanted it to be, but when I tell people this they assume wrongly that I love it because it's so gay. The gay area in fact is a very small area called the Castro and basically takes up a couple of blocks – don't get me wrong, though, it *is* very gay. We saw a man there casually walking down the high street naked with a cock ring and a balaclava – well, it was a bit nippy. No, believe it or not, it was the other parts (of the city – not the man) that attracted us. Being a huge fan of *Vertigo* I spent days following where Kim Novak's character would have gone in Alfred Hitchcock's masterpiece like a really really late stalker, so I obviously made a visit to the Palace of Fine Arts and that jetty underneath the Golden Gate Bridge where she tossed herself off.

We then travelled to Sonoma and Napa Valley, all sunscreened up, you'll be glad to hear. My skin had thankfully gone from beetroot to terracotta in the few days we had been in San Francisco. Sonoma and the Napa Valley are the cutest places you'll ever see and are famous the world over for their wines – or as I like to put it, Disneyland for pissheads. We'd be walking around a flea market in the square, minding our own business, and then we'd hear a 'psst psst'. I'd look round and my eyes would settle on a stuffed moose and I'd think, 'Alan – you must stop drinking.' But behind the moose there would be a vintner (posh word for winemaker) trying to get our attention, waving a bottle of wine and saying in hushed tones, 'Do you like Pinot Grigio?' Yeah – duh! 'Then follow me' – and we'd be off down some back street, all very clandestine, to sip some wine. It's like *Scarface* but with Sauvignon Blanc. We'd spend the whole day getting leathered and buying all their delicious wine, because naturally there's no such thing as a free piss-up.

It's dangerous being pissed all day, for health reasons of course, but also for making judgements when shopping. All over the Wine County there are these quaint little markets and fairs – I promise you, I'm not being paid by the Sonoma tourist board, it's just that they are really cute. Don't get me wrong, there is a lot of shit being sold too – if I'd turned up on *Antiques Roadshow* with this one-armed Victorian doll with matted grey hair Fiona Bruce would have pissed her knickers.

Feeling that mid-afternoon slump one day – that's what happens when you have your first 'tasting' at half ten – I went to relax by the pool (okay, I was face-down on the slats of a sun lounger to stop my head spinning), leaving my partner, Paul, shopping unsupervised. Next thing I know I'm being rudely shoved awake.

'What the . . .?' I groan.

'Alan, Alan, look what I've bought, oh my God, oh my God, I can't believe it – only twenty dollars. I rushed out the shop as soon as I bought it so she couldn't take it back.' As my eyes refocused in the Californian sunlight I could see Paul triumphantly holding up Van Gogh's *Sunflowers*. In Paul's defence, it was at least to scale.

'You woke me up for that? A bloody copy of Van Gogh's *Sunflowers*?'

'How do you know it's not genuine?' he answered back sharply.

'Well, firstly the real one went for over sixty million pounds and secondly, this one's got Van Goff written in biro on the back.' I mean, I know Van Gogh had some disturbing mental issues but give him his due, he could spell his own name.

Typical Paul, he digested this information and, still refusing to admit that he'd wasted twenty dollars, said indignantly, 'I'm going to get it valued.' He didn't. I think he had a quick browse courtesy of Wikipedia and saw that the chances of our *Sunflowers* being genuine were very slim – I noticed it wasn't packed in the car as we left our hotel. So we drove on, a painting lighter and sadly sixty million pounds poorer.

We spent the last few days of our holiday in a scorching Palm Springs. The place was almost other-worldly; all the colours seemed heightened and juxtaposed against the barren desert landscape and we couldn't really decide what to make of it as we walked the streets. Judging by its inhabitants, it seemed both elderly and yet full-on homosexual. Basically, if Sir Ian McKellen was a holiday destination he would be Palm Springs. Sad that our holiday was coming to an end, my travel wallet depressingly empty, my head full of memories, my suitcase jam-packed with dirty washing (you know the score), we decided to head to Melvyn's.

Melvyn's is a restaurant and lounge bar for ever associated with old Hollywood history. Frank Sinatra, Rita Hayworth, Debbie Reynolds and Liberace have all walked through Melvyn's legendary doors for a beverage or two; well, they can add Northamptonian National Treasure Alan Carr to that list now. It was like walking back in time – in a good way, not like walking into a British Home

Stores. If the Rat Pack had suddenly jumped on the stage and sang 'Ain't That a Kick in the Head' they wouldn't have looked out of place, if you see what I mean.

Something I did not know, which came as a pleasant surprise, was that Melvyn's is also where the Apple Martini was invented, or so the waitress told us, so of course it would be rude not to. I'd never had an Apple Martini before, so what an amazing opportunity for me to pop my Apple Martini cherry. Hmmm! You know how some people have a certain drink that when they drink it they go a little bit doolally tap? For example, with my friend Matt it's High Commissioner Whisky – he once picked me up and put me head first into a wheelie bin. Until that fateful night in Palm Springs I hadn't realized that my drink was Apple Martini. I don't know what Melvyn put in it but I turned big style – not only did my Apple Martini give me superpowers (superhuman stamina and a relentless appetite for more drink), it also gave me amnesia. I woke up in our chalet and at first I thought we had been burgled – the burglar had tipped the coffee table over, pulled my clothes out of the wardrobe and flung them across the room. I didn't feel good at all. I went to the bathroom, looked in the mirror and saw that I'd got a black eye – oh my God, I'd been in a fight. I went to the bed and rolled Paul over. His face was bruised too and he had what looked like the imprint of a flip-flop sole on his forehead. Unbeknownst to me, we'd had a fight the night before. After we'd left Melvyn's I'd turned into a wild man and lunged at my Paul in the street, attacking him with a Havaiana flip-flop. The only way he could get me off, he said, was punching me in the face. Who knew something as innocent as an Apple Martini would be for me like bath salts in a glass.

We went down to breakfast and were met by the frosty eyes of everyone in the hotel. It was only a boutique hotel so thankfully there weren't too many people, but there were enough combined glares to melt the ice cubes in our Tropicana. We had never had a fight before so it was all a bit awkward. We had meant to visit the Sinatra Estate where, yes, you guessed it, Frank Sinatra lived after visiting Palm Springs in the late 1940s and falling in love with it. Apparently there is a chunk missing from the sink where Frank threw a bottle of champagne at Ava Gardner – maybe he'd had an Apple Martini at Melvyn's too, who knows. But both being hungover and in a foul mood we decided to just stay put. It was sad that such a lovely holiday had ended on such a downer – and that feeling wasn't about to improve. We still weren't talking to each other until Paul, surprisingly, spoke (it's usually me that speaks first – well, I guess I am *Chatty Man*).

'Oh no!' he said.

'What?' I asked, pretending not to give a shit, suitably abrupt but with enough interest to glean the information from him.

Paul showed me his phone and there it was, an email from Kanye West.

Hey, are you guys in LA yet?

SHHIIIIIIIITTTTT! Oh my God, I didn't think he was genuine. Why would I think he was genuine? We were on our way to the airport.

'Shit, Paul, we've just snubbed Kanye West, one of the biggest stars in the world.'

When Paul had told me Kanye had put his email address in his phone I'd assumed he was just going through the motions, like you do – *I'll just pop you in my phone – yeah right – under AVOID!* We were so gutted. The only positive was that it had at least got me and Paul talking. Well, that would be the last we'd hear from Kanye, I predicted. Wrongly, as it turned out.

Which takes us back to the beginning of the chapter – it wasn't just Kanye coming on *Chatty Man* this time, remember, but his wife, Kim Kardashian, too. I was nervous, but a weird kind of nervous. When you're dealing with an A-list pop singer or Hollywood star you sort of know how to deal with them – you get on to their latest film or album, rave about it and have a bit of a giggle; sometimes if the guest warrants it you have a look at some of their earlier stuff for a bit of sepia-tinged nostalgia – but with Kim, what could I do? 'Let's have a clip of you – in your sex tape.' I can't see her getting all watery-eyed about that (although the penis was quite big). With Kim it was different, she was from this new breed of superstars, these media manipulators *extraordinaire* whose change of hairstyle can knock a terrorist attack off the front pages. Everything with Kim is so overblown you can't quite get your head round it, a bit like her bum.

She and Kanye turned up with hardly any entourage, in fact they were refreshingly low-key – no unicorns on their rider, nothing, they were a real pleasure. Not only was Kim really nice, she was unbelievably attractive; last time I'd seen eyes like that they were on Bambi. She was willing to have the piss taken out of her and she even asked whether I'd like to touch her arse – well, I had to, didn't I? It was like being asked if I'd like to meet the Dalai Lama. I approached it tentatively, as if a dangerous dog had a child's toy and wouldn't let go of it. How can I describe her arse? It was surprisingly firm to the touch, not unlike a Babybel or an Edam. I didn't probe any further, it was just a slight caress. I felt it would be wrong to finger, particularly when her slightly intense, hot-headed rapper of a husband was no more than ten feet away, sitting in the audience. If he'd got angry and stormed the stage the St John Ambulanceman laden down with barley sugars wouldn't have stood a chance.

Kim was introduced to the other guests, who included *Britain's Got Talent* winners Ashleigh and Pudsey the dog. Ashleigh started showing everyone Pudsey's tricks, including his most famous one when he stood on his hind legs and walked. We all stood up and then Pudsey gravitated towards Kim's arse, maybe mistaking it for a couple of juicy hams under a tablecloth – well, Kim grabbed my hips and we participated in a conga. It was fun and the audience just loved it. Little did I know that her people had stormed into the gallery demanding it be stopped. It wasn't in Kim's contract that she would be conga-ing with a dog – I mean, who has that written in their contract?

You usually find that these big stars are actually all right with most things and are game for a laugh; it's the people around them terrified of losing their jobs that implement these guidelines. I remember when we had Justin Bieber on and I was trying to break the Guinness

World Record for running in high heels – don't ask – and we were strictly told that he would NOT wear high heels and we were NOT to ask him under any circumstances. The word stiletto did not pass my lips but once he saw me breaking records with my killer heels, totally ad hoc he said, 'I want to try,' and to the delight of the audience he wore them and beat me – the bastard – ha! And it was the same when Kim conga-ed with Pudsey: the audience roared, Kim enjoyed the reaction, I enjoyed watching it and even Pudsey's lipstick came out, so it has to be said that EVERYONE had a good time.

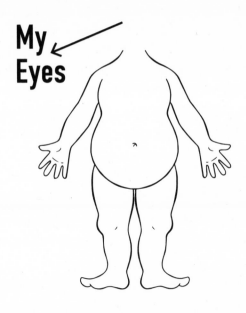

My Eyes

In 2009, after Paul and I had been living together for a couple of years, we decided maybe it was time to try somewhere other than Holloway. Instead of heading up and over the hill to Crouch End we thought it would be exciting to try a whole new area. Paul had some friends in Notting Hill so we'd had drinks and dinner there and it had won me over. It was also round the corner from *The Friday Night Project* offices where me and Justin used to mooch about getting a sandwich, and we would always see a celebrity. I remember a car screeching dramatically to a halt and Kate Moss jumping out and hot-footing it into a shop – it all felt so glamorous. Justin and I pressed our faces to the shop glass to have a look but we were waved away by the shop assistant – I don't know if it was because we were intruding on Ms Moss's shopping or because I had smeared a bit of my egg sandwich on the glass but we shuffled off nevertheless. Notting Hill had a definite allure, posh yet edgy, architecturally conformist yet bohemian in attitude. It's no wonder that it has been used as a backdrop for numerous films such as *Alfie*, *Performance* and, er, *Notting Hill*.

I really wanted to live there – it had been a dream of mine to live in a townhouse just like the ones in *Mary Poppins*. We started searching for our future home and after we cut through all the estate agent guff – compact (tiny), traditional (chintzy) interesting (dirty) – we finally found one on Ledbury Road. I was so excited – it was perfect. I loved the house the moment I saw it, what with its columned doorway, high ceilings and glorious sunshine flooding through the huge sash windows; big, chunky Victorian fireplaces only added to the appeal and the cherry on top of the cake was a roof terrace which was so high up that save for a couple of mean-looking pigeons it wasn't overlooked by anyone – it would be just perfect for my favourite hobby, naked sunbathing. I'm jesting, I obviously don't sunbathe naked – I strap my privates down and shove them in an empty Calippo tube.

I told the owner I would take it, we exchanged pleasantries, I complimented him on his beautiful abode and asked him what he did. Well, how was I to know it was cricket legend Mike Atherton! Yes, there had been a lot of cricket memorabilia, a smattering of bats and some trophies here and there, but it hadn't clicked, and as you all know, sport isn't my forte. Besides, I was house-hunting, not filming an episode of *Through the Keyhole*. If Mike Atherton's heyday had been before 1988 then I bet I would have recognized him. When my dad was trying to wean me on to sport in the early days he bought me the 'Question of Sport' board game the Christmas of 1988 and my admittedly limited knowledge of sport came solely from the picture round. Evonne Goolagong and Geoff Capes were like old friends, I could spot them a mile off, but anyone after 1988 I would pass in the street without a second glance.

Obviously if you are shallow enough to choose to live somewhere because it's been in some films and because you might get the chance to bump into supermodels in your local corner shop then the superficial sheen you've applied is inevitably going to start peeling off pretty sharpish. I had no regrets about leaving the Upper Holloway area although as we drove the removal van down the street I did see Dr Legg looking despondent, standing at the Crouch End clock tower in the rain outside a closed-down Woolies – it made me feel a bit sad and I wonder now whether it was a sign.

Things took a dramatic turn shortly after we'd actually moved in: we saw a woman get mugged across the road, and then the very next week as I walked home from the shops mid-afternoon, minding my own business, I came upon a woman performing a sex act in a driveway. I don't know what was more alarming, seeing the act itself or the fact she tried to strike up a conversation with me mid-bob – 'Isn't it getting cold?' Well, I think that's what she said, but she had a cock in her mouth. Her mother obviously never told her not to talk with her mouth full.

I winced, grabbed my pearls and carried on my way. I was beginning to see a seedy underside to this place I'd just moved into. I had thought I'd be rubbing shoulders with Gwyneth Paltrow, not rubbing out one with sex workers, but then again didn't that just serve me right for being a snob? Evidently Notting Hill was all fur coat and no knickers. I could either embrace the colourful street life or stand there tutting behind my nets. I decided to get out there and take it on the chin, a bit like the kneeling lady I'd had the pleasure of coming across just that afternoon.

I also found out pretty quickly that my wonderfully full sash windows on every floor not only let the sunshine in, they let prying eyes in too, and of course when you are new in the area, let alone – dare I say it – 'a celebrity', those eyes tend to pry a little bit deeper. I came down the stairs one morning to find someone shouting through the letterbox, '*Celebrity Juice* man, *Celebrity Juice* man – lend me a tenner.' I turned on my slipper and decided to have a few more minutes in bed. If you're trying to goad a celebrity, at least have the good grace to get the right celebrity.

Sometimes it wasn't me that was the object of fascination; a good-looking female friend of Paul's who happens to be a personal trainer was taking a shower in our bathroom when we suddenly heard a woman's voice over the back fence shouting out to her son, 'Stop it now, I know what you're doing.' I rushed to the window, saw the slats on the blind in the house opposite slam shut and a boy run up the stairs doing up his trousers being chased by his mother. Whether the mother would watch me showering, caressing my soapy body with a shower mitt, I never found out, but my heart sank. And let's hope she didn't own a periscope once the news of my naked roof-top sunbathing got out! But seriously, was it always going to be this weird?

Don't get me wrong, there were fun times there too and for the two and a half years we lived there it was a party house. As my good friend Scott says, 'It was the best free nightclub in West London.' I once found my friend Julie behind the settee under a tea towel two days after a party ended, lying there like when cats go away to die. Due to its location our house was perfect for a late-night drop-in and seven days a week the doorbell would ring and drunken waifs and strays would pop round. We had everyone in that house, singers, fashion designers, actors, Spice Girls, you name it – people of all walks of life popped in for a bevvy, and subsequently my social life (but not my liver) had never looked so healthy. I remember at one party Julien Macdonald the fashion designer pulled down my curtains, cut holes in them and made ponchos – oh, how funny it was, mincing paralytic up and down my hallway like a catwalk model, showing off my new Julien Macdonald poncho, in sharp contrast to the next morning when I was weeping and wondering why there was so much light being let into my lounge. It was a lot of fun and I do smile when I look back on those days – as always, remembering the corks popping and the wine glugging rather than the head throbbing and the self-loathing.

It was in the upstairs bedroom that Adele stayed when she was at her lowest ebb. The album *21* had just taken the world by storm although you would never have thought it with how miserable she was. Although she had purged her feelings in *21* she was still really cut up about her ex and she was completely inconsolable. She turned up at the house all upset and I think what with the promotion of the album she was just exhausted, physically and mentally. We told her to go upstairs and get some rest in our spare room. We would gingerly go up the stairs and leave her a fresh cup of tea or a sandwich outside the door and then tiptoe back downstairs. She was quiet as a mouse, so quiet in fact we forgot she was up there, and it was only after a couple of days that I realized we hadn't seen her or heard a peep out of her.

Paul said, 'Adele is upstairs, we better go and see if she's okay.'

'I daren't!' I said. 'What if she's dead?'

We looked at each other. Just out of interest, if the world's biggest star dies in your house, does your house price go up or down? I'm asking for a friend. I'm not going to lie, my brain went into overdrive. Would we get a plaque? Could we turn it into a museum? Would we have busloads of Adele fans tying wreaths to our knocker? Who knew, but all these questions flooded my head. First things first, we had to check whether she was dead after all. Paul and I walked up the two flights of stairs and there she was, sound asleep and thankfully alive (yay!), but you probably knew that already unless Adele's record label has been doing a *Weekend at Bernie's* for the past five years.

It was a weird time for me while she was staying with us, I was living this dual existence of complete uber-fan and yet friend too. She was hurting, and ironically

'Someone Like You', the song about that hurt, had become THE single of the year, played over and over on the radio – an instant classic, both sob-inducing and catchy in equal measure. I'd be happily wiping down a surface and suddenly break into 'NEVER MIND, I'LL FIND . . .' Then seeing Adele scowl at me from across the table, thinking I was taking the piss, I would quickly change my tune to the Eurythmics and take out the bins.

Although a lot of my Notting Hill neighbours decided to leave town that last weekend in August we always stayed for the Carnival – to have such an iconic festival literally on your doorstep and then choose to leave when it's on doesn't really make sense to me. So every year we would get our drinks in, invite our friends over and watch all the colourful chaos ensue from the window – we had a little balcony and we would go out and dance on it to the soca music, looking exactly like the people I would see when I used to go before I was on telly and say to my mates, 'Look at those posh wankers.'

Our friend the interior designer Kelly Hoppen had gone away for the weekend and as she lived down the street she had asked us to keep an eye on her house. We told her that the house was fine but there was a man standing in her garden next to her taupe (what else?) pots holding a sign saying 'URINALS 50p'. She believed it for a millisecond and then knowing what piss-taking bastards we were told us to piss off! But the reality was that people did literally take the piss in your gardens or worse. I'm all for let's have a party but no one wants to find a human poo on their welcome mat. Once bored of their boggling, people would relieve themselves in my bush.

Well, we started filling up buckets of water and drenching the dirty bastards before they'd even unzipped – I mean they were so off their heads they probably thought they'd been caught in a freak downpour but I was ready for them.

Once the noise had subsided and most of the party people had gone back to their homes I would take my dogs out for a well-earned walk. No lie, the street would be knee-deep in chicken – you could not see the tarmac for chicken wings and goujons. Well, my Bev, a greedy bitch at the best of times, nearly gave me whiplash as she dashed out of the gate. I swear I saw her look up to the sky and say 'Thank you, God.' She must have thought she'd died and gone to heaven. Usually when I walk her I will pull her away from such things but we were just wading through bones – it was like I was stuck in a chicken graveyard – and she was going mad, hoovering up chicken like a Dyson.

Like the Carnival, all good things sadly must come to an end and whereas many a night we'd had a riot inside the house, it was the night of the riots that occurred outside the house that made our minds up about leaving. It was in August and I was coming to the end of the warm-ups for my Spexy Beast arena tour that would scarily be happening that coming autumn and winter. I was doing my thing in the seaside town of Great Yarmouth, being blown off (and not in a good way) at the end of the seafront by a very blustery east wind. It was sad that the weather was so miserable because I had spent so many summer holidays on that east coast. It was the closest place to anywhere

beachy if you lived somewhere as landlocked as Northampton and each summer we would drive the 140 miles
or so. Nostalgia played her mischievous part as I drove
there – of course it was glorious sunshine every day in
Great Yarmouth, of course all I ever did was laugh and
skip along the beach, of course I never trod in dog shit –
so, I can't lie, it was a bit of a disappointment as we drove
round the coastal road only to be greeted by torrential
rain and a very sad storm-battered theatre.

There had also been a storm a-brewing back in London and like the rest of Britain I'd been watching on telly
what had at first been a disgruntled community in Tottenham simmering with anger slowly metamorphose into
a violent seething mob. This anger would overflow from
Tottenham and eventually bleed into the neighbouring
boroughs until it became a free for all. Something had
been in the air for a couple of days now. I had come off
stage buzzing, they had been such a great crowd, and got
a phone call from Paul, who was back in London.

'They're outside,' he whispered.

'Oh, piss off,' I said, wanting to get back to watching
the news – assuming he was on the wind-up I dismissed
it with 'Don't even joke.'

'They're outside,' he said again and suddenly I could
hear tension in his voice. 'They're going up and down the
street.'

He held the phone to the window. I could hear shouting,
smashes and very loud noises that I couldn't identify – we
would later find out they were cars being turned over and
bins being shoved about and set on fire.

Shit! This was actually happening. They had broken

into the restaurant across the road and smashed their way into my local pub, the Walmer Castle, and nicked the till.

I didn't know what to do and neither did Paul. Would turning off the lights attract attention, would making the house look empty be a good thing or would that signal a house ripe for burgling. What to do? What to do?

I so enjoy touring and travelling around the country doing my stand-up comedy but it's times like these that frustrate you when you are away, out of the loop and out on a limb – I should really have been there protecting my home and my partner and my bitches (the dogs not some ladies). Only in a moral support kind of way, I hasten to add; I am in no way insinuating that I would have gone outside as a vigilante Batman kind of person and fought them all with nunchakus, I know my limits – my get up and go got up and went a long time ago. I just felt a bit useless and I suppose helpless.

Well, I stayed on the phone as long as I could and just hoped that the gang would move on to terrorize another street. Paul had phoned the police and they hadn't picked up – obviously overstretched – so he went upstairs. It was only when he was in the relative safety of the living room that he heard the kitchen window downstairs slide open. He relayed this back to me over a cuppa when I got home and even hearing it second-hand made me shiver and the hairs on the back of my neck shoot up. He had clamped his hand over the dogs' mouths to stop them barking (totally going against the whole point of having dogs – but I would have done the same!). He could hear them rummaging through the downstairs, opening drawers and tipping things over, but thankfully they never came up the stairs and after what felt like for ever they finally slipped out the window and away. Paul said they had slowly pulled the window down as they left as if to give the impression we had not been burgled – bless.

After very little sleep, the dawn came and, like a lot of people living in London, Paul woke up to find scenes of chaos and destruction on the street. As it happened, we had only had a laptop and a camera stolen; sadly, some had lost their livelihoods and/or homes, so we counted our blessings. Communities all over London came together to sweep up and try to restore their streets and I suppose in a way their sense of community. It was only when I got back and wanted to go for a drive that I realized something else was missing: I couldn't find my car key. Then it dawned on me – 'Someone has stolen my car key!' – followed by the inevitable – 'Someone has stolen my car!' Cheeky bastards – in all the drama and the sweeping up we hadn't noticed it was missing.

The police found it a week later on an industrial estate – it had been used in a ram raid on a Carphone Warehouse! Why they would use a Mini Clubman to ram-raid I will never know – maybe it was the shape of it, they are quite elongated, I suppose. I remember waiting at a pedestrian crossing once on a sunny day with the window down and I overheard someone say, 'Look, a dwarf's hearse.' Rude, mean and politically incorrect. I drove on.

I didn't want the car after that – memories of me pootling along with the dogs in the back had been sullied and I wanted rid. Thankfully there had been nothing personal in the car apart from a spare pair of glasses in the glovebox and for a split second I had the fear that they might have popped them on and driven through the shop window pretending to be me, screeching 'Look, it's me, *Chatty Man*,' and that once the old bill had scoured the CCTV they would knock on my door and arrest me – I had seen *Making a Murderer* and wanted no part of it. I just hoped and prayed that the burglar hadn't been camp.

Once the car had been interviewed and put in a police line-up – this didn't really happen – we cleaned it and tried to sell it, uploading it on various websites. Eventually someone bought it, but not before I saw on said website written in bold underneath the photo of my mini 'PREVIOUS OWNER ALAN CARR!!!' Really, does everyone have to take the piss?!

Once the rioting drama had subsided we could get on with our lives and find a new house – but first I had to get the slight inconvenience of a thirty-two-date arena tour out of the way, which was looming ominously in the autumn. The tour was going to take me around the country, performing in some of the biggest auditoriums on offer. As soon as I started the shows I quickly realized that arenas weren't for me – tellingly, it was the first time I had ignored my gut feeling and said yes to doing an arena tour. Every comedian worth his salt was doing them and so the logic went that I should do one too but that's not really how you should make those kind of decisions. You and your stand-up tour are like a marriage – you are going to spend a hell of a lot of time together so you better make sure you get along. We did and I was incredibly proud of the Spexy Beast tour but I soon found to my dismay that these cavernous venues were not really cut out for my whimsical and sometimes quite frankly silly witterings. It felt hamstrung; any personal or private comment seemed inappropriate in such a large venue and it felt like my jokes were getting lost.

Personally, I do prefer the older theatres. Call me a stage-door Jeremy but when you're performing in these older buildings that have been there for centuries, you get a sense of inheritance, of being a part of something that has gone before, that you are a kind of conduit. Up there treading the same boards as Laurel and Hardy, Harry Houdini, Abbott and Costello makes the performance feel a little bit magical for me. Whilst I was waiting to go on stage at St George's Hall in Bradford, the door lady spotted my Charles Dickens biography poking out of my bag and told me to come with her. I went to her office and with a yank she pulled down a battered dusty tome from a shelf. She opened it up and showed me that on 28 December 1854 Charles Dickens had performed for the first time a reading of *A Christmas Carol* on that very stage. How wonderful is that?

Arenas are fine and all that, but you just don't get the same sense of history following 'Tweenies On Ice'. And it soon dawned on me that any audience interaction would be impossible due to the actual size of the room – what Bob does for a living in Row A, Block 1 is going to mean jack shit to Rita out of earshot in Row Z Block 999. Sometimes the weekend shows would go cray-cray, and I would have to leave my act behind and do a bit of crowd control; an arena full of drunk people can easily slip from audience to mob and you've got to remember it's just me with a microphone – if people start kicking off at a Beyoncé gig she can whip out 'All the Single Ladies' to snatch their attention back.

Having said that, when it worked, it really worked, and the dates at Cardiff, Manchester, Dublin and the final shows at the O2 in Greenwich were real corkers. I was buzzing, I got a glimpse of what being a rock star felt like and I loved it. Standing there getting the applause from 12,000 people (at some of the gigs I even got a standing ovation too), I had these extreme feelings of elation, my shuffle turned into a swagger and I felt 'king of the world'; I was so high on confidence and bravado that if someone had said to me 'Let's invade North Korea,' I would have said 'Let's go for it!' The downside is you can't get to sleep till three in the morning; my blood would turn to Sunny D and be literally fizzing in my veins. It was only the fear of having to do the show again the next night that finally calmed me and brought me back down to earth with a bump.

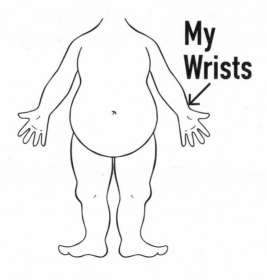

My Wrists

It was not only on stage in these huge arenas that I was feeling giddy; my personal life had me in a spin too. I had become an uncle. My brother, Gary, and his wife, Carly, had had a son, Max, in early September so finally my parents had been delivered of a grandchild (apparently my two red setters Bev and Joyce stood for nothing) and there was much excitement in the Carr household. This was swiftly followed by a little sister for Max – Isla. Two grandkids – I thought my parents were going to spontaneously combust with love, which was great news for Gary and his wife, but not so much for my dogs. The relationship between my dogs and my parents has deteriorated so much since then that they have been reduced to 'Bev and Joyce who?' I have stepped up to the challenge of unclehood and you wouldn't recognize me now, honestly, I've turned into Nanny McPhee – and don't say I've already got the teeth. I keep my swearing to a bare minimum, and keep my anecdotes 'U'-rated rather than '18', more *Hungry Caterpiller* than *Human Centipede*.

My brother tells me that people come up to him asking him if he's jealous of my success. Of course, what they are actually revealing is about themselves, that they would feel pangs of jealousy, but Gary isn't jealous and I can say that hand on heart. We are an incredibly supportive family and my dad is the first to shout 'Twat!' if there is a nasty review or comment in the papers. If anything, I'm jealous of Gary's family life, the kids, the wife, the stability; their two gorgeous children have completed their family and it's so nice to see. I know these days gays and lesbians can become parents so the option is there, but it's not for me. I wish it was, but it's not. Being gay is like being in the world's biggest girl group – in front of the curtains we are all-singing, all-dancing, backslapping and all smiles, but behind the curtains, it's cat fighting, bitching and backstabbing. It's a pity because it doesn't really have to be like that. Whilst I watch with envy other minorities closing ranks and pulling together when under fire, the gay community can't or won't do that. Ironically, the most homophobia I get is from the gay community, and I understand why – it's the campness, the effeminacy, that winds people up. You're made to feel that you've let the side down. Half the time people think I put it on, but I ask you – do you think I want to talk like this? Do you think I want to squawk? Admittedly, it has given me my biggest Hollywood role to date (don't get too excited, I'm playing a seagull, but more on that later) but do you think I want to be so obvious? Hands on hip is my default pose, my arms flap like I'm swatting non-existent gnats and I mince down the street like my pelvis is made of cheesy string – believe me, I'm not fucking happy about it either!! Sometimes I get annoyed with myself and have a word, and then before you know it I look down and there it is, my hand on my hip, looking like an angry teapot – irritating or what? Campness has always been the grit in the eye of the gay community, to be straight-acting is the key, the ideal factory setting. If you don't act gay then you've hit the jackpot. It hasn't dawned on anyone that being told NOT to act gay is THE most homophobic thing ever, and if it came from the mouth of a right-wing leader or a preacher then every-one would be up in arms.

When soldiers and rugby players come out they are branded 'brave' and all the gays rejoice, and yes, I agree they are, but so are the effeminate gay kids, the butch lesbian kids and transgender kids who go to school every day and face bullying, beatings and abuse the minute they step into the playground – I know it's not a rugby pitch or a battlefield but it might as well be for them. Let's cheer on *their* bravery, not just your muscle-bound squaddies or your sporty jocks because let's remember that the gay community's motto has always been 'I am what I am' and not 'You aren't who we want you to be.'

Since becoming an uncle I've realized that bringing up children, although rewarding, can be incredibly tough too. A lot of my friends, especially the ones who are new to the parenting lark, do look like shit. I will meet up with them for a coffee in the high street and I can see the blatant ecstasy in their eyes at the fact they are actually spending time with someone not under the age of three. I'll say to them 'You do know you've got sick on your shoulder?' 'Is that Cow and Gate on your shoe?' or 'You know that balaclava is on back to front?' but as long as I'm not Peppa Pig and they're not in the Night Garden they don't care – is it too early for a wine?

I always seem to put my foot in it with parents. When they tell me that little Joey said his first word today or Emma took her first steps, I always start going, 'Well, my Bev ate a whole bag of Wotsits that I hadn't put in the cupboard properly' and then I see their face change and I'm like, shit! Alan, having dogs is not the same as having children.

With children, just like with certain strains of TB, as you get older your body gets less resistant to them. Before you know it, you're smiling at them in post offices, simpering over their outfits in supermarket queues and offering them an Opal Fruit in a service station (I know they're called Starburst but I refuse to comply. Cif will always be Jif in my house and while we're at it I still call Iceland Bejam, but that's me for you). However, my new-found love for children was pushed to breaking point earlier this year when I filmed a celebrity version of *Child Genius* for Stand Up To Cancer. I have been involved with Stand Up To Cancer from the outset, since the launch of it with Gwyneth Paltrow back in 2012, and whenever I can do anything to help publicize it or raise money for it, I'm there.

A few years back I did *Deal Or No Deal* for Stand Up To Cancer where I basically spent the whole show crying. I always enjoy going on other people's shows: firstly, it's nice to see how the other half live, and secondly, the pressure is off, they are the host, they have to read the script, and all you have to do is rock up and be a contestant. Alan Carr National Treasure becomes 'Alan Carr is pushing forty, likes reading and Zumba and is a TV personality from Northampton.'

Come to think of it, I used to love it when Channel 4 did those TV mash-ups, where Channel 4 'talent' would get the opportunity to host another show on Channel 4 for a day. People on *Countryfile* would call it cross-pollination. Initially, I wanted to host *Embarrassing Bodies* but apparently that show was off limits as it was a serious medical programme focused on finding solutions to people's discreet medical problems. Channel 4 were basically saying I didn't have enough gravitas – well, that is charming! However, I did get to wrestle *Million Pound Drop* out of Davina's hands and to be host for a celebrity special, where whatever money the celebrities won went to their chosen charity. The celebrities were the Loose Women versus *Pointless*'s Alexander Armstrong and Richard Bacon. You would think for a charity special that the atmosphere would be all puppies and butterflies, but not in the least – contempt was so thick in the air, I felt like popping waders on just to walk through the green room. The day hadn't started off well, when the producer had whispered in my ear that the actual *Million Pound Drop* set was so flimsy that we could only allow one Loose Woman on at a time, maximum two – basically I had to treat the

Loose Women like naughty schoolgirls in an inner-city newsagent. Well, there's never a good way to say to a lady 'Sorry, love, you're so fat that if you step on our set it will implode and you could kill us all.' For the record I think it was only the design of the set that prevented multiple Loose Women – it wasn't anything personal I'm sure, and besides, I'm hardly pencil thin and I wasn't warned. The atmosphere got worse when one of the Loose Women got a question wrong – it was quite an easy question but anyone who has taken part in a pub quiz knows that a question is only easy if you know it. Not only did they get a question wrong but Alexander Armstrong exchanged 'a look' with Richard Bacon, basically implying that they were thick; one of the two Loose Women separated in the green room spotted the look on camera and kicked off whilst the other one got emotional and started crying. Ooh, you could have cut the atmosphere with a knife, and me, of course, spotting a contretemps brewing, went into emergency St John Ambulance mode, grabbed my first-aid kit and waded in – separating the rival teams, handing out hankies and barley sugars, calming the guests down.

My next mash-up was thankfully less dramatic and went a tad more smoothly. It was with TV presenter, estate agent and professional skip rummager Kirstie Allsopp and I replaced Phil Spencer to co-host *Location, Location, Location*. I love that show, I even watch those repeats on More4 where all the pricings are wrong. A central Manchester terraced house for two and six? I'll pop that in my basket, thank you very much. We had the unenviable task of finding a young professional woman a pied-à-terre in central London for £250,000 – well, I spent the first five minutes wiping my cappuccino off her face where I'd spat it out after she'd told me her budget. £250,000? In central London? And she wanted a second bedroom – I thought, love, with that budget you'll be lucky to get a window. I know that people who don't live in London will be thinking 'A quarter of a million and you can't get a flat in London? Really?' Yes, really. We had our work cut out traipsing all over London looking for something I thought didn't even exist but Kirstie did her magic, rang round a few estate agents and, what do you know, we found that girl a two-bedroom flat in Maida Vale. Admittedly, the second bedroom was so small you would have to put air holes into the wall so you didn't suffocate to death, and basically the lounge served as the hall, kitchen, reception room and wet room too, and was so small that if you opened the microwave door everyone would have to duck.

Anyway, I digress. As I was saying, this year for Stand Up To Cancer I got the chance to do a celebrity version of *Child Genius*. For those who don't know, *Child Genius* is a Channel 4 TV show hosted by Richard Osman where the nation's most super-smart children go head to head through a series of quiz rounds to see who is the cleverest of them all and who will ultimately be crowned 'Child Genius'. I turned up to the Royal Institution, a very grand and solemn pillared building in Mayfair that apparently is the 'home of science' and went in, the butterflies in my stomach beginning to awaken. We were taken into this musty book-lined room to meet the children that we would be quizzed against. Like I said, now I was an uncle

235

and had acquired copious amounts of godchildren, I'd got better at being around them. I'm not so awkward any more, I don't patronize and I talk to them like I would like to be talked to.

Not so long ago I would have been clueless. I cringe sometimes when I remember having Miley Cyrus on *Chatty Man* for the first time. With her being so young I thought we might get some sweets, or 'candy' as Americans like to call it, in the globe for her to nibble on or maybe some fizzy pop to ease her gently into the show – obviously I didn't realize there was the brain of a forty-year-old businesswoman inside a sixteen-year-old girl's body. She was so confident, so driven, so focused – lovely and all that, but watching her sitting on the couch, full of self-belief, I couldn't help thinking we could be staring at a future female president of the United States of America.

When Miley returned to *Chatty Man* two years later she was older, obviously, but this time more relaxed, and I felt that this was the real her – she seemed more comfort-able in her skin, even if the new her was openly courting controversy. Her stage performances had become more and more outrageous and this had come to a head at the MTV Awards when she had rubbed up against Robin Thicke sexually and touched herself with a sponge finger (like the ones you used to see in the audience on *Gladi-ators* in the 1990s, not the Mr Kipling cakes). Her notoriety was set to continue on *Chatty Man* when she announced she would perform her new single 'We Can't Stop' with a dwarf band. The record company and Channel 4 were concerned about this: was it exploitation, was it politically incorrect – who was to know? While everyone was waiting around to see if it would go ahead, the dwarf guitarist asked where the canteen was. I said, 'Come with me,' and the entire dwarf band followed me along the corridor – if a couple of bluebirds had flown along with some cups and plopped some sugars in the tea it would have been just like *Snow White*. Well, panic over, the performance went ahead and the wait was worth it – it was an amazing performance from Miley and the band. One of the dwarves stole the show with her twerking. Miley told me that she was a huge supporter of the 'dwarf community' back in LA and hoped to integrate them more into pop music in a dignified way, which I thought was really noble of her – although as a lot of the instruments they were playing weren't 'plugged in' and were from Fisher-Price I thought there was still a long way to go.

Anyhow, back at the 'home of science', we all filed in to see the children. Although we would be on opposing teams I thought I would try to put them at their ease. After all, they were only eleven and the prospect of appearing on television is scary enough, let alone answering really hard questions in front of an audience. So I went on the charm offensive. I stepped into the room, all smiles, only to be greeted with 'GOD, ALAN CARR – YOU'RE SO LOUD AND ANNOYING – I CAN'T STAND YOU, YOU'RE NOT EVEN FUNNY' shouted in an imperious voice. The rest of the children laughed and looked disdainfully at me. If no one had been looking I would have twatted the little shit round the head with his 'Eggheads' lunchbox. They then huddled in a group and looked over at *Countdown*'s Rachel

Riley. 'She's nowhere near as good as Carol Vorderman,' they stage-whispered. But it was poor old comedian Aisling Bea who bore the brunt of the little cherubs' mockery: 'Look at your nose – you big Irish witch. You DO know you're not allowed to use SORCERY in the quiz?' the ringleader chipped in, cackling and pointing towards her (for the record) medium-sized nose. If this is intelligence for you I would rather be thick as shit. It was like being in the playground all over again. I tried to be polite.

'What's your specialist subject?'

'The paradoxes of Zeno of Elea,' came the reply from one of them – for a minute I thought he was referring to *Xena: Warrior Princess* on Channel 5 but actually he was *of course* referring to the Greek philosopher Zeno and the set of philosophical problems he created to support Parmenides' doctrine. 'What's yours?' he asked inquisitively.

'The Life and Times of the *Golden Girls* Season Four to Season Six.'

'What's the *Golden Girls*?' he said suspiciously.

Great, I thought, now I feel thick AND old! I tried to explain the *Golden Girls* but he ended up looking at me in the same way I'd looked at him when he'd said Zeno, so I decided to leave it be.

To be fair, it was quite a fun day after all; once the children realized it wasn't a matter of life and death and chilled the fuck out, the day passed without event. *Child Genius* is set to hit our screens this autumn, and hopefully it will raise lots of money for Stand Up To Cancer – we all of course donated our fees to the charity and I really hope you enjoy the show. I won't offer up any spoilers to you,

you'll just have to find out yourselves who left with their heads held high and who ended up with egg on their faces – but you can probably have a bloody good guess.

Stand Up To Cancer is a biennial event (once every two years – yes, I learnt that from those clever kids!) and it is a real privilege to be asked to present it along with Davina and Dr Christian. On the one hand I look forward to it because it means raising lots of money (mainly thanks to your generosity) to help fight cancer but I also dread it because invariably I end up sobbing throughout the night, listening to all the stories and the battles, some won, some sadly lost. It is such an emotionally charged event – I don't think I've ever been involved in anything so filled with energy and laughter one moment and then tears and snot bubbles the next. I remember we had broken the record set two years earlier and the whole team was buzzing with the enormous amount donated by the general public – I awoke the next morning still walking on air, foolishly patting myself on the back for a 'job well done'. It was then that I went to my laptop and checked my mail and saw it there in my inbox – an email from the parent of a lad who had been in contact with my agent and was due to come and see my stand-up tour telling us he had lost his battle with cancer the night before. Stupid, I know, but you sort of think no one's going to die when you're doing a charity fundraiser, as if we could stop this awful disease just through positivity alone. We had raised all that money and yet we were too late to save him. Well, I just burst into tears – it had highlighted the horrible reality, this awful sobering thought that we can't give up, the fight doesn't stop once the telethon does, we have got to keep going. There are always going to be people who need our help and so the battle must continue and let's hope this autumn Stand Up To Cancer raises even more money.

As you can imagine after all the trauma in Notting Hill, I had started missing Manchester. Yes, I had joked about Scally Karen in Stretford and how rough around the edges the Drum pub had been and how the barmaid had laughed at me when I asked for a wine list – 'A what list?' – but they'd never been weird. And I'd never felt uneasy up there – the people were too friendly. I was mid-reminisce one day when weirdly I got a call on my mobile with the 0161 code – ahh, Manchester!

I had been renting out my flat in Stretford – the property boom had flat-lined and the assurances that the Salford Media Village which had just been constructed around the corner would become the epicentre of the Media World and that my humble abode would triple in value hadn't really materialized. This news was compounded by the discovery of a body in the park that was spitting distance from my flat. Even Phil and Kirstie would struggle to put a positive spin on that. The Manchester phone call was from my letting agent in Stretford. I picked up, instantly curious.

'Hiya, Alan, it's Dawn here, just letting you know, the police are outside your property in Stretford and they want to smash your door down – would you be okay with that?'

'What? The police?'

'Yes, they want to knock your door down.'

'My God – what's happened?'

'I'm afraid your tenants, Mr Awolowo and Miss Chuk-wuemeka, have been using your flat as a cannabis farm and the police want to arrest them.'

Excuse me – cannabis farm? No, not my lovely flat, it was so innocent and unassuming. I couldn't believe for one minute it had got involved with drugs.

'Can the police go in?'

'Er, yes, go ahead.'

'We'll keep you posted,' trilled Dawn cheerily, hanging up, as if I'd rung up and asked her to tell me the latest goings-on in *Big Brother* or something.

Dawn did ring back and filled me in. They'd smashed the door down and Mr Awolowo had jumped out of the window over my Juliet balcony and run to the park, but thankfully he had been arrested trying to get on the Metro. Miss Chukwuemeka was not at the flat and had apparently gone rogue and disappeared under the radar, which is no mean feat with a name like Miss Chukwue-meka, but anyway.

At first I couldn't believe it but then I could. This kind of weird shit always happens to me so I'm sort of used to it – do you know what I mean? There is always 'something', and here's another example. Me and my friend Sam, who you might remember from Stand Up To Can-cer survived throat cancer, we bought a narrow boat together. We'd had a lovely weekend in Bath cruising up the canals there, tipsy on lager, cranking open the locks, chatting merrily to all the other canal-boat owners; it felt so relaxing and liberating bobbing along and, like Victor Kiam, I loved it so much I actually bought a barge, as you do. Once we had transported it back to London, enamoured with our new purchase and thrilled with our new road-free utopia, we sailed along the Regent Canal into a body wedged in a suitcase in the canal – yes, a fucking body in a suitcase. The police were called and Sam was questioned (she was innocent, thank God). I was on stage in Croydon on my Yap Yap Yap tour at the time – honest, check the dates and everything – but nevertheless my boat was all over the news bedecked in 'Police Crime Scene' tape. Thankfully they caught the poor girl's murderer – it was her boyfriend who had killed her. Like the cannabis farm, my agent told me not to tell a soul, which as you can imagine for me was so hard.

'How's that barge you bought?' my mum would say.

'Fine, just fine,' I would say, shuffling nervously. If I saw two youths smoking a spliff I would imagine them saying 'This is good shit – pure hundred per cent Stretford' – well, maybe that's an exaggeration but I was nervous and back then I was scared of the press. My agent was right though about keeping it all under my hat and away from the journalists. As newspapers migrate to more online pastures, the news is condensed into sound bites – they are called clickbaits – to draw you in to 'click' on the story. You find people don't actually read the articles (but will gladly comment on them). I know it wouldn't have been headline news, but still, the last thing I needed to see was 'Carr's Barge of Death', or worse, a mocked-up head of me with a Rasta-hat and superimposed doobie, headlined 'Alan Carrnabis'. So there you go, I've finally come clean – who'd have thought you'd be reading about drugs and murder in an Alan Carr autobiography. Who knows, there might even be a sex tape later – but then again, you've got to have sex first.

I went back up to Manchester to visit the flat. It was so upsetting; it was totally wrecked. It stank like Bob Marley's ashtray, they had stubbed cigarettes out on the carpet, wardrobes had been smashed up and the fridge was bent double where it had been kicked in. I left that day with a heavy heart and, weirdly, the munchies.

Not long after that I moved up to Blackpool – well, sort of. My agent had received a call asking if I would like to have my good self turned into a waxwork dummy for all to see at none other than the world-famous Madame Tussauds. Of course I leapt at the chance and obviously with me living in London it would be no hardship nipping up to Baker Street to check out my waxwork likeness. But it wasn't to be in London, as it turned out, it was going to be in the Blackpool Madame Tussauds. Oh! My dream of rubbing wax shoulders with Gandhi and the Queen Mother melted before my eyes like, well, like a waxwork that's been left next to a patio heater. I'd once nipped into the waxworks in Blackpool when it had started raining, at a loose end waiting for my father, who was manager of the local football team, to come back from training. The waxworks looked shoddy and with their gozzy eyes and manic grins, some of them were more terrifying than the serial killer dummies in the dungeons below. I don't want to bore you with business details but apparently, since then, they'd been taken over properly and Madame Tussauds had invested loads of money, which was plain to see when I went back there. It had had a complete makeover and there I was alongside Keith Lemon, Simon Cowell and Cheryl Fernandez-Versini.

The process of making a waxwork was an interesting one, which took place not in Blackpool but just outside Hammersmith. I met up at their headquarters, a large multi-roomed warehouse full of ghostly white heads and bodies all in different stages of completion – half a Russell Brand here, a quarter of Ant and Dec there, all frozen in time waiting to be touched up (aren't we all?). Sadly, some waxworks were looking a bit dejected, waxworks whose namesakes have lost their fame or done something naughty and therefore have to be taken off display. Forget all the gossip columns, it's here that you can see who is in favour and who isn't. Popularity made real and set in wax.

I foolishly assumed that getting my likeness made would be quite simple, I would just stand there naked and then Madame Tussauds would tip a whole bucket of wax over me, a bit like being gunged; it would cascade over my body and set in every nook and cranny and then, once hardened, they would chisel me out and by and by I'd be allowed to go home – job done. No, it was (obviously!) more intricate and professional than that. You have to stand on what can only be called a huge lazy Susan and then you're told to 'Strike a pose!' a typical pose that would represent you. Once you have chosen your pose, you are then slowly rotated, inch by inch, while they take your photo and measurements with some very futuristic lasers, making sure all the time that you are still in your chosen position. How much you then want to put into the process depends on how realistic you want your waxwork to be. I wanted mine to be perfect and was very hands-on. It is so strange when they bring in a huge drawer full of eyeballs and then a huge drawer full of hair samples and you sit there choosing which one perfectly matches your own – it is a narcissist's dream. I actually ended up donating my own clothes and spectacles. The end result looked very realistic, I was so impressed.

Madame Tussauds Blackpool chose my waxwork to be an interactive part of the tour – if you go there you can see they have recreated the *Chatty Man* set and I am placed in the centre, just waiting to be interacted with. Anyone who pays the entrance fee can just walk over to me and do whatever they like – and they do. Not a day goes by where I am not shown a photo of someone having their wicked way with me. Touched, fingered, bummed . . . my wax cock has been grabbed so many times the crotch is beginning to look threadbare. I might be made of wax but I'm like a piece of meat. Sometimes if I've had a bit of a night out and roll over in bed and check my Twitter, I have to double-take at the photos on my timeline to make sure it isn't in fact ME who has grabbed that woman's tit – oh, thank God, she placed her own tit in my waxy hand. One of the things that has always perplexed me is that although I am probably one of the least sexual people you will ever come across, people do try to have their wicked way with me. Maybe that's part of the appeal – I am like Kenneth Williams and the general public are like Hattie Jacques, pulling me squirming to their ample bosom. That poor waxwork has been subjected to more groping and depraved indecency than a full-time sex worker.

In the early noughties the city of Barcelona peppered

its Ramblas with brightly coloured fibreglass cows which proved a big hit with the tourists, so my home town Northampton decided to emulate this by erecting lions all over Northampton town centre. I was honoured when it was decided to decorate one à la Alan and there it stood in Northampton town market in all its magnificence, guarding the fruit and veg; well, it wasn't long before someone had nicked its glasses, snapped its teeth out and tweeted a photo of someone bumming it. Now I know how Banksy feels when someone throws a pot of paint over one of his creations.

Sketches have always been a big part of my oeuvre (whatever that means), whether it's *The Friday Night Project* or my annual *New Year Specstacular*, and I recommend anyone to watch at least one *Specstacular* before you die. It's like CCTV from an 18 to 30 holiday – it makes *Geordie Shore* look like *Downton Abbey*. That dreadful footage filmed in Magaluf a few years back of the girl sucking those fifteen men off so as she could get a complimentary cocktail was so close to an actual game on *Specstacular* that I had to speak to my lawyers. Have you ever seen that BBC natural history programme *Earth* with David Attenborough? Do you remember the episode where those barnacle geese goslings are stuck 400 feet up on the side of that mountain and they need to learn how to fly so they just leap into the unknown and plummet downwards, ricocheting off the side of the mountain, smacking their heads against the granite as they bounce down, only to land with a thump, sore and battered but alive and well? That's like me on a *Specstacular* record: I swig some champagne, go out on to the stage and plummet – I just freefall through the show, bouncing merrily off whatever I hit, all six hours of it.

We have such good guests on that show, Justin Bieber, Bruno Mars, Ellie Goulding and James Corden to name but a few, and whether I like it or not, it's always a riot. Sometimes it's hard to tell who are the more pissed, the celebrity guests, who all evening have been slowly pumped with alcopops, beers and Prosecco, or the audience, who all evening have been slowly pumped with alcopops, beers and Prosecco. You see, comrade, everyone is treated the same on my *Specstacular*. By part eight, it's basically crowd control; people are getting off with each other. Jimmy Bullard, fresh from his 'success' on *I'm a Celebrity*, pulled off his trousers and sat on my face; another year one celebrity got fingered during a crowd surge and poor old Danny Dyer went through every alcohol stage during the six-hour record, from fun drunk to silly drunk, morose drunk, angry drunk and slumped drunk, and ended by flashing his surprisingly large ball-bag at me and Mel B.

Considering my outfits and wigs for the sketches are ropy, historically incorrect and downright itchy, the locations that the team pick are always surprisingly excellent. There is someone who is dedicated to finding these locations for filming the sketches and, as you can imagine, they have to be spot on – they can make or break a scene. You wouldn't film *Wolf Hall* in an NCP car park, do you get what I'm saying? I have rocked up to film my *Specstacular* sketches in some absolutely beautiful places, including Hever Castle, the Methodist Central Hall in

Westminster and many lovely churches and stately homes. Some things, however, are out of the location manager's hands. I turned up to one location, a woman's house near Golders Green, and I was going to be Kerry Katona. To be honest, the sketch was a bit harsh and unnecessary. I was going to have trotters and a curly tail – yes, I was cruelly going to portray Kerry as a pig. I feel so bad because I've met her since and actually she's really sweet; like everyone, I'd seen her in the papers and thought I'd got her sussed. Anyway, I came through the door hooved and snouted, with my cute little tail poking through the back of my terry towelling dressing gown. I was greeted by the aghast homeowner screaming, 'Get out, get out of my house!' I was like, what? It turns out she was an Orthodox Jew and any depictions of pigs or anything remotely porcine were strictly forbidden in her house. Well, my cute little curly tail was out the door quicker than you could say 'pork scratchings'. I was then ushered away to wait in the car by the production manager as another maybe less religious household was found.

Believe it or not that wasn't the quickest exit I have made from a shoot. We were doing a pastiche of Quentin Tarantino's *Django Unchained*, ours being called *Tango Unchained*, where we focused on the oppression of fake-tanned, orange people from Essex in 1880s Romford (unlike *Django Unchained*, our adaptation sadly got overlooked by the Academy). Never letting a good pun get in the way of dubious historical facts, we searched for a house that would conjure up that colonial feel of mid-1880s Texas – and anyone who knows the budget on a *Specstacular* will know there was no hope in hell that we

16. Lost for words for the first time

17. (*right*) Hawaii 2014

18. (*below*) Bev channelling
Joan Collins

19. Yes, we wear matching pyjamas – do you have a problem with that?

20. JT and some very unimpressed Irish Setters

21 and 22. Our dressing-up box is to die for

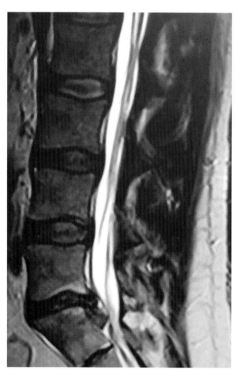

23. Paul's back injury

24. *Yap Yap Yap …*

25. (*above*) ... at the Hammersmith Apollo

26. (*left*) My first ever *Chatty Man* promo as Little Alan

27. Getting my *Specstacular* started

28. (*above*) Brucie showing me how it's done

29. (*right*) Clay You, Clay Me

30. (*above left*) Taylor Swift blatantly using me to boost her Instagram followers

31. (*above*) Helping Gaga with her ra-ra

32. (*left*) Bradley Cooper flirting outrageously with me

33. (*below*) UnBelieberable

34. (*left*) Carly looking gorgeous – me and my brother looking like we work at the deli in Morrisons.

35. (*above*) Silly Bowles

36. Celebrating my 40th with friends

could afford to visit 'The Lone Star' to get a more authentic feel, not unless it was on a Megabus route and sadly it isn't. Much to everyone's surprise the location manager excelled herself and found the ideal house on the outskirts of a sleepy village in Suffolk (obviously). It was just perfect. We filmed in the garden all day and were supposed to be out by 6.00 p.m. sharpish. We were running late because the weather had been against us so the director went to speak to the owner of the house and asked if we could we possibly extend the filming till 7.00 p.m. She agreed, but by 7.00 p.m. we still hadn't finished. Cheekily we carried on till 8.00 p.m. She must have looked out of her window and seen we were still there because she came out of her porch. I thought, what's that in her hand? Shit, it's a gun! 'Get off my fucking land!' came the cry and she fired the gun into the sky – well, let's just say we got the point. Every man, woman and child legged it to the van; using a runner as a human shield, I managed to clamber to safety behind a bush, where I waited for the gunshots to die down, and then raced from cover and threw myself into the back of the van. What I feel bad about is that (Equity, cover your ears) we left some of the supporting artists (extras to you and me) still shackled together in the field, and we had to watch them hobble over to us, desperate not to be shot.

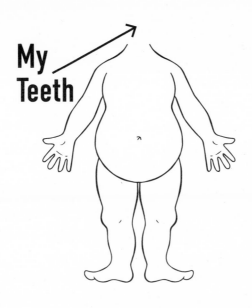

My Teeth

'Alan, why haven't you broken America?' asks no one – ever. Well, let me tell you why. Mainly down to the success of Russell Brand, Ricky Gervais and more recently James Corden, a new question has now materialized on the journalist's notepad: 'Would you ever go and find work in America?' Of course, I would love to, and believe it or not I've had my moments. Whoopi Goldberg after coming on the chat show reached out to me for a potential show idea in America. My agent rang me up as I was about to go on stage in Ipswich at the Regent Theatre.

   'Whoopi Goldberg wants your email address – can I give it to her?'

   'Errr, yes!'

To the people who came to see that Ipswich show in 2011 – apologies for being so giddy on stage that night; sitting in my dressing room with the rain pelting at the window, I had been touched by Hollywood – finally. I was a-buzz in the wings – what could it be? What could she want with little old me? *Sister Act 3? Sister Act 4?* I could look good in a habit – or maybe a monk . . . Anyway, my thoughts of tinsel town dissolved as I strode on the stage with purpose – 'Hello, Ipswich!!!!!!'

Once my giddiness had subsided, we swapped email contacts and before long we were chatting via email. After meeting me, she had come up with a possible TV idea. It sounded promising, with real potential, and she asked me to come over to see her in New York. Unfortunately I was in the middle of my Spexy Beast arena tour and a *Chatty Man* run, and finding two consecutive days off in the schedule for me to fly over let alone that would fit in with her jam-packed diary was nigh on impossible. Maybe we could have rearranged a *Chatty Man* recording day but you can't start cancelling arena dates – you're essentially pissing off 12,000 people who just happen to be your fans – I just wouldn't do it. Reluctantly, I said I couldn't see her until after December – and before long the communication fizzled out, which was gutting. She probably saw it as a snub but it wasn't, I love her and I was so honoured that she came on *Chatty Man*, let alone got in touch afterwards.

I'm not one for regrets, but sometimes if I'm on my way to some shithole to do my stand-up or preparing to speak to a guest on the show who isn't particularly nice or inspiring, my mind does drift to 'what might have been'.

I dream of a different 'me', a me that is having a wheat-grass shot with my personal trainer whilst squatting in Central Park, my teeth whitened and straight, bald spot mysteriously AWOL . . . ahhh, 'what if', the two saddest words in the English language. When I go to America it's usually for pleasure rather than business, which is significantly less stressful and ultimately more fun. I'm lucky to have made some wonderful friends in the good old US of A and we don't see them as much as we'd like to but when we do it's a hoot.

We have two wonderfully talented friends, Claire and her husband Justin who, when not touring the world and playing guitar for Pink, live in LA. One summer they announced they were getting married at the family ranch in Virginia. This beautiful ranch was just perfect for a wedding, the weather knew it had to be on its best behaviour and glorious sunshine bathed the happy couple. There wasn't a dry eye in the ranch as they got wed down on a jetty overlooking a beautiful lake that seemed to just twinkle – it was gorgeous. At least it was until someone introduced 'moonshine' into the proceedings. In the Bruno Mars song 'Moonshine', he equates drinking moonshine to kissing a woman and once intoxicated it takes him to a special place. Well, I don't know what was in his moonshine, but the only special place I was going to was A&E. Boy, it was strong. Claire's gran's teeth fell out and we started looking for them in the grass. I found them and picked them up, then Pink took them from me, washed them in her rosé and gave them back to Claire's gran, who shoved them back in her mouth and continued to dance – it was one of those nights. I was already a big fan of Pink but after seeing her do that I loved her even more.

As is the wonderful nature of this job, you get to meet a lot of people and some of those people work or gravitate to the States so whenever I do go over to America, I always end up staying in Los Angeles and catching up with friends, staying at their beautiful Hollywood homes and going green with envy. One of the perks of going to America is that no one knows me and I can have a certain amount of anonymity over there, plus there's always someone more famous in the vicinity and who's going to give a shit about me when you've got Cher in the next aisle buying cotton buds.

Recently, though, my American dream of anonymity has been threatened – unbeknownst to me an employee at Virgin may have passed on my personal details to the paparazzi in Los Angeles. They seemed to know the flight I was on and when I would be arriving but not, sadly, what I looked like. When you get off the plane and you are mildly famous you expect a bit of pushing and shoving, a scrum if you like of paps jostling to get that all-important photo. When I got off the plane, instead of 'Alan! Alan!' it was 'Alan? Alan?' One paparazzo – ONE?!! He kept holding up an A4 piece of paper with my face on it, looking at it then looking up again to check – 'Alan? Alan?' It was so embarrassing and of course I didn't have a limo waiting, I had to stand in the queue for a taxi. The pap looked pissed off and to be fair I wasn't really showering him with stardust. He walked off in a huff. I don't know whether the employee got paid but I don't think they'll be getting any more money for my details.

Don't worry, though, my ego got a well-deserved massage later in the day. LA is very industrial city and whereas European cities have a heart, a hub that defines that city, be it a palazzo, a park or a palace, Los Angeles just lies there sprawled out like some kind of grey jellyfish. To be honest, it's not my favourite place, especially for someone who loves a bit of history and having a wander. Americans, who drive everywhere, look at you in horror as you actually walk around; they assume you are homeless – why would you walk, you crazy dumb ass, they're probably thinking as I mince along, spluttering. When you think about it, they are probably right. I decided to walk along Mulholland Drive, only because I knew a film was made about it so it must have some historical merit, but it's basically a motorway. I was walking along a motorway, breathing in petrol fumes, slowly getting a shadow on my lung just because it felt vaguely famous. Can you imagine if you had someone to stay at your house and they said, 'I'm going for a walk up the M6, okay?'

'Oh, enjoy – you're just going to love the Wild Bean Cafe at Warwick Services.'

Madness!

So I was walking along Mulholland Drive, and I don't know, maybe it was the constant coughing or the way my eyes were burning with the fumes, but I fancied a nice cold, refreshing beer. The only place I could find was this cowboy-themed bar. It actually looked quite fun: waxwork Apache Indians manned the saloon, and there were lots and lots of plastic cacti and waitresses in gingham bras, daisy dukes and cowboy boots greeting every customer with a mighty fine 'Howdy, partner.' Okay, it was fucking tacky – but I needed a beer, back off with your judgements. I grabbed a seat outside and a beer and watched the cars go by. Five or ten minutes must have passed when I heard a Scouse voice: 'Is that who I think it is?' My ears pricked up – no, it couldn't be, I must be hallucinating with all the fumes, or maybe it was the rusty saloon door creaking on its hinges (sorry, Scousers). 'It is, it is,' came the Scouse voice again. I looked up. It was a whole busload of Brits on a Hollywood Homes tour.

'It's Alan Carr, look! Alan! Alan!'

By now the whole group was not only waving but taking my photo. Even people who weren't British who didn't know who the hell I was started taking my photo just in case. There's a certain kudos in having your photo taken in Beverley Hills if you are in your garden or on a balcony in your mansion, but not sitting by the side of a motorway next to a slowly deflating cactus – it's embarrassing. But on the plus side, it was nice to be recognized and seeing the bus gave me a lift. Not literally, I carried on walking, but it was nice to get such a warm welcome so far away from home, a ray of sunshine pulsing through the smog.

Whether I'll ever make it in the US, I don't know. If it happens, it happens, and if it doesn't, it doesn't – I guess I'm not really that driven. Mind you, I have flirted with film, albeit briefly. I've graced the silver screen twice in my illustrious career; admittedly one of those times was as an animated seagull but nevertheless it was the silver screen. I'll save you the time of going on Wikipedia, it was *The SpongeBob Movie: Sponge Out of Water*, released in 2014 and grossing a mammoth $323.14 million at the box office – some people have called it the 'Alan Carr effect' but the film's not about me and I digress.

The first of my two films was *Nativity!*, written and directed by the lovely Debbie Isitt; it's a really warm, charming Christmas film about two competitive schools putting on rival nativity plays and because it's so un-ashamedly Christmassy it's shown every year on the telly, yes, you guessed it, at Christmas. Just like the only two certainties in this life are death and taxes, for Christmas viewing it will for ever be *Nativity!* and *Carry On Camping*. It warms my heart every Christmas because I always get people coming up to me, maybe people who wouldn't normally watch *Chatty Man* or my stand-up, saying how much they like it – it's sweet and gives my Christmas an extra shot of good cheer.

Like anyone who spent their Saturday afternoons going to the local cinema, I still get dazzled by the movies and the thought of actually being in one and being up there on the screen is so intoxicating that I tend to say 'I'll do it!' before I've even read the script (which probably explains that low-budget animal porn flick I did in the late eighties that thankfully went straight to video). I got asked to meet up with Debbie to talk about *Nativity!* at the BAFTA headquarters in Piccadilly over a cup of tea where, after a smattering of polite chit-chat, they offered me the role of a bitchy gay theatre critic, Patrick Burns – I know, reader, a bit of a stretch (how long would I have to be in prosthetics, I wondered). I pretended to think about it – some of my best acting – and then after a minute I squealed, 'Yes, I'll do it!'

You soon learn that the actual nuts and bolts of making a movie are so boring. Everything takes for ever. Yes, they call it the 'art' of film making and they genuinely treat it as an art. They say that a minute of every movie takes a day to film and they ain't joking. I was blissfully unaware that filming would inch forward at a snail's pace. Everything is meticulously analysed and examined and filmed over and over till it's perfect. I had come from the spontaneous world of stand-up and the erratic fly-by-the-skin-of-your-teeth nature of light entertainment where there is literally no time for such blatant fannying about. I remember chuckling to myself as I spent hours with the wardrobe mistress, pondering over whether a theatre critic would wear a camel-coloured jacket or a more textured taupe hue – just the week before on telly I had been wrapped in a bin liner which was then staple-gunned to my body as a makeshift blouse and for the bottom half they'd cut two holes in a bag for life for my legs to fit through which was then labelled a 'miniskirt'. My outfit, worn in front of millions of people, was worth £1.10 and here I was in this huge costume department fingering through literally hundreds of racks of jackets; it was like being in a very sombre TK Maxx. It was real luxury to actually have clothes that fitted me, not itching, not bunched up, the utter joy of having the security to move without hearing the 'ping' of a safety pin popping out – *Shit! My trousers are slipping off – now – on telly – oh my God, I can feel the breeze on my thighs, I'm in my pants. Fantastic. Camera! Action!*

I will always be thankful for the whole *Nativity!* experience, not just for giving me the opportunity to appear in their film but also for giving me the chance to see what I would look like with a tache. I've never been able to actually grow a moustache due to my dangerously low levels of testosterone – seriously, if I do Movember I have to start in April – so for me to finally see what I would look like if I had one was alarming and quite frankly scary – I looked like a sex offender.

As we filmed mainly on location in Coventry it meant I could stay over with my parents in Northampton, which was nice as it had been a while since I'd really spent any quality time with them due to my busy schedule. I spent the majority of the first night in their spare room tossing and turning. Anxious about what my first day 'on set' would entail, it didn't help that the cast were all stalwarts of the British acting profession: Martin Freeman, Ashley Jenson, Pam Ferris, Jason Watkins and Ricky Tomlinson have probably acted in some of THE most popular programmes on television.

Filming on location is fraught with problems: not only do you have the weather, which could turn at any moment, but a plane flying overhead, a car honking its horn or an overzealous member of the public who wants to upset the proceedings. During the heartbreaking moment whilst filming *Who Do You Think You Are?* when I was told my great-grandad had deserted his wife and six kids to escape conscription, a white van driver had pulled down his pants and pulled his arse cheeks apart at a T-junction in the background.

There are two things that will draw the general public

out of their houses and they are skips and film cameras. Lie in the street screaming, 'Help, I've been mugged – get help!' and not a sausage, but stick a skip outside your house and I promise you within five minutes you'll have people milling around and staring in it, or if they are particularly brave, popping their hands under the tarpaulin like it's some kind of industrial lucky dip. When renovating my house up in Holloway I popped a skip outside for all the rubble, plasterboard and junk that I had accumulated over the years and I had a better turn-out from my neighbours than when I'd held a coffee morning. I could see them, bold as brass, having a rummage, holding up chipped jugs and three-legged tables, making a comment and then popping them back. The same is true for film cameras. People see a film camera and will leave whatever they are doing and just stand there staring, zombie-like. Some people will have so little faith in the director that they will actually start filming the proceedings themselves on their iPhones just in case the director's footage isn't up to scratch. Some of my scenes had to be redone because after looking at the footage there were so many people staring from round corners and in between fence posts that it looked less like a film and more like an extended episode of *Dickinson's Real Deal*.

It was when we filmed indoors that I really became aware of the painstaking lengths it took to film anything (I'd thought you just took the cap off the camera and pointed it). I hadn't thought to bring a book, a laptop or anything. I would have looked out the window if there had been one. Also, I had assumed that we would have

Winnebagos. I distinctly remember seeing a behind-the-scenes feature on *E! News* and I swear John Travolta had an indoor cinema and a hot tub. Well, I spent hours and hours sitting in a cabin – well, okay, a Portaloo with a desk – twiddling my thumbs. There was no script to learn as it was all improvised. I would have to come up with my own lines, which believe it or not is actually harder, for me anyway, than learning an actual script. I felt my stomach twist like a stopcock. I tried sleeping to pass the time but my Portakabin was next to the animal enclosure; for the finale, filmed within the bombed ruins of Coventry Cathedral, the nativity would include a whole menagerie of animals, donkeys, sheep and a camel, and they were in a pen next to my dressing room – testament to how far down I was in the acting pecking order. The animals were closer to make-up and the canteen than I was.

I was surprised at how long the hours were – for the final scene, we didn't finish filming till 2.00 in the morning. Listen, I'd never go up to a nurse or a miner and go 'Phew, I'm pooped – I've been overacting for hours on end here,' but I saw a different side to acting. Admittedly, the scene had overrun and I heard a poor researcher outside my dressing room having to do the unenviable task of ringing up all the parents, asking if their child could stay till the early hours of the morning to do some essential filming. I heard the researcher ask a parent 'if Jemima could partake in one last nocturnal scene' and at that moment a donkey started hee-hawing – the parent must have thought, 'What the hell are they doing to my daughter?!' I had a flashback to that film in the late eighties.

When you get offered a part in a film and the name of your character is actually what you are, and followed by a number, then it's probably not worth you clearing shelf space to make room for an Oscar. So when the role of Seagull Number One dropped on my agent's desk it's safe to say I wasn't that excited. But when I heard it was for a SpongeBob SquarePants movie and I would be acting with Antonio Banderas I couldn't help getting all unnecessary and of course I squealed (again), 'Yes, I'll do it!'

I read the script, which admittedly didn't take long, on the way to the actual recording studio and panic set in. I had quite casually assumed that it would be okay for me to just rock up; I hadn't practised let alone researched the role, but then what could I do? Go to the seaside and eyeball holidaymakers, hang around a tip, nick some pensioner's chips? I just had to hope that the director wasn't going to get all Daniel Day-Lewis on my ass. Anyway, I was still cock-a-hoop that I would be meeting Antonio Banderas and sharing screen time with him. I arrived at the headquarters of Paramount all excited and was greeted by a woman at the door with a clipboard.

'Of course your portrayal of Seagull Number One will just be exclusive to Great Britain as you're not famous anywhere else in the world,' said the woman and followed it up by telling me that, 'Antonio obviously filmed his scenes in America. One of the joys of being a cartoon seagull is you don't actually have to be in the same room, as you and Antonio can perform your lines anywhere.'

'I sort of assumed anyway that Antonio wouldn't be here in this basement in Soho talking to little old me,' I lied, popping my Sharpie and *Evita* DVD back into my carrier.

It was a very strange experience for me – sitting there with the script trying to fit my words into the animated beak of a seagull. And it dawned on me mid-session – I had been chosen to voice a seagull because I actually sounded like a seagull.

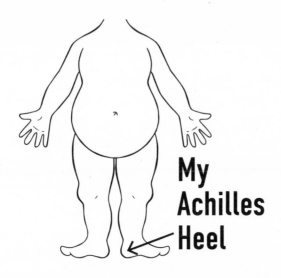

My Achilles Heel

People like Chris Evans and Dermot O'Leary choose to have 'open talk back' when they're recording a show: that's where you can hear the whole gallery through your earpiece – every mutter, every comment, everything that is going on in the studio transmitted straight to your ear. I choose not to have this – as I've said before, I have enough on my plate keeping up with the conversation I'm having with the guest let alone hearing 'Oh, Pippa, get me a panini,' 'God, they're boring,' 'What an awful dress!' Sometimes they accidentally leave the 'open talk back' on and you can hear them slagging you off. ME! On my own show! On a few occasions I've heard, 'Oh, get on with it' or 'Oh, please!' if I've come up with a different question.

Dawn French was on once and she mentioned that she went abroad to a villa to write her books. My producer commented, 'Oooh! All right for some,' speaking right over her so I missed her next few words. Unprofessionally, I came clean and told Dawn what the producer had just said. 'Well, maybe he'd like to come out of the gallery and say that to me down here,' she said. I could hear panic in my ears and a door opening and shutting quickly – somehow I didn't think he was on his way down to speak to Dawn.

Sometimes, though, your producer's guidance can be invaluable – I remember interviewing the gorgeous film star Bradley Cooper, and I kept hearing my producer's dulcet tones, 'Ask him a question! Ask him a question!' I'd just been there playing with my hair, spinning coquettishly on my swivel chair for five minutes, my eyes drawn lasciviously to his size 13 shoes, all dreamy thoughts of Rob Lowe evaporated.

One thing I am a stickler for is research. I have been a chat show guest myself many a time and it does piss me off when people don't do their research. I read all the books, I watch the films, I listen to their CDs, I sniff the perfume – I do whatever is needed as a courtesy to the guests, big or small. You have to – they have chosen your chat show so it really is the least you can do, don't you think?

I find it so depressing when you're interviewed by someone and they've just got all their information off of Wikipedia. Nowadays Wikipedia takes itself a bit more seriously, even asking you to pay for it (yeah, right!), but back in the day, Wikipedia and in fact the internet itself was a free-for-all, it was bandit country – you could write whatever you wanted about whoever you wanted. I've sat down in many an interview and been asked what was it like having Lionel Blair as a dad. What? Or 'I can't believe you started out as the voice of Zippy on *Rainbow*.' Pardon? Then the penny would drop and my eyes would spy a highlighted Wikipedia photocopy on the desk opposite – ahh, I see, they've gone to Wikipedia.

Doing research is also good for avoiding any potential social faux pas – you really don't want to be forcing a Disaronno down the throat of a recovering alcoholic or making a cheeky sexual joke to someone who just that week has been involved in a cocaine-fuelled orgy with a farmyard animal. You normally get taken aside by their agent and told not to mention certain things – sex tapes are often on the list, although I remember Colin Farrell decided to bring his own sex tape up and chat about it openly even though we had been warned not to, which I was impressed with – him being open, I mean, not the sex tape. Good for him, I thought, everyone had seen it so why not just mention it. Drug scandals and alcoholism are a no-no, which I suppose is understandable. With Ariana Grande there was a woman's name that I couldn't mention, I can't really remember it but it was a really mundane name, something like Becky Tadlock. 'Do NOT mention Becky Tadlock to Ariana' – I didn't even know who Becky Tadlock was/is and whether she was famous or not, I'd never heard of her. Of course, as soon as you get told not to mention something it sticks to your thoughts like chewing gum – I got myself in a right state about it and I started to panic. I was dreading her coming down the *Chatty Man* stairs and instead of asking if she'd like a drink I would just scream 'Becky Tadlock!'

I remember one occasion when a certain star graced the *Chatty Man* sofa and we were told in no uncertain terms by his PR not to mention or look at his hair. What? Well, as soon as he came down the stairs, I swear I could not take my eyes off it. Was it fake? It didn't look fake. I spent the whole interview staring at his head like a nit nurse. Was it a syrup? I couldn't tell.

Sometimes the PR people tell us to specifically mention things, like their charity work or forthcoming tour dates, especially ones that aren't selling, and sometimes we even get told to mention things that the interviewee doesn't want to talk about. This happened in the Lindsay Lohan interview. We were told by her people that Lindsay wanted to come on *Chatty Man* and set the record straight — the drugs, the alcohol, her rumoured lesbian relationship with the DJ Sam Ronson, she wanted to get it all out in the open — the only problem being they hadn't told Lindsay that. She thought she was coming on to talk about a people-trafficking documentary. Oblivious to this, I started to get excited. This is going to be good, I thought, this is what chat shows are made for, good old juicy titbits straight from the horse's mouth. I really admired her for doing it; how brave of her and what a wonderful 'up yours' to the gossip mongers and the tabloids. We sorted out the questions beforehand and they were to the point, fair but not too harsh — we made sure there was enough scope for her to open her heart and do herself justice.

She arrived on time and was really friendly in the make-up room, chatting to everyone and patting my red setters. The only telltale sign of her partying lifestyle was her gruff voice, which sounded the spit and dip of Marge Simpson's chain-smoking sister Selma.

With certain guests on the show you can feel a frisson in the audience, a buzz of anticipation running through them. This is normally reserved for the likes of Justin Timberlake or Lady Gaga but for this specific show the buzz was for Lindsay Lohan. She came down the stairs and as per I offered her a drink from the globe. She insisted on 'just water' and the audience tittered as that morning she had been photographed coming out of a nightclub at 4.00 a.m. with a coat over her head. I asked her about the open letter that the director of her latest film had written, criticizing her partying, but she was having none of it – she said she was always on time. I then asked about the partying – apparently she rarely partied. Okay, this is going well, I thought, and then I asked if she was dating.

'That's none of your business,' she snapped.

Fuck it, I thought. 'Are you Arthur or are you Martha now?'

'You bastard!' she rasped. We eventually moved on to people-trafficking but the atmosphere stank. She was naturally wary of me and rightfully so, I had inadvertently gone all Paxman on her ass. I don't want to be too harsh on her because, to be fair, she hadn't been briefed properly and neither had I. Journalists are obsessed with her – that interview was way back in 2010 and it still gets mentioned now and they always want to know 'What was she like?' I feel sorry for her because people do have it in for her – they want to think the worst of her – and actually once people have an idea of you it is unbelievably hard to shake that image.

Lindsay came back on the show in 2014 and what a transformation! She seemed 'on it' but in a really, really, good way. She was focused and in good spirits. Obviously people were disappointed that she wasn't a hot mess but I was pleased. She came along to support Stand Up To Cancer too, she just turned up unannounced to help with the fundraising, which I thought was so sweet, such a lovely gesture. It's nice to see people getting better.

Sometimes the guests on the show aren't even human – sometimes they are simply puppets – but they can still make an audience gasp when they hear they are on. We had Kermit from the *Muppets* on one series and that blew my mind as I am such a huge fan. Along with the rest of the world I grew up with the Muppets, had the books, watched the movies, I even had the *Muppet Show* album. I wasn't the only one super-excited, so was my best friend, Michelle, who until a phone call on the day was probably the only person in the world who didn't know they were puppets.

'We've got Kermit on *Chatty Man*.'

'Oh my God, I've got to come down and meet him – do you know if he'll be in the green room after the show?'

'Er, I hate to be the one to break it to you, but he's more likely to be in a carrier bag, stuffed in a holdall, my love, but I can check . . .'

I wouldn't mind but she works in telly! I was tempted

to say I was having a power lunch with Big Bird and would she like to join us just to see her reaction but I held my tongue.

We do bend over backwards for our guests and we always give them a favourable edit. They can rest assured that the anecdote that went down like a cup of cold sick in the studio on the day will sure enough have a huge belly laugh on the end of it by the time it leaves the editing suite later that week. We will often film out of order to accommodate the stars, sometimes grabbing a guest, filming them, keeping them under wraps for weeks and then putting them out just before their blockbuster drops at your local Odeon. It's a great way to get a good line-up on your chat show but it does have its flaws, such as continuity. Sometimes the filming is so out of sync, I've put on weight, my hair's changed length or I've suddenly got a tan. There was one interview I did where once the poor sod had finished his chat, it looked like his interview had been so boring I'd actually grown a beard. I had two weeks' growth! I interviewed the late great Sir Terry Wogan when he was promoting his book on Ireland, and we had filmed him earlier too so the show would coincide with the release date. We hadn't realized that it was going to be the weekend of Remembrance Sunday, so for all my other guests I wore a remembrance poppy and then for his interview it was noticeably absent. It was like mid-show I had completely changed my moral stance on World War I and its fallen heroes. Do you know what? I don't want to remember them after all. Oh yes, the perils of continuity.

Everyone gets their knickers in a twist when we have a

big film star on, but sometimes it's the stars of the small screen who can provide the most entertainment. I'd be lying if I said I didn't want THE biggest names on the show but I must say it irks me a bit in the world of chat shows that an interview with an A-lister grunting one-word answers can trump a scintillating chat with someone a bit further down the pecking order. One of my favourite chat show guests has got to be Phillip Schofield, I always have the best time when he is on, and it's not just because he brings tequila with him, oh no. Every time he comes on, we always end up getting totally smashed. However, the big difference between me and him is that he doesn't mix his drinks, he sticks to tequila, and if you get the hundred-per-cent-agave one, allegedly there's no hangover. I say allegedly, but I don't have the willpower to stick to one drink; sooner or later I will drift on to red wine and that is a toboggan to hell, which goes some way to explaining why I'm found the morning after face down in a skip while Phillip is up bright and early, chipper as you like, discussing feminine dryness with Holly Willoughby. I was once so twatted on the show that not only did I forget I'd interviewed the very funny Romesh Ranganathan but I'd also mentioned his lazy eye. I don't know what I said because I am so ashamed I can't bring myself to watch the interview but apparently I said he had one eye on dim, one eye on dazzle. Oh the shame. However, it did not stop there. When I woke up the next day, my body refused to move on to the hangover phase and I was all a bit giggly still. Any dog owners reading this know that dogs do not care how rough you are feeling, if they need a walk, they need a walk, and they will not stop mithering you until you are in that park, anorak on, throwing sticks and poop-a-scooping. So taking advantage of having a hangover-free hangover, I ventured out with the dogs to Hyde Park.

Everything was going well until we got to the Serpentine, the lake that curves so majestically through Hyde Park and Kensington Park Gardens. My eldest dog, Bev, had found a ball in the undergrowth and, wanting me to throw it, dropped it at my feet, whereupon it rolled into the Serpentine. I leant forward to grab it, but then it was as if all the tequila that I'd drunk the night before flooded forward to the front of my head and, becoming top heavy, I toppled in head first. Now I've seen news reports where animals have jumped in selflessly to save their masters from rip-roaring rivers and lakes, but no, not my two dogs; they just stood there wagging their tails, thinking it was a game. I managed to crawl out as luckily the Serpentine is not actually that deep, it's just slimy and you can't get a good footing. No one would be mistaking me for a swan any time soon. Seriously, it could have been a lot worse – say I'd hit my head and gone under! Can you imagine being pulled out of the Serpentine, dead with a tequila worm in my mouth – very *Silence of the Lambs*, don't you think? Of course, once I'd managed to get out of the lake I had to get home across the park. I was absolutely sopping wet and it looked like I'd pissed myself. As I walked back, I actually did that thing they do in the movies, where they take off their shoe, turn it over and all the water tips out. Because of my wet clothes and quite frankly slimy appearance it was obvious that I had become 'the man' – mums were holding on to their kids' hands saying 'Come away from the man.' And to add insult to injury, my hangover had moved on to the thumping head stage and I just wanted to get home. Most people splash a bit of water on their faces to wake themselves up after a heavy night but only I could choose a whole lake.

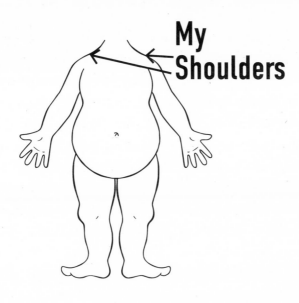

My Shoulders

It's one thing having your own chat show and interviewing all these celebs, but it's quite another going to award ceremonies and rubbing shoulders with all the stars at once. And when it comes to award shows you can't beat the Brits – I just love their drunken randomness. You listen to an album all year and then you get to meet the people who sing the album and you just gush. It was there I first met Adele. It wasn't the best of meetings – I waved at her across an after-party, then trying to look cool I did a Del Boy. Not at a bar like he did so fantastically well in *Only Fools and Horses*, but against a wall. I leant back on what I thought was a solid wall, but was actually a lift door that was in the process of opening. I leant backwards into the lift, getting no resistance from anything solid, until I fell flat like an ironing board on to the lift floor with such a thud that I had to check in the mirror to make sure I didn't have 'Otis' stamped on the back of my skull.

I've given away a total of three Brit awards and I'll be giving my fourth one out this year. One year I was actually in the running to host the Brits but it failed to materialize. Mind you, even if the television executives had decided to go for me I think I would have turned it down – it's such a thankless job. You go out there and you're greeted by a wall of noise; hardly anyone is listening and the ones that are, are off their nuts. It's better to just give an award out and then you can get on with enjoying the bevvies.

Although it's fun to see the performances it's always nice to have a nose-about backstage and the great thing is that because you are part of the show you get armed with an 'Access All Areas' laminate. You can go anywhere and everywhere and believe me I do. So, you'll just be there having a beer and Harry Styles will saunter past or Lady Gaga will be having a chat with a Pet Shop Boy. I was walking down the corridor one time and Rihanna was coming towards me. She stopped and pointed at me. I stopped and racked my brains, flicking manically through my cerebral Rolodex of insults, thinking, shit, have I slagged her off?!

'I taught you the dutty wine!' she squealed.

'Yes,' I said, 'on *Chatty Man*.'

'Of course, I remember,' she said and she rushed over and gave me a huge hug and then we both proceeded to do the dutty wine in the corridor. It was one of those magical moments that just makes me love her even more.

I also remember dancing with Florence Welch from Florence and the Machine in a flurry of confetti as Blur played. I don't know where her machine was but these kind of things just don't happen to me. The whole of that night was literally a blur and me and Paul woke up in Adele's suite at Claridge's the morning after wondering if the night before had actually happened.

If you want to know where you are in the hierarchy of celebrity then such showbiz events as the Brits are just perfect for finding out. It's not just the applause you get from the crowd as you exit your limo, but also where you are in the seating plan. When I was a guest of Adele's in 2012 and sat at her table I was so close to the stage I could have retuned Chris Martin's guitar with one hand and poured myself a glass of Prosecco with the other; obviously when I wasn't with Adele I was at a table in Zone 6 with Sonia. You get to know your place very quickly, and it's the same with the after-parties. It can be all very hit and miss: sometimes you'll get whisked in as the doorman recognizes you instantly and your feet won't even touch the red carpet; other times you'll be standing there for ten minutes in the freezing cold relaying your CV and waving an Access All Areas laminate in their face.

I was invited to the MTV Awards and greedily said yes, before it was revealed to me that it was in Frankfurt not Los Angeles. Like I said, you get to know your place. What they didn't tell me till I got there was that I would have to walk the red carpet. Fine, I thought, I've walked a red carpet before, you just shuffle up behind someone more famous – all the autograph hunters and fans go wild for them, the journalists lunge forward with their microphones ready to ask them a question and then you spot your chance and like a cat burglar slip inside under the radar and head to the bar. Result! Sadly, not this time. I would be walking the red carpet – individually – after having my name called out. What? But no one's heard of me in Frankfurt – it's *Chatty Man* not *Chatty Herr*.

Well, there I was outside this modern concrete building (like the one Prince Charles calls a carbuncle) on an industrial estate. The red carpet thrust out of the front door like a lolling fat tongue and my name gets called out via a tannoy like I've been separated from my mother in the Arndale: 'ALAN CARR!' Not a cheer, not a whoop. I'd been in louder libraries. I walked in silence along that red carpet while the paparazzi actually looked away and started chatting. I plodded onwards, the carpet feeling a mile long, until finally a group of girls screamed at me and started talking in excited German. They beckoned me over and I soon realized that at last someone had recognized me. My German isn't the best, but even I could understand '*Chatty Man*' and 'One Direction' – they had recognized me from my show and from having the World's Biggest Boy Band on. I confirmed that I was he and they screamed as if Harry Styles had just materialized before their eyes. They grabbed my hand, touched it, looked at it, admiring it like an artefact in the British Museum – my hand being the very hand that One Direction must have gripped at some point during *Chatty Man*. I had unwittingly become a conduit for a boy band – these girls were in the throes of ecstasy through osmosis. It was

278

sweet to watch them giggling and admiring my hand but I decided I'd better move on before one of them whipped out a circular saw to take it home as a souvenir.

Sometimes I don't think I get the most out of fame. Sometimes I get serious FOMO when I'm flicking through those celebrity magazines. Pages and pages of parties that I haven't been invited to, wall to wall beautiful people, models, Hollywood starlets and superstar DJs having the time of their lives in these exclusive clubs. Most of the time I will let it wash over me but every once in a while I will snap and say, 'Paul – get your coat! We, my dear, are getting a piece of that' – jabbing the society page in *Hello* magazine. Glad rags will be put on, *Come Dine With Me* will be switched off, and we will go out.

One time, we headed out midweek and typically nothing seemed to be open or remotely 'happening'. We were just walking past Claridge's feeling that we had made a big mistake leaving our cosy living room when we heard the sound of some music floating from a sash window of Claridge's ballroom. If my ears did not deceive me there was a party going on, and quite a good party judging by the number of posh cars lining the streets and the crowd of people idly milling around outside, rubber-necking at every twitch of a curtain and silhouette on the door. Plus there had to be celebrities inside due to the handful of autograph hunters outside, all buttoned up, the grey of their anorak colour coordinating with their auras. Determined to wring some life out of this dreary midweek night I approached the scowling lady at the door, who was gripping a clipboard.

'Alan Carr plus one for the party.'

'Alan Carr?' she said, casting her eye down the guest list.

I did the same, muttering 'Alan Carr, Alan Carr' – if my name had actually been on that list I probably would have passed out.

'I'm afraid it's not down – you can't come in,' she said dismissively.

I was going to kick off and say that someone had mistakenly forgotten to put my name down and I would be speaking to them first thing in the morning, but then it dawned on me, I did not have the foggiest idea who or what the party was for. I was only after a free drink so I thought I'd better not push it. I was just about to give up when I caught sight of a bronzed leg protruding from a limo. Who could that be? No, not David Dickinson, but Kate Hudson – who had just that very week been on *Chatty Man*.

'Hi, Kate.'

'Hi, Alan.'

'Oh, Kate, they don't seem to have put my name down on the list.'

'Just come in with me.'

'Okay, Kate.'

I linked arms with Kate, which looked a bit weird as she was already linking arms with the baseball player A-Rod, but anyway, needs must, and in we went to the party, which just so happened to be the after-party for her new movie *Nine*. It was a musical and although musicals were sort of having a renaissance it didn't really grab cinema-goers' attention, but who cares – 'I'll have a free drink, Mr Weinstein – make it a double!' Nicole Kidman,

Penelope Cruz and Judi Dench were there, along with the Hollywood uber-producer Bob Weinstein.

Bold as brass, Paul went straight over to Judi Dench: 'Excuse me, Ms Dench – can I please introduce Alan Carr to you?' He totally missed the point that you have to actually know someone yourself before you can introduce randoms to them. She was sweet but I didn't know what to say to her. 'Do you reckon *As Time Goes By* will ever come back?' popped into my head but I thought better of it. 'I loved the film,' I lied and quickly kowtowed over to Tamara Beckwith, who was probably on the same celebrity plateau as me and who I could relax with. After we drank the bar dry we decided to head home – life a little bit shinier after a slice of Hollywood on a rainy Wednesday night.

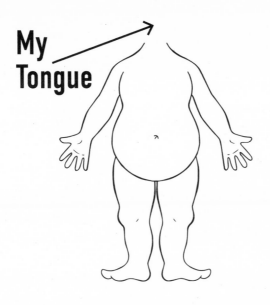

My Tongue

The musical performances on *Chatty Man* are a real treat for me because a) I get to see these huge stars singing so close up on *my* show and b) it means it's the end of the show and I can have a (nice) drink. These performances are usually done twice so that the artist can pick which one vocally is better. Obviously we do our best to sell the song and light it beautifully – in fact, our lighting man actually won an award for it – but sometimes that is not enough. The producers got an angry phone call one Saturday morning from a certain star's manager, complaining that from the filmed performance it looked like he was miming. He WAS miming!! What more could we do? Do you want me to crawl across the stage and poke his lips up and down with a stick so they fit the lyrics? C'mon, please – meet us halfway.

We've had some really memorable performances on the show, including Rihanna's 'Rude Boy', Justin Timberlake and his on-point horn section; Katy Perry doing a stripped-down version of 'Unconditionally' blew me away. Lady Gaga decided to do two songs for us and that was fine by me – both were amazing. Honestly, there are times when I have to pinch myself to make sure I'm not dreaming. Sometimes the stars like to hang around afterwards, which is a lovely compliment. There was a lovely piece in the *Mirror* once saying that on my birthday Adele and J-Lo had surprised me with a cake and they had all sung 'Happy Birthday' to me – all bollocks but I ain't going to correct it, it's nice to have something in the newspapers that paints me in a good light. I remember Kylie stayed and had a whisky that was basically as big as her – who knew Kylie drank whisky? She's so cute and petite, you imagine that even a quick gargle of Listerine would have her 'Spinnin' Around' – ha ha, I'm on fire today!

My dogs are a real honey trap when it comes to celebrities; my Bev's milkshake brings all the boys to the yard and Justin Timberlake was no exception. Outside his dressing room he saw Bev and instantly fell to his knees, smitten with the ginger bitch, and how could we resist taking a photo? It's on our mantelpiece: Justin is smiling, looking dead cute as usual, and there's Bev, completely oblivious, mesmerized by a squashed pastry on the floor. This is one of THE biggest stars in the world and Bev is more

interested in a discarded vol-au-vent – I guess not everyone can love you, Justin.

Grace Jones is one of my favourite ever guests on *Chatty
Man*. My idea of 'diva' is very much rooted in 1920s Hollywood. If you are fortunate enough to be a star then at
least bloody act like one, be fabulous, be other-worldly,
and this is exactly what Grace is and I bloody love it. She
is a handful but a glorious handful at that. Her head is
always covered, unlike her long, long legs, and she is
always wearing a Philip Treacy hat – the first time she
was on she had this hat with huge antennae poking con-
spicuously off her head and I didn't know whether to kiss
her or hang my coat up on her. Our meetings hadn't
always been so friendly. A while back I had been very
kindly invited by Julien Macdonald to see Grace Jones at
the Roundhouse in Camden Town – he had designed a
few of her outfits and so we had been invited to see her
perform. What a treat. It was such an amazing night and
reconfirmed why I love Grace. Why just perform a song
when you can perform that song rotating a hula hoop
round your neck wearing a bowler hat with your left tit
out? 'Come and meet Grace,' Julien trilled in that lyrical
Welsh voice he has, and we were promptly whisked (once
you get famous you never just walk) to her dressing room.
So we stride past the queue of trendy Roundhouse Cam-
denites to the front and with a flourish Julien knocks on
her door. It is opened by Simon Le Bon no less, and we
enter. I must have gone in first as Julien was behind me.
Grace Jones spins round on her heels, wearing nothing

but a black minotaur hat and a sheer top (I'd only seen her left tit on stage and now I caught sight of the right, so in an OCDish way I felt happy I'd 'got the set' as it were – I felt a bit like those antique experts on *Antiques Roadshow* when they are presented with two matching vases). She glares at me. 'Get out, get out!' she spits. She grabs me by the shoulders and in one fell swoop I am spun round and flung out of the dressing room on to my knees – in full view of the queue. It must have looked like that bit where the goat is lowered into the cage at Jurassic Park and then once devoured the remains of its corpse are discarded. I brushed myself down and hobbled off. Perversely, I was quite chuffed, because you kind of want that from Grace Jones, you don't want to meet celebrities and coo about how wonderful the night has been, fawning over them whilst they sip tea politely, nodding sagely – no, you want to be manhandled aggressively, thrown about like a rag doll. Well, maybe.

When Grace Jones agreed to come on *Chatty Man* her rider was slightly alarming; she requested an expensive bottle of red and copious amounts of oysters – great, I thought, she's going to come on stage pissed AND horny. But we were more alarmed by the fact that she was always notoriously late, which had us all sweating. This is naughty and I hope Grace doesn't mind, but we basically lied to her and told her that *Chatty Man* filmed at 1.00 p.m. in the afternoon – she turned up at 7.00 p.m., which was actually just when she was meant to be arriving at London Studios so it was the promptest she'd ever been.

The meeting was a bit friendlier than our previous one, but still eventful – this *is* Grace Jones we are talking about. Now, how can I put this? I got off with her. I know, I know, I shouldn't have, but I'd been mixing my drinks throughout the show (as always) and the tequila shot (as it always fucking does!!) had pushed me over the edge. As my tongue playfully toyed with her tongue, our mouths invigorated by the instant hit of tequila, I wondered to myself, what would Michael Parkinson do? At least Russell Harty only got twatted round the head when he interviewed her, I was being emotionally assaulted too. Half of me was thinking, Wow, I'm getting off with Andy Warhol's muse, model superstar, musical sensation Grace Jones, and then I remembered she was sixty-seven and if this was undercover footage recorded in a nursing home I would probably be arrested and/or put on a register. Anyway, it was something to tell the grandkids, wasn't it? That's what makes life a little bit more interesting. She'd come down the steps flashing her knickers, crawling on all fours, swearing and being outrageously flirtatious, not just with me but with a horrified front row – but I'd rather have that than some flash-in-the-pan singing sensation wittering on about how their album has upbeat songs and slow songs and how there is something for everyone on it – oh, bore off! As I came off stage everyone said, 'Was she hard work?' No, give me that any day.

People like to pretend to despise these divas and the ludicrous demands they come up with, but I think if we are honest we actually love them for it. Come on, admit it. When I hear an outlandish, outrageous demand being made by a superstar my eyeballs start to roll but I can feel the anecdote forming in my head like an embryo and I just know it will be ready to be given birth to at my local pub over a pint of lager and a packet of salt and vinegar crisps. You must remember that riders are not proportionate with talent or star power – that's something you soon learn. Taylor Swift, Katy Perry, Kylie, Justin Bieber, all good as gold. I couldn't believe how approachable Lady Gaga was. I remember I got a knock on the door from Bradley Walsh, who was filming his quiz show *The Chase* in the next studio. He wanted Lady Gaga to sign a CD for a children's charity.

'Would she do it?' he asked.

'I don't know,' came my (honest) reply.

We tiptoed up to her dressing-room door like we were playing 'Celebrity Knock Down Ginger' and tapped on it – she answered wearing a purple sperm on her head if my memory serves me correctly and Bradley explained about the charity. She just signed the CD, no 'Speak to my agent!' or 'Don't you dare knock on my dressing-room door, you Z-list oiks.' No, she was very sweet, and watching her make Bradley's and the charity's day I thought, I've got a lot of time for you for doing this – someone so outlandish in dress on stage, yet so down to earth in real life. On her rider I think she only wanted a bottle of Jameson's whiskey. She loves whiskey and had a few too many on the sofa and really needed a wee, dashing upstairs to her dressing room after the show. She couldn't get out of her costume quick enough and ended up having a piss in a bin – something I loved her for even more!

Like I said, star power is not proportionate to riders and demands. *Made in Chelsea* personality Mark-Francis

Vandelli Orlov Romanovsky refused to get in the complimentary car we put on for him as he 'doesn't do diesel' so we got him a taxi instead to take him home. He wafted off in it and disappeared home to most probably Chelsea, leaving everyone scratching their heads, for taxis – as we all know – run on diesel. Anyway, each to their own. Still, one thing I was not happy about was that I had offered the *Made in Chelsea* gang an Iceland buffet on the show and, well, you'd think I'd offered them a dog turd wrapped in a sanitary towel. The shade! They declined, asking, 'What is Iceland?' Coming off stage, always ravenous, I had gone to nibble on a prawn ring in the green room to curb my hunger. Gone! The ravaged trestle table looked like something on the *Marie Celeste*. The *Made in Chelsea* lot had popped all the Iceland grub in their handbags and hot-footed it back to Mayfair! Robbed, we was, robbed, and you know when you've set your heart on a chicken tikka lasagna – well, I could have cried.

At *Chatty Man* we always provide a car home, but sometimes the guests can be a bit cheeky – the *Only Way is Essex* gang diverted the car to a nightclub, partied all night, then went to a drive-thru McDonald's where Arg had a wee up against it. Well, I can't really get on my high horse about pissing; I can't in one breath condone Lady Gaga's piss-bin-gate going, 'Ooh, what's she like,' and then condemn Arg for relieving himself too – I have to be fair, I am an equal-opportunities gossip.

As you can imagine, we were all intrigued when we heard that Jennifer Lopez 'Queen of the Diva Demands' was making an appearance on *Chatty Man*. J-Lo (as I call her when I'm hanging around 'on the block') was an absolute delight but her rider – what a disappointment! I had literally legged it through Soho, desperate to see all the outrageous demands. 'What was on her rider, tell me, tell me everything!' Well, my little heart sank. Bottled water? Just bottled water? Just B-Wa for J-Lo? Where were the black orchids, the pygmies showering her with rose petals as she sashayed down the corridor? 'Where're the fucking bottles of Cristal?' I cried, shaking the celebrity booker.

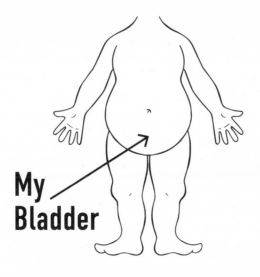

My Bladder

2015 was one of the busiest years I have ever had – looking at that year from the relative quiet of 2016, I probably did bite off more than I could chew and that wasn't necessarily a good thing. A 200-date comedy tour, Yap Yap Yap, that would cover the whole of Great Britain and Ireland, plus a chat show run and all the extra baubles that hang on the glittery Christmas tree that is my life, like radio, press, weddings, funerals and births, and let's not forget the Christmas *Chatty Man* and the comedy behemoth *New Year Specstacular* that haunts my December every year like the ghost of Jacob Marley. It was a lot to take on, but I felt ready for it. I was really pleased with my Yap Yap Yap tour, it had been going down a storm in the warm-up tour and there was a 'buzz' about it, whatever that means.

I'll interrupt the dialogue for just a second there – do you like a bargain? Ahh, now you're interested. Lean in, I have something to tell you. Comedians don't just start a tour, bang, when it says so on their tour poster, oh no, they need to work it all out on stage, hone it, sculpt it, find all the funny bits that will eventually (hopefully) be manipulated into a comedy routine – and if you are savvy and quick enough, sometimes you can get to see a comedian warts and all, up close and personal, sweating in a tiny little arts centre for maybe as little as a tenner. I've seen some of my favourite comedians do this. I was once in an audience and Harry Hill popped up to try out ten minutes. Sometimes it's nicer to see a 'work in progress' night when it's a bit rough round the edges because not only are you getting a good night out but you are also supporting your local arts centre and community spaces – so next time you see 'See Alan Carr Live at Tring Working Men's Club – £5', don't sneer 'Oh, look how the mighty have fallen', say 'Ooh, I might give it a go.'

Anyway, I digress. There I am, it's the first night of my Yap Yap Yap tour and I go on stage, it's going well, laughs in all the right places, then all of a sudden, oh my God, I'm wetting myself. I can feel it. It's coming out. I blurt something at the audience – I can't remember what, I was too busy clenching my urethra shut – and run for the Playhouse toilets. In fourteen years of stand-up this had never happened before. I went back on stage and continued the show and didn't think too much about it. In the car on the way home I blamed first-night nerves and the urn full of Yorkshire tea that I will drink throughout the day even if by 4.00 p.m. I am shaking like a shitting dog. I love my tea and, believe it or not, Jägerbombs and tequila are not my favourite drink – oh no, it's the good old-fashioned cuppa that floats my boat, and as the monkey in the beret said, pushing the piano up the hill, 'It's the Taste!'

The next evening I go to step on stage, buoyed up by the night before's reception, chomping at the bit. I step out and there it is – the sensation. I need a wee so bad I can neither explain it nor contain it; my bladder is not a bladder any more but a box of wine with a faulty nozzle – drip, drip, drip, oh no, it's flowing down my leg, is that a puddle I see before me? Help! Of course it wasn't and, like the previous night, when I finally got to the toilet I couldn't go. Obviously, dear reader, you don't want to hear about the goings-on of my bladder and I wouldn't even have included it in this book if it hadn't affected me so badly. For me, the sensation became The Sensation. Every public performance, every episode of *Chatty Man*, even something as uplifting and joyous as walking one of my best friends down the aisle, The Sensation would be there. The little blip on 1 February 2015 in Weston-super-Mare had become a daily, all-encompassing nightmare.

By March, The Sensation had become a fully fledged panic attack. I had palpitations, I was vomiting, the fear of going on stage would be so intense that it would literally grip me. All this at the beginning of a 200-date comedy tour – *Really body, really?!* This is going to ruin my life, I thought, and it did.

Listen, I'm sure a few of you are tittering away at the idea of me cross-legged on stage trying NOT to think of waterfalls and dripping taps and yes, I get that there is something intrinsically comic about your waterworks – I still giggle about Gangi Bhabuta wetting herself over the packed lunch boxes when she did an ill-advised cartwheel at middle school – but it was genuinely awful trying to suppress this wave of discomfort while my mind was telling me that every laugh I was getting on stage was due to a massive growing piss stain on my crotch. I started turning down work because the fear was too much – I couldn't handle it. I was even turning down birthday invitations and friends couldn't understand why. Little did they know and how could I tell them something so embarrassing? I'm not coming because I don't want to rain on your parade – well, it's more piss on your parquet but you get the gist.

There is a part in the stage show when I ask the audience what food they consider 'sexy', what kind of food turns them on. Well, one man in Coventry said 'trifle' and I felt a pang in my undercarriage (can your penis snap?). I felt the floodgates (literally) open – *oh no, I'm wetting myself!* – and I grabbed my crotch. 'Oh, does it turn you on as well!' I said. Well, the audience burst out laughing. I had to do something, I was becoming a wreck. Enough is enough, I finally told my private parts, and I rang up my doctor in tears. 'There are some wonderfully discreet adult nappies available on the high street,' came the voice down the line.

'Whoa whoa whoa, I'm not actually pissing myself! It's the sensation!' I shouted back. Well, the last sentence was a bit hushed – a woman in the next aisle had looked up.

That was the biggest irony: if I was wetting myself on stage I would just buy nappies – hey ho, pop them on, piss away, and if anyone asked why my nether regions were getting wider and wider during my act I could just blame it on feminine bloating. Done – problem solved. But it was more than that.

The doctor put me on to a urologist who spent a whole afternoon testing my bladder, kidneys, liver – in fact, any internal organ was tested that might have unloaded this misery on to me. Whilst we waited for the results I went into a little anteroom and spoke to the nurse. With head tilted to one side, she proclaimed, 'You know, there are some wonderfully discreet adult nappies available on the high stree—'

'I'm not pissing myself – oh, I give up.'

She then went on to tell me that she had a patient who was fine all day until she arrived home and stuck the key in the lock, whereupon she instantly had an uncontrollable urge to urinate. Well, it's all right for her, I protested, she can pop her 'Welcome' mat into the washing machine – what do I do? I can't stand on stage at the Hammersmith Apollo with a mop.

Meanwhile the results had come back – I closed my eyes and prayed for the best. Nothing wrong, tip top, perfection, impeccable, sublime, in fact the doctor said that you could eat your dinner off my prostate – well, he didn't, but you could tell he was thinking it.

Woohoo, I thought, nothing wrong – get in, my son! But then it dawned on me that if the problem wasn't downstairs, that meant there was something wrong upstairs. Oh dear – that prospect actually filled me with doom. Understanding the cause and effect of anxiety was like nailing jelly to the wall. Where do you even begin? Well, I tried everything. I didn't drink liquids after noon – apologies to people who saw my Yap Yap Yap shows in March through to April, I wasn't drinking water and that's why my lips stuck to my gums and my tongue kept flicking out and licking my eyeballs like a lizard! I tried more therapeutic paths of enquiry, including meditation, healing and Reiki. I even tried 'cupping', but my genitals kept falling out. Okay, the last one was a joke but you get the gist – I tried everything. One bloke believed that it was anxiety creating a ball in my stomach that needed to be 'broken down'. Already totally upset and feeling ill at ease, I sat on his couch.

'I'm just going to massage your colon,' he said, pulling the blinds down.

'You are not massaging my colon,' I said, pulling the blinds UP. 'No way, love.' I made a swift exit.

The only therapy I did not flirt with was hypnosis. I've always been wary of it. I know for a fact it works and I've seen people 'go under', but I wouldn't go near it with a shitty stick. It's the staring-in-the-eyes part that gets me – let's just say I will not be skyping David Blaine anytime soon. I just didn't want hypnosis to start effing with my head. You never really know the long-term effects, do you? I would just worry that in years to come I might hear the opening bars of the 'Birdie Song' and start taking my clothes off or doing the funky chicken.

In my time off the stage, mainly while writing this, I am hoping that The Sensation relents and the anxiety goes. Maybe the break will not only nourish me mentally but physically too. I've always been an anxious, nervy person, always, and it has manifested itself in all kinds of ways throughout my life causing a relentless relay race of health misery. Migraines in the playground and through university, and psoriasis all through my twenties and early thirties until recently when the baton has been squarely passed on to IBS. I know, the number of times on *Chatty Man* I've joked about having it and then I get it, which just goes to show you should be careful what you wish for. Nausea, vomiting, bloating, distended abdomen and the worst wind ever.

All my blood tests came back fine as I knew they would – it was bloody stress, which wasn't helped by the doctor's next suggestion: 'We are going to have to perform a colonoscopy' – a camera stuck up your jacksie. Now I was getting really anxious and my mind was whizzing. The cameras on *Chatty Man* were huge and sometimes they had to be assisted by a man carrying a cable – surely it couldn't be one of those that got shoved in? Of course, because of my sexuality people assume I will have no problem with things being thrust up me from behind. As if I'm going to be bent over a table and turn to give the doctor a cheeky wink as he pushes it in – please!!

Why does my body hate me? Even sleep failed to provide any relief – I started getting night terrors. Well, I must ask you – have you ever had a night terror? Just imagine having the scariest dream possible but you are wide awake and you're being sat on by a fat person. My first night terror was, er, terrifying – I was lying in bed, fine and dandy, trying to sleep; I'd just placed my *Puzzler* on the bedside table and closed my weary eyes, blissfully unaware of the *Nightmare on Elm Street* scenario that would soon unfold. Suddenly my eyes were drawn to the landing where the light had come on. Strange, I thought, it was only me in the house, Paul was out with friends. Oh my God, it must be a . . . I would have screamed but I was frozen, nothing could move, I found myself totally paralysed. My mouth wouldn't even open to let out a whimper. The door slowly opened and this 'thing' – for I do know not what it was or how to describe it – this thing came in through the door, circled my bed, then leant in and came about a foot from my face, staring at me with these cold eyes. No part of me could move. I managed to utter through a clamped-shut jaw, 'What are you?' and then it pulled back, circled round the bed and out of the door, and with the flick of the landing light going off, I woke. Even though at last I felt I could move, I daren't, just in case this 'thing' came back. It was the oddest experience I'd ever had and it really shitted me up – those dreams of walking naked around a shopping centre were small fry compared to this!

If anxiety isn't putting the willies up me whilst I'm alone in my bedroom, it's always there manifesting itself in all kinds of ways and more often than not at the most inopportune moments. For example, I was covered in psoriasis on the day of my *Tooth Fairy* DVD cover shoot – the poor make-up artist, Sue, was at one point contemplating paintballing Touche Éclat at my face and hoping for the best – seriously, my skin had the consistency of flaky pastry.

Maybe all I need is a rest, a chance for my body to

reboot, but I am disappointed in it. At the time of writing my body and I are now estranged and I only see it at the weekends. After the year I've had, I have so much sympathy for anyone who suffers with anxiety attacks and its crippling side effects; I feel your pain, brothers and sisters. And if anyone comes up to me in the street and tells me they've endured the same bladder complaint as I have, I will take them to one side and say to them from the bottom of my heart, 'There are some wonderfully discreet adult nappies available on the high street.'

I wasn't the only one in 2015 having a tough time. Paul was having a very personal battle of his own that year and it all began with a pair of stilettos, an oversized bra and a couple of condoms.

Adele was having a birthday party (does anyone have a Hungry Hoover, I seem to have dropped a name?) and the theme of the partay was 'Come As Your Hero'. Adele always throws a good party and everyone puts in an effort, so when we saw what the theme was, me and Paul decided to have a really good think. If you're going to dress up you should pull out all the stops – no sticking a sheet over your head and turning up as Casper the Lonely Ghost, you need to put the work in. My heroes are Wonder Woman and Prince so it was a tough call. Both had their positives and negatives. Wonder Woman would make more of an impact and yet red strapless corsets are so unforgiving on me and as for the star-spangled shorts – forget it, I'm a classic pear. So Prince it was. I decided to go for the *Purple Rain* era – classic Prince – rather than the bumless trouser look of 'Gett Off'. I rang up Angels, the costume hire company, asked for the said outfit and had it delivered to the *Chatty Man* offices. I slipped my trotters into the shiny purple pixie boots, squeezed into the purple sequined trousers, the ruffled shirt, the tousled black wig, and drew on the pencil moustache – *ta dah*, I thought as I stepped out on to the office floor. 'Ooh, Charles the Second,' said the receptionist as she passed by with a handful of files. Maybe it needed a bit more work.

My fancy-dress dilemma was nothing compared to the monstrosity that met my eyes when I walked through the door at home. Paul was in high-heeled boots, a pencil skirt, a plunging V-neck, a perm so tight it squeaked and a bra wedged with water-filled Durex. 'Who are you supposed to be?'

'My mum,' came the reply.

'Your mum isn't Jeremy Clarkson!' She really isn't. His mother was his hero, which I thought was unbelievably sweet, but little did he know that it would be his downfall. Oh, how everyone at the party laughed when he turned up swinging his massive breasts, swinging them left, swinging them right, swinging them in opposite directions. Wasn't it funny as he was slut-dropping in his heels and body-popping, throwing his humungous breasts here and there.

A great night was had by all. Adele turned up as George Michael – I mean dressed as him, she didn't drive through the wall with a steering wheel round her neck. Paul and I laughed all the way back home in the taxi. What a party! What a scream! What the fuck are you doing writhing around on the bedroom floor, panting and yelling for painkillers? All of a sudden Paul was in complete agony and we needed to get him to a doctor, A&E, anything. He was contorting himself into these animalistic shapes and crying – it was awful to watch. I decided to take him to A&E, well, once I'd got him out of the women's clothes. And I had de-Princed. Knowing my luck, they'd be filming an episode of *24 hours in A&E* and the last thing you want is: 'It's 2.05 a.m. and Prince has just wheeled in a screaming Jeremy Clarkson.' Anyway, to cut a long story short, while he was necking shots and slut-dropping at Adele's party, waving his tits around like an out-of-control swingball, all the vertebrae in his back had been yanked out and it was only when the alcohol had worn off and the breasts had come to a standstill that we realized he had done something absolutely devastating to his back.

Those first weeks when he was bed-bound I had to do everything for him, and I mean everything. Overnight, I had to take on the role of carer – God, it was boring. You like to think that when a loved one is in pain and is reliant on your help there is a pit of emotion dormant inside of you that will awaken, and you'll plunge into it and it will give you limitless patience and empathy. Well, sadly for me that pit had been filled in. The novelty of bringing up bowls of soup on a tray soon wore off and when the piti-ful voice fluttered down the stairs – 'I need to go to the toilet, can you please help me?' – especially if it was dur-ing one of my favourite shows, I would turn into Kathy Bates in *Misery* – 'What now?! What more do you want from me?! You're loving this, you cockadoodee!' stomp-ing unenthusiastically up the stairs. That was when I started crushing Nytol into his food. I'm not proud of this but he was in so much pain I thought it was for the best, for him and me. Only with sleep would healing come, I told myself, as I ground the tablets into his soup. How could I wash him and nurse him on zero hours' sleep? Every time he moved, bless him, a spike of pain would shoot through his body. I wasn't prepared for this and, quite frankly, I didn't need it – I was on stage every night, stopping myself from having a piss, and here was my partner taking the piss.

The worst thing of all was that due to the huge scale of the tour and the chat show – which had now been extended to seventeen weeks – I had to leave him for the West Country leg of the tour. It broke my heart, and I still feel the guilt now. There never is a brilliant time for back pain but the timing that year was exquisite; he was lying on the sofa screaming and I was pottering around a gift shop in Taunton trying to kill twelve hours till I could get home to look after him. Thank God for his friends, who really helped out – I owe them so much.

I came back from the tour to find Paul recumbent on the sofa, lying on a nest of *Chat*s and *Bella*s, looking as you'd expect – bloody awful.

'Alan, does my leg look all right to you?' he muttered pitifully.

I looked casually down. 'I can't see your leg, it's covered by a thick mottled purple support stocking. Whoa! That is your leg!' His leg was not only twice the size but it looked like he'd stuffed a couple of morbidly obese Ribena berries down a pop sock.

'We need to get you to a doctor!' I surmised quickly

and as it happened correctly for as we bounded in to A&E the doctor did a carbon copy of my first reaction – a kind of 'Whoa!' – and he diagnosed that Paul had developed deep-vein thrombosis from not being able to move around. We had got there just in the nick of time.

Sadly, it wasn't our last visit to A&E that summer. Paul and the dogs had decided to join me while I was in Bournemouth on my tour. (It's always hard finding good dog-friendly hotels and more often than not once my dogs have stayed there – stealing Cumberland sausages off of breakfast plates and jumping enthusiastically and unwashed on to the duvet – the hotels aren't always dog friendly when we leave.) After complaining of not feeling well and of a tightness across the chest, during the night Paul suffered a pulmonary embolism and yet again, frantic, we rushed to A&E. (Do hospitals do loyalty cards? The amount of times I was there in 2015, I deserve a complimentary bed bath or something.) Anyone who has had a loved one in hospital knows that the A&E ward is one of the most unsettling places ever, and it's even more unsettling on a Friday or Saturday night when not only do you have the fear that this could be your loved one's last moments but you have to share those last moments with pissheads covered in blood slumped in wheelchairs and ravers shaking off the effects of hippy crack. It was all very tense.

We finally got a bed, in between a drunk handcuffed to a gurney who was threatening violence and an elderly man with a bloody bandage wrapped tightly round his head. The nurse was asking him questions like 'What day is it?' 'Do you know where you are?' It was frustrating for me because I knew all the answers and wanted to shout them out – I do love a quiz – but I felt it would have been unhelpful to the nurse and the poor gentleman. The nurse recognized me but could see I was upset so left me alone, which I was thankful for; a few years back I was staying with a friend who had to be suddenly rushed into hospital (who am I, the angel of death?!) with meningitis, and the nurse there recognized me and took me around the ward to meet people like Diana used to do. I didn't know what to say to the patients – some of them really didn't want to see me, not because they were in a lot of pain but because they just really didn't want to see me – so I shook some hands and did some head-tilting. What could I possibly do for them?

'My back's broken.'

'Here, have an anecdote.'

I was about as much use there as a one-legged man in an arse-kicking competition.

They did a number of tests on Paul and asked him lots of questions: 'When did the symptoms start? Point on your body where it hurts. Do you have a headache?'

'He hasn't,' I said, 'but I do!' – eyeballing a janitor who had at that moment decided to wash around our curtained-off area with a mop and a bucket of neat bleach.

Paul was looked after handsomely and the staff were an absolute godsend. When I went on stage that night I threw myself into it more than ever, enjoying the release and just thanking my lucky stars for my health – slightly undermined by my phantom waterworks but nevertheless my distracted mind and lethargy soon vanished when I stood on that stage and it was just what I needed.

Once the panic was over we went back to London, relieved that the clot hadn't reached his lungs and thankful that no permanent damage had been done – we were out of the woods at least for now. Unbeknownst to me, however, a series of events had been put in place right in front of my very eyes and I was too blind to see it.

There is a common thread running through this book and no, it's not loitering around Accident and Emergency wards – it's alcohol. As you've probably already realized, the demon drink has played a part in most of my life adventures; it has enhanced some really boring evenings and totally ruined some perfectly wonderful ones and to say I enjoy a drink is hardly noteworthy, but it was in 2015 – *that* year – that I got a genuine taste of the real effects of alcohol, a lesson that even the worst hangover could never have taught me.

Paul and I had always drunk and we could easily match each other drink for drink, but after his cross-dressing-induced back injury, his DVT and embolism he had been drinking that little bit more. I didn't pay much attention to it, I just thought, well, if I'd been through what you've been through – you go for it. Being away on tour, I couldn't keep an eye on him. He sounded a bit slurred some nights and there were other nights when I couldn't reach him, which I didn't think much of. When I did come back to the house I saw how many bottles had been consumed. I wasn't particularly worried about the wine, it was the empty bottles of spirits, gin and vodka, which I found alarming. I started to worry – it was getting to the point where I would have to decant some of the empties from the recycling bins to leave a manageable (read 'socially acceptable') amount and take the surplus to the recycling centre to avoid malicious gossip from the neighbours and severe back pain for the dustman who would have to lift the bloody thing. I soon found out he had been drinking in the mornings. I took a sip of his 'water' from his side table and my body instantly repulsed as the recognizably harsh taste of vodka kissed my lips.

All of a sudden he started asking me to drive, which was strange in itself because he can't stand my driving, and he's right, I'm not the best driver. I'm all right with certain manoeuvres, that's fine, it's just that my brain connects anger with speed. Does anyone else get that? Basically, when I'm angry or have angry thoughts I lose myself and the anger shoots down my leg, causing my foot to press harder on the accelerator. It's the weirdest thing. I remember when Isis were beginning their destruction in Syria I was so fuming that I jumped a red light and nearly ploughed into a Debenhams window display. It's my nerves, I am always thinking the worst. You know those signs that you get in the countryside, 'Concealed Entrance', they fill me with fear – I start looking everywhere, sometimes even the sky, terrified that a vehicle will appear from out of the blue. Why do people have to conceal their entrances – what's wrong with a bit of bunting and neon? Oh and roundabouts, I will never understand them. I never know who you give way to and when – what if they are already at the junction? What if you arrive at the roundabout at the same time – who let's who out? It's etiquette hell. To avoid any embarrassment or unnecessary tooting I just wave my hand and whisk everyone across the roundabout, whether it's right or wrong: 'You first, kind sir, please, after you; no, madam, after you.' I'm like some Walter Raleigh of the Round-abouts, with elderly people mouthing through the windscreen, 'What a lovely young man.' Little do they know, I don't know what the fuck I'm doing. Don't you feel safe that there are people like me on the road, dear readers?

Anyhow, as you can imagine, I instantly saw through the 'Why don't you drive, honey?' bullshit. I could smell a rat and I could smell whisky, which was worrying as I could also hear the opening bars to *Lorraine* wafting out from the lounge. He was pissed – again.

We set off on holiday to Barbados with me hoping that a few chilled evenings with friends accompanied by a couple of socially acceptable pina coladas as the sun set could induce in me a feeling of peace and serenity, both mentally and spiritually. However, this wasn't to be as I could see that Paul's drinking had got out of control. It culminated in him drunkenly pulling a monkey's tail and trying to steal its banana in an animal sanctuary. The monkey went crazy as you can imagine, and we left Paul to his own devices. I really wish we hadn't because five minutes later we saw him picking up a turtle out of its pen and kissing it. The turtle, thinking 'What the fuck?' then shat itself all over Paul's top. Well, there were angry looks at lunch that day – mainly due to his behaviour and also the pong that was rising from his shirt.

While we were in Barbados we were invited to have dinner with Sir Cliff Richard, but I couldn't bring Paul, not in his current state. The last thing anyone needed was Paul breaking into a rendition of 'Millennium Prayer' in a fish restaurant. I said to Sir Cliff he was ill – which, if truth be told, he was.

I don't understand alcoholism even though there have been times when I've thought I actually was an alcoholic. I know now that I'm not and, seeing it first-hand, I realize I was nowhere near to becoming one. You start to understand that alcoholism isn't really about drinking, it's about control, habit, self-worth, depression, escape, a whole myriad of trigger points that can be set off at any moment. Alcoholism is like jet lag – you never really have much sympathy for it if you haven't got it yourself. I was hugely inconsiderate with Paul at the beginning. I thought he was being self-indulgent – 'You CAN stop, you've just got NO will power.' I foolishly used to be the same with eating disorders – 'Oh, shut up and have a cake.' And depression – 'Cheer up, go and see *Cats*. Let your hair down.' Boy, has that changed now. The guilty pangs of when I was dressed as Amy Winehouse came back to haunt me again – God, what must she have been going through?

The trouble was, Paul was a functioning alcoholic and I don't know if that was better or worse for the whole situation. You see, one of the side effects of his drinking was that he would dress up and wander about and do things. There were times when I thought, why can't he be one of those drunks who sits in the corner of the pub boring people to death, or just lying in the park enjoying the sunshine, feeling sorry for himself? But no, he couldn't stay in, he'd have things to do and he would often get dressed up. I remember the neighbour saying, 'I've just seen your Paul dressed as a geisha,' and there he would be, staggering along in wooden shoes, off to do the weekly shop.

Paul ended up in rehab a couple of times. The first time, I put him in there, though I felt bad doing it – it seemed like a betrayal, but what could I do? Without being overly melodramatic, he was killing himself before my eyes – his skin was grey and he was incoherent most of the day, staggering, talking in tongues. The second time in rehab was different, he actually asked to put himself in there, which I knew took real guts. He was walking around the garden with one shoe on, crying and visibly disorientated. I came out of the back door, our eyes met and he said, 'I need help.' It was heartbreaking to see but I was so proud of him – this brave first step could only lead to a better place. Something needed to be done because our relationship was breaking down – I used to only kiss him so I could tell if there was alcohol on his lips.

We sat down in the kitchen and I went online to look for a place to send him. It was grim and the only light relief came from Bev. As Paul was crying, I saw out of the corner of my eye her paw slowly pull his plate across the table and his mackerel omelette slide effortlessly down her gullet. Yes, even at our lowest ebb, be it man, woman or beast, someone will always be there to take the piss.

I carried on with the tour and the chat show, I had no choice. The clinic didn't allow him visitors, which was tough on both of us, and there was no point in me just sitting at home fretting. Believe me, the irony of me pouring those disgusting drinks from my globe, forcing my guests to drink them whilst my other half was locked away for alcohol abuse was not lost at me. I thought, if he's sitting watching this, this is not helping! Another irony that I became aware of was that *my* alcohol intake was going through the roof; the stress of the whole situation was nudging me towards the bottle rather than propelling me away from it. I would find myself on the way to the office popping into a pub: 'Glass of Pinot, please – large!' Taking the dogs for a walk, I'd nip into my local: 'Give us a pint, Craig.' I would actively seek out drink when I needed relief, and fast.

I remember the final *Chatty Man* of the series – well, I don't actually remember, this next part has been compiled from eyewitness accounts, police reports, CCTV footage and folklore. The last thing I do remember is them wheeling in a vodka luge. After the year I'd had, it was a lethal combination. We ran out of vodka to pour down the luge and so we moved on to the contents of the globe. I'm gagging as I write this but apparently I was loving it at the time; my mouth was so tightly clamped to the ice that my lips had inflated and looked like Kylie Jenner's.

I woke up on the floor in my dressing room; I must have passed out. Oh God, I thought, I'd better get home. I grabbed my bag and coat and went to ask Antonia in the office to book me a car home. 'Antonia, Antonia!' The office was empty and the lights off. I looked at the clock – 3.25 a.m. – everyone had gone home. I was locked in London Studios, and I tell you, nothing sobers you up quicker than the realization that you are locked inside a building alone and no one knows you're in there.

I wandered the labyrinthine corridors where a few years back they used to have photos of TV legends on the walls and you'd always find the exit by turning right at

Michael Parkinson. These had been taken down and replaced with random, colourful depictions of London landmarks. I was staring up at this turquoise outline of St Paul's Cathedral, not knowing where the hell I was. I stumbled along the corridors in a daze, like those people in pyjamas in the *Poseidon Adventure* who are walking aimlessly and refuse to go with Shelley Winters and Ernest Borgnine. I had access to all the studios and in my drunken haze I thought, ooh, I could have my own show – and then it dawned on me, I did, and that's what had got me into this mess. Eventually I found the entrance and the kind security guard dialled me a taxi. I thought that my kip on the dressing-room carpet would prevent a hangover, because I was already having it, wasn't I? I'd had my sleep and this was the hangover so the next time I slept would be a normal sleep and when I woke up – no hangover – right? Wrong!

I woke up stinking. I didn't know which were puffier, my eyes or my lips, which were frozen with chilblains after getting off with an ice sculpture for half the evening. I quickly rang up Jon in the office, who was busy doing the edit for the upcoming show. Gingerly, I posed the question, 'Did everyone have a good time last night?' my finger poised to press 'end call' if there was any hint that the conversation was about turn to my drunken indiscretions, but no indiscretions came. Jon was fine, nonchalant even, I'd just got leathered. I was out of the woods. Then . . .

'You must be buzzing after meeting your hero last night!'

'Pardon, what hero?'

'C'mon, you remember, Harrison Ford.'

'What?'

'Harrison Ford, he was filming with Jonathan Ross in the next studio.'

I could not remember a thing, goddamn, and I love Harrison Ford.

'Was I all right?' I asked, fear only slightly creeping into my voice.

'I'll send you the video, one of the cameramen filmed it.'

Shit – there was video evidence. Oh my God, I was having palpitations now.

The video came over and it took me thirty or forty minutes to press play – I was terrified. When I used to dream about meeting Harrison Ford, it was not like this.

I pressed play. There I was round the back of London Studios, copious amounts of empty and some quite full bottles of wine on the table, singing the *Indiana Jones* theme tune to a bemused Harrison Ford. I go up to him and fling my arms round him, telling him 'I love you,' and he says, 'Boy, I need to have a few to catch up with you.' Fair play to Harrison, he could have had me tasered. I imagine a drunken me rolling towards him must be slightly less scary than that boulder in *Raiders of the Lost Ark*.

Well, as I was considering maybe popping into rehab myself, my lovely Paul has come out and he's a different person, a better person. With alcohol you are never yourself – there was party Paul, hysterical Paul, upset Paul, morose Paul, exuberant Paul. Nowadays I get just Paul and I like it like that.

*

The Yap Yap Yap tour was slowly coming to a close and I felt quite emotional that this show I had been touring for well over eighteen months would finally be no more. The tour went swimmingly on stage but, as you have read, it was the off-stage dramas that had taken their toll on me. Panic attacks and alcoholism, surely that was enough to be getting on with as well as the hours and hours of motorway loneliness – but apparently there was more to come.

We'd had an amazing run of gigs up in Liverpool, they really are some of the best audiences ever – they get me and they get it, so much so that I wanted to celebrate. It was a Saturday night and I didn't have a show the next night. I thought that if I couldn't have a good time in Liverpool, I might as well throw myself in the Mersey, so I headed out. I found a lovely little tapas place near the city centre and had some delicious small plates and half a bottle of Malbec with my tour manager, Elliott, what a lovely evening. My belly full and my head woozy with mild intoxication, I turned left out of the tapas place and stumbled back to my hotel. Why then was I sitting in A&E at 6.00 a.m. the next morning with a tour manager covered in blood with a broken leg? Because I turned right, didn't I! Yep, I turned right instead of going left like a good boy, the infamous second wind blew down Wood Street and took me with it and I spent the night drinking and cavorting with random Scousers at various night-spots around Liverpool. At 4.00 a.m. I got hungry and queued up for a Maccy D's with my tour manager – well, the next thing I know, a fight is breaking out between my tour manager and the bouncer at McDonald's. Of course, in hindsight, if a fast-food restaurant has to have a 'doorman' then it's probably not the best place to drop in and have a drama-free bite. Elliott was dragged outside and his leg stamped on so brutally it broke. He was white as a sheet and obviously in distress as he lay there on the ground, though this didn't stop me from trying to pop a chicken McNugget in his mouth – I had queued up for them #justsaying. Before I knew it, he was being put on a stretcher and we were both put into an ambulance and taken to the nearest hospital. I tried to be as helpful as someone as pissed as me could be. I stayed until he was sedated, took some selfies with the nurses – they asked to, not me – then went back to the hotel, thinking all the time, 'Did that just happen?'

Severely hungover, I took the dogs out and texted Elliott to see how he was, feeling guilty for not being more help. Then a police officer very kindly came to the hotel to check that I was okay and to verify my statement. Statement? I'd made a statement last night? I couldn't really remember saying anything. She opened up a black folder, pulled out an A4 piece of paper and started reading: 'It was 4 o'clock in the morning. I was in McDonald's in Liverpool City Centre with my tour manager waiting for some food. I noticed out of the corner of my eye that my tour manager was being dragged out by the neck and being repeatedly punched in the face – I didn't go to help him as I was starving and my chicken McNuggets were nearly ready—'

'Whoa whoa whoa!' I interjected, my hangover suddenly dissipating. 'Excuse me, Juliet Bravo, you can't put that down, I sound like an idiot, a selfish, mean, greedy pig!' Admittedly, it was the truth, and yes, I was starving, but I'd look a right arsehole in court. I could see the jurors shaking their heads and tutting, 'Dropping a friend for a Big Mac meal, and he looks so nice on the telly;' I could see my Pride of Britain Award disappearing into the distance before my eyes. I felt awful but what could I do? It was the truth – am I an awful human being, reader? Please say no.

Poor old Elliott had to have six tough weeks off with his leg in plaster to get his leg mended and also, more importantly, to recuperate mentally – it had been such a vicious assault. I carried on the tour without him, hoping no more shit would go down. Seriously, I thought, enough with the dramas, what was happening to me? I felt cursed – I kept checking through my tour book to see if I had done a gig on an old Indian burial ground or something. Earlier in the tour we had stayed at a hotel up north and whilst having post-performance drinks the hotel manager, quiet tiddly herself, had pulled out a Ouija board and we had started contacting the dead. I wondered if I had angered any spirits and if this run of bad luck could have been brought about by meddling with things from the other side. Mind you, looking back, we weren't terribly successful. At one point, we asked, 'Is there anybody there?' and the duty manager, who had nodded off at the table, started talking in his sleep – we hadn't contacted the dead but we had contacted Jim. Well, anyway, drama like this makes it easy to write autobiographies but not so easy on the nerves.

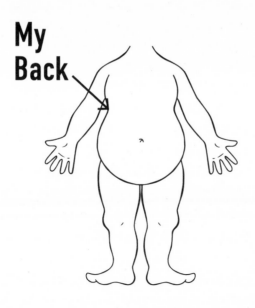

My Back

After saying at the end of 2015 that I was going to relax and enjoy some quality 'me' time, 2016 has proved to be the complete opposite – isn't that always the way? A succession of very exciting projects that I hope you will see very soon on your TV screens has had me beavering away, loving the chance to step back from the chat show for a bit and display a different side of me. These projects, however, have been bittersweet for me – it's the first time I have taken on anything without being under the watchful eye of my manager, Addison Cresswell, who I mentioned earlier in the book. He took over my career in 2005 and changed my life beyond recognition – I owe so much to him. Ask anyone who knew him, he was a tornado, a whirling dervish of enthusiasm and ideas. The phone would ring at 2.00 a.m. in the morning: 'You know that show we were talking about – what if we set it on a cruise ship and all the guests are shipped in on inflatable bananas?!' If anyone rang at that time I knew it was either Addison or my Nan had died. Half asleep, I would try to piece together what the hell he was on about – 'Er, yeah, I think that would be a good idea, eh?' – but then he would flitter off, I would say like a butterfly but he was so nocturnal I guess moth would be the best simile. Comedy was his life and he just had this sixth sense for knowing what would work and what wouldn't. He transformed stand-up comedy with his *Live at the Apollo* series; before that stand-up had been filmed in an almost apologetic way, above a pub or in a smoky back room with a solitary mike stand looking sorry for itself. *Live at the Apollo* made stand-up comedy sexy, it was flash, it was rock and roll, and it introduced the general public to a load of fresh new stand-up comedians that you might never have come across, John Bishop and Micky Flanagan to name but two.

The show mimicked his energy and enthusiasm so it was a complete shock on 23 December 2013 when I got a call to say that he had died of a heart attack in his sleep at the age of fifty-three. Totally unbelievable. This guy was so restless with ideas and schemes and plans I couldn't even imagine him sleeping let alone dying. There was a horrendous storm that night, the trees were swaying violently past the window and our recycling bins were playing kiss chase across the lawn. Then, to cap it all, we were plunged into darkness courtesy of a power cut.

Knowing what Addison was like, I could just picture him cackling away, moving objects around my house, slamming doors – and of all the people on his books it would be me he would take the most pleasure in haunting. Addison would make the best poltergeist and if you'd met him you'd know exactly what I mean. Sitting there in the pitch black, the only thing showing any life was the burglar alarm that for some unknown reason had started up and was wailing across London. Unable to get a technician out so close to Christmas, we had to put up and shut up. Yes, needless to say it was the most miserable Christmas ever.

Addison had saved me when I was at a confused time in my life, at a crossroads, miserable, unsure, uncertain of the future, and had put me on the right track. I miss him and his ability to make everything all right; in a notoriously flaky industry, he had my back. I even miss all those early-morning calls when I would grunt under my breath as I fumbled for my mobile on the bedside table, 'What does he want now?' What I would give for him to give me one last call, just so I could hear his voice again . . . Addison – I miss you so much.

I love Channel 4, without them I would be nothing. They have supported me and given me work for the last ten years and for that I will be for ever grateful. But as much as I love television, I detest television politics, those behind-the-scenes goings-on where someone upstairs has made a decision and you being a 'name' or 'face' of the channel have to endorse it whether you like it or not. It happens at all channels and is by no means exclusive to

Channel 4, but you soon come to the sorry realization that you are actually the monkey and not the organ grinder. Whether it's a blanket ban on mentioning, say, a reality show that involves celebrities plummeting down a ski slope and ending up in a wheelchair or a neck brace – I'm just thinking out loud here – or maybe a show that a Channel 4 commissioner passed up on and subsequently turned out to be a huge hit for a rival channel, well, understandably as a paid-up employee of Channel 4 I'm not going to start raving about it. However, there are times when you find yourself caught in the crossfire and everything is out of your control and you have to sit there powerless, feeling the pegs being slipped slowly down the back of your shirt as you are hauled up upon the washing line and 'hung out to dry'.

I used to be a features editor for *More* magazine, now sadly defunct (don't look at me!) and I liked *More* because it was positive, no one was pilloried, it wasn't bullying, it wasn't sensationalist, it was the kind of magazine that if I had a teenage daughter I would like her to read – it was one of the good gals. No one got treated like a paedophile if they had a handbag that didn't match their shoes and if you were fat no one gave a shit. Every week I would go to meet a 'celebrity' and chat to them and have a few photos taken with them, usually with me dressed as a gimp – but hey, it paid the bills. Well, one week I was meeting the stars of Sky's hit dance show *Got to Dance*, Kimberly Wyatt, Ashley Banjo and Adam Garcia, at Covent Garden's legendary Pineapple Dance Studios. I turn up there with my Dictaphone, notebook and pencil, and what every prospective journalist needs, a red setter (I think Paul must have been working – anyway, I digress).

I headed into Pineapple Dance Studios and how can I describe the vision that met my eyes? There was a camera crew filming and this homosexual pirouetting around the foyer like a lazy Susan on speed – I stopped in my tracks! 'Welcome to Pineapple Dance Studios,' he lisped hysterically, putting one leg into a pointe and resting the other on the reception counter – this man made me look like Chuck Norris. I laughed nervously and went into one of the many dance studios where I did my interview, thinking what an odd little man – obviously this was before *Pineapple Dance Studios* became such a big hit and the whole world was introduced to that fabulous camp human whirlwind Louie Spence. The penny dropped as I was watching it: 'So that was the show they were filming – oh, I get it now.' I was actually excited that I was going to be on *Pineapple Dance Studios*.

What I didn't know was that Channel 4 had turned the series down the year before and it had gone to Sky 1 and since become this hit show that everyone was talking about. Channel 4, feeling a tad irked, had implemented a ban on any Channel 4 talent being on the show. But I'd already been filmed on it, what could they do? Channel 4 stood fast and denied permission for me to be seen on *Pineapple Dance Studios*. Please, when you've finished reading this book, go on to YouTube and watch the clip – it's so ridiculous you can't even get annoyed. I am completely pixilated, along with my dog, pixels so big they look like Stickle Bricks, and my voice has been autotuned

HIGHER! The only thing they didn't autotune is my laugh – so you can tell it is me instantly. As I come through the door the narrator, Michael Buerk, comments archly, 'Sometimes international superstars drop into Pineapple Dance Studios – this one refused to be filmed.' What!? Arseholes – I'd been stitched up like a kipper! The humiliation of it all. But what could I do, what could I say? Did anyone really care about the commissioning process of *Pineapple Dance Studios*? Not really, but social media had their say (of course) without bothering to get the whole story (of course): 'Too big to go on *Pineapple Dance Studios*, are you?' came the accusations; 'International superstar – I don't think so.'

God, I felt a right dick and although my ego was bruised, it was a great leveller, a little reminder that you are a small cog in a bigger machine and that sometimes things are out of your control, you are powerless. This surprises some people because they think celebrity equals power, but sometimes that just isn't the case. I assumed that once on the telly in the comfort of my own chat show format I would be brimming with confidence, I would feel bulletproof, I would be striding down the street, chest puffed out, cockiness personified. Oddly, I've found the opposite to be true; if anything, it has undermined my confidence in a lot of ways. Instead of soothing my anxieties I think it has added to them, but then again I worry too much and I know this. You create the show or the stand-up routine and like a parent you send your child off to school and hope it doesn't get too bullied and picked on. *Why do you do it then?* you ask. *Give up, let someone else have a chance if you hate it so much, you big old misery guts!* Well, it's the buzz, isn't it? All the time I'm on stage I am getting the biggest thrill – it's the other bollocks that attach themselves to the process that do my head in.

The problem is that celebrity is mistaken for wisdom. I remember a female DJ saying something ill-judged on the radio and she got a barrage of abuse. She apologized and everyone forgot about it – that's the reason I'm being vague because she's moved on from it all so I don't want to dwell. (And besides, this book is about ME! If you want to know about her scandal, read her bloody book!) Commentators, social media and anyone with an opinion basically said, 'She's in the public eye – she should know better.' This has always perplexed me – WHY should people in the public eye know better? How do *we* know better than you? What *is* better anyway? Perhaps people assume that once you get a show on television you are whisked off to a ladies' finishing school, lobotomized, fitted with a chip and shoved back out with all your opinions sanitized and politically correct – believe me, you aren't. I am fumbling along, trying to make sense of it all, like the rest of you.

The only guidance I ever got was a couple of hours of media training at Channel 4 headquarters, where a woman who was a dead spit for the Governess on *The Chase* quizzed me ferociously on camera in a mock interview, pelting me with journalistic curveballs, flustering me and leading me down conversational cul-de-sacs. I then watched it back and she went through my answers with a fine-tooth comb, highlighting how things could be taken out of context, homing in on what was quite an innocent reply and how that could be manipulated to say the complete opposite – it's true you can draw poison from the clearest of wells. She then told me conspiratorially to avoid certain nightclubs and bars as newspapers and gossip magazines had paid informants (her words) that would be listening into your conversations. She said, 'Taxi drivers, doctors, police, court clerks, nurses, bar staff, cabin crew – all sell stories so don't say anything incendiary around them that could be used against you.' Fuck, as I left the building I looked behind me to check whether I had in fact wandered into MI5 instead of the Channel 4 offices.

Filled with fear, the taxi ride home was like a minefield.

'What you up to today?' said the cabbie.

'Nothing!' I replied, scanning the cab for bugs – desperate that my 'Big Shop at Asda' would remain off the front page of the *News of the World*.

I read a lot of autobiographies, both for pleasure and for *Chatty Man*, and I know there is nothing more boring than a celebrity moaning about the awful press intrusion, especially when you see them on the front of every magazine, gurning spread-eagled on their kitchen island, legs akimbo, letting the press inside 'their home'. 'Their home' is in inverted commas because a lot of the time it's not their home at all and is rented or hired for the photo shoot, which makes the whole pantomime even more ridiculous. I get on with journalists, I've got some that are my mates; we always have a good laugh and a gossip and you can bet your bottom dollar that gossip will be with them until they die. Having said that, some journalists aren't nice – then again, some celebrities aren't nice.

I'm proud of how well *Chatty Man* has done, but it

wasn't always like that – it got slagged off badly in the early days. The *Sun* ran a piece saying it was going to be axed after **JUST ONE SERIES** – they changed the font and put it in bold just in case you didn't quite understand the words. I can laugh off that shitty article now from the safety of my sixteenth series, but it stung at the time. They'd followed me and taken a photo of me holding my head looking miserable in the street, because if you find out that your series has been axed after **JUST ONE SERIES** I don't know about you but I tend to go out and just stand in the street holding my head. The show then kept getting moved around in the listings, which isn't ideal – if your audience can't find you then how can it grow? It's been moved again this year to a Thursday, which I actually think is a good move on Channel 4's part; at least the comparisons with Graham Norton's chat show directly opposite on a Friday might stop (which has the most frighteningly amazing celebrity line-ups each week!). Wherever you move it, of course, some people still don't get it or enjoy it and that's fine. 'Chatty Man? More like *Batty Man!*' the wits cry. I know, that's why I called it *Chatty Man*, it was a deliberate subversion of the homophobic term. Jeez!

Still, I am determined this is not going to be one of those moany books all about poor me being slagged off. I had my journalistic epiphany on *Chatty Man*, believe it or not. We had Karl Pilkington on, a boy band you might have heard of called One Direction and Lady C – a bonkers hermaphrodite aristocrat fresh from her stint on *I'm a Celebrity . . . Get Me Out of Here!* – don't ever say *Chatty Man* doesn't give you variety!

During the interview Louis Tomlinson's phone had gone off and out of politeness he said, 'Sorry, Alan, oops, should have turned it off,' and slid it across the floor. The audience, full of Directioners, cooed in unison, their hearts melting at such an act of kindness, and the interview continued drama-free. We had to record a couple of songs because One Direction had very kindly said they would sing a song for my Christmas special too – the sweethearts – so the record was taking longer than normal. By the time Lady C came on well past 9.00 p.m., the Directioners, who had been outside the studio from 9.00 in the morning so as to get good studio seats, decided quiet understandably to go home. The show was all wrapped up by 9.30, I had a few glasses of wine with the team and we all congratulated ourselves on what a fun show we'd had. So imagine my surprise when I read in the paper the next day that Louis had thrown his mobile across the studio in a fit of rage and the audience, so outraged at what Lady C had said, had stormed out – I thought maybe someone had spiked my Cinzano. None of that had happened, it was all bullshit. I get so protective of my show that I felt truly aggrieved. It was a load of bollocks. This was a betrayal by the press, I spluttered to my agent down the phone, shaking my fist – probably. Then the next day when we got the ratings in, I had my epiphany. You stupid idiot, Alan – you've missed the whole point of this chat show lark. The newspapers got the headlines, the band got the publicity, the newspaper readers got the gossip and I got the ratings – and before my eyes blazed the reciprocal ring of celebrity. Who cares if it's not true, everyone got what they wanted and I was the last to understand it – what an idiot I was. I had to get it into my big, thick, naive skull that this isn't charity work, love, it's showbiz. What a revelation.

Still, it has to be said that press intrusion is not always so flippant; sometimes it can take a more sinister turn and there is one incident that I do need to mention that really shook me up. It was my first taste of the 'dark arts' of the tabloids.

I got a call out of the blue from my mum, asking me frantically, 'Are you okay? Are you okay?'

I put down my croque monsieur. 'Yeah, why?'

The drama unfolded. A journalist had come to my parents' neighbours' house and told them I had been in a serious car accident and that he needed to contact my brother, Gary, to let him know. 'Would you have his phone number or address, it's really urgent?' he said. My parents' neighbours, obviously in a panic, gave him my brother's address and the journalist went off. Of course, once at my brother's, there was no mention of me being involved in a serious car crash; however, if Gary wanted to sell any stories on me he would be handsomely rewarded. He told them to 'fuck off'.

Apparently it's called 'doorstepping' and it's quite common with tabloid journalists, but whatever it's called it was pretty low behaviour and it put not only my family but their neighbours in a right state. I think even the most 'celebrity-hating' reader, with their predictable catch-all 'if you don't like it get a job at Tesco', will feel slightly unsettled at that story. A line had been crossed and it felt sinister. I'm not going to start pointing fingers and moaning about the press; we are all to blame because we are the ones who want the gossip and we want it now and we want it fresh. I have spent hours chewing the fat with friends, discussing X's career or Y's love life, when my own home life or career has been less than rosy. I guess it's easier, and safer, to sort someone else's life out than your own. If you start picking at your own life, I think we'd all feel a bit scared at what we might find once it started unravelling.

Don't worry, I am not going to stop you gossiping, it's just that I want you to all gossip responsibly. I think gossip should be labelled, like food. Seriously, ask yourself when you're chatting with your girlfriends at your weekly coffee morning, where has this juicy titbit come from? Apply the same thought process that we do with food. Oh, this chicken was corn-fed in a beautiful farm with all its friends in the Cotswolds – oh boy, do I feel good about myself, yum! This gossip is lie-fed and was obtained by doorstepping a pensioner and lying about a serious car accident. Oh, I don't think I want this gossip now – I'll pass. This meat came from a puppy farm in Korea – no thank you. This gossip about a pop singer who was involved in a lesbian orgy actually comes from the singer herself because her album isn't selling very well and it needs a boost. Lovely – very tasty. You get the gist.

Although I can be quite curmudgeonly about social media, I can't be too down on it; the ability to view snippets of comedy routines or shows on the World Wide Web, and not only to like them but to share them far and wide has given me the opportunity to perform my stand-up all over the world. To be able to travel not only to Europe but to the Middle East and to such far-flung destinations as Australia and New Zealand and for people to know you and to 'get' your comedy still to this day blows my mind.

I gigged for the first time in Scandinavia this year, once in Oslo and once in Tromsø in the Arctic Circle, and as the taxi driver collected me from Tromsø airport he asked if I would be doing the TripAdvisor joke. There was me a bag of nerves on the plane, wondering if they would even understand me, and here they were making requests, whatever next. As it happened I had nothing to worry about, the gigs went so well I even got a standing ovation in Oslo. I was soon offered more gigs in such places as Amsterdam, Stockholm, Denmark and Iceland (the country, not Bejam), which made my day.

Travelling is one of my favourite things ever and yet bizarrely I have never been offered a travelogue *cough* sort it out Channel 4. You will often see me whizzing round the hotel's revolving door at some ungodly hour, anoraked up, compass out, ready to take on whatever a city has to offer. Whilst in Tromsø, seeing the northern lights was right at the top of my to-do list, so after the gig a lovely Norwegian man drove me for an hour even deeper into the Arctic Circle to catch a glimpse of the Aurora Borealis. Frustratingly, we waited nearly an hour in the roadside car park, looking up to the heavens with some other hopeful tourists, but alas the northern lights failed to materialize, not even a little green twinkle from the skies. The temperature dropped to minus ten and regretfully we decided to call it a day, hopped in the car and drove back south. I can't even take comfort in the photographs, me standing there anxiously in an anorak, cold and uncomfortable in the headlights of a Cortina – it looks like I'm dogging.

The next morning was very weird for me, walking around the city of Tromsø; it's so small and compact that I soon realized everyone had been to see my gig the night before, not because I am so hugely famous up there, probably more due to the fact that there is nothing really to do once the skis have been popped away for the evening. 'Hello, Alan' floated from every car window that passed. People waved at me from across the street. I went into a coffee shop for a much-needed brew and a croissant and I swear the whole shop turned and said, 'Hello, Alan.' The waitress behind the counter said, 'We loved the gig so much and we were all hoping you would come into our coffee shop.' I thanked her and told her mournfully that after the gig I had waited an hour to see the northern lights but that sadly I hadn't seen them.

'It's only green in the sky,' she said with a wink, 'get over it,' and with that she plopped my croissant down and served the next customer.

Bloody forty, eh? Wait there, I was born in 1976 and this year is . . . 2016 – yep, I'm forty, goddamn it. Where has the time gone? What have I achieved? Who's this old bloke in the mirror? Even worse, on the gay scene I have transitioned from 'twink' to 'bear' in the blink of a jockstrap. But, you know, when you start thinking about how depressingly sad 2016 has been, I just have to thank my lucky stars that I've been able to reach forty in the first place. I had always poured scorn on all those people who cried, panicked and froze in fear at reaching forty; get over yourselves, I thought, rolling my eyes as maxims like 'Life begins at forty' and 'Forty is the new twenty' fell from their mouths. Foolishly, I thought I was immune until my Paul came in one evening the day before my fortieth birthday and found me literally sobbing on the settee, cuddling my dogs and, inexplicably, my neighbour's dog, Morris, who had somehow got through the fence. A half-empty bottle of gin stood on the table. Yes, the gin had been my tipping point but obviously the fear had been lying dormant – why else would I be sobbing 'I don't want to die!' my face all red and swollen, Morris acting all cool yet still trying to lick off one of my snot bubbles. Paul thankfully sedated me and put me to bed, but do you know what? My fortieth birthday came, hung around for a day and then went – I didn't die, nothing fell off, nothing prolapsed. In fact, I had a bloody amazing party down in Brighton to celebrate. The theme was 'Life is a Carrbaret' (get it?). Think 1920s decadence, Berlin, art deco, *The Beautiful and the Damned*. Everyone, and I mean everyone, dressed up. It was such a fun night, I even came down the stairs and performed in a bowler hat and suspenders as Sally Bowles to a thrilled/appalled audience – it's my party and I'll make people vomit if I want to. Some wit said I was more 'Silly Bowels' – but I had them thrown out.

I sort of understand now why people say 'Life begins at forty'; of course your life doesn't begin but you MAKE your life begin at forty, you kick-start it. You say, 'Look, you're lucky to be here, you're halfway through – make the rest count,' and that's what I've been doing. People on social media had been asking me to take my stand-up tour to New Zealand and Australia for the past year and I had been non-committal but now I said to my agent, 'Book it in – Yap Yap Yap's going down under, baby.' I wanted to give something back, so I became the proud patron of Neuroblastoma.org.uk, a children's cancer charity that is just so brilliant at what it does and it's my goal to raise its profile and hopefully thousands of pounds to help these poor kids and their families. But hey, don't worry, I'm not getting all Mother Teresa on your ass, I had some personal ambitions of my own. Glastonbury, arguably the biggest festival in the world, was an itch I had wanted to scratch for ages, and this year let's just say I scratched at it so much I needed a skin graft – to this day I still don't think I'm over it. What a weekend. I had done festivals before but only appearing at the Comedy Tent – being ferried there on a milk float, collected after the performance and then driven home – but this time I was to camp over for THREE nights in a tent, with just a groundsheet between me and the mud. Now before Bear Grylls reads this and thinks he's out of a job, I have a confession: I helicoptered in. Yes, I know, I know, I was a helicopter wanker. My lovely partner had bought the flight for me as a birthday treat. Judge away, call me a wanker if you must, but as I hovered over the miles and miles of traffic jams I was a smug wanker. I tell you, though, the smug look soon left my face as we started our descent. I don't know about you but I just assumed the helicopter pilot has to hand a whole smorgasbord of knobs and buttons, longitude and latitude statistics, state-of-the-art technology to guide him in, but just as our helicopter began its descent, the pilot squinted, leant forward and said, 'Keep your eyes open for a windsock.' What? All you're looking for is a windsock? Shit! We could land at a car boot sale!

Thankfully it was the right windsock and we landed majestically in a beautiful green field in Somerset. Little did I know it was the last time I would see green that weekend. Everything was brown from then on in. Brown, brown, muddy brown, brown inside the tent, brown outside the tent, everything was brown. As it turned out, it was the wettest, muddiest Glastonbury ever – of course it was, I was going. Did I really expect it to be glorious sunshine? I still had an absolute ball, though of course, sod's law, when you are in a state you keep bumping into people you know. One hundred and seventy-five thousand people over 1,100 acres and I run into an electrician who bodged up my wiring three years ago, but anyway, it wasn't the time or the place. In fact, I saw so many people I knew – Grimmy, James Corden, Niall from 1D – that for me it was like a really muddy works do.

I also met one of the nicest people in showbiz, Dermot O'Leary, who looked the business as always. 'How are you, buddy?' he said as he glided over the mud wearing Ray-Bans, a tight T-shirt, beige chinos and miraculously clean Hunter wellies. Beige? Chinos? At a festival? Without a single splatter of mud on them? If I wore them, I'd be caked, I'd look like a skid mark. I'm always envious of Dermot, he is so effortlessly cool – how does he do it? My friend Julie had knocked a pint of cider over my crotch and someone else had accidently tipped a glass of red wine over my obligatory hat, doing nothing to quell the rumours that I was three sheets to the wind. What with the dustman's jacket and red leggings, people were pointing and screaming at me, thinking one of Mr Eavis's scarecrows had come to life. Even though me and my three mates and fellow campers, Ross, Elliott and Julie, only saw sunshine the whole weekend between 4.32 p.m. and 4.36 p.m. on the Friday afternoon we had a blast – what an experience. Would I do it again? Never in a million years!

So, it's time to put the scalpel down, wash your hands clean and replace the sheet over my body. The autopsy is drawing to a close and you've pried and poked and inspected my whole body from top to toe as I've laid myself out on the slab. I know parts of me like my hips and hairline might not be what they were a few years back but I hope my body hasn't let you down like it has me – hey, bladder!? This one's been easier to write in some ways than my first book, *Look Who It Is*. The memories are fresher so they are easier to remember, and yet writing about television, the hall of mirrors that is celebrity and the whole absurd business that is fame is much trickier. Everyone has their own opinion of these things so it's hard to pin down, to find a truth that everyone agrees with. My first book was all about my childhood and growing up and it felt secure and solid – it was there, crystallized in Northampton, and all I had to do was chip away and the fond and not so fond memories would ooze out and I could dip my nib in and write away to my heart's content. This one was a different beast because I've been writing in what is in effect 'real time'. Of the people I started writing about at the beginning of the book, some have died, some have changed from hero to monster, some have gone up (or down) in my estimation and some have disappeared off the face of the earth so it's hard to know where to anchor yourself. It's all about perceptions, I guess, and I'm sure in the future I'll look back at this book and my perceptions will have changed yet again.

And what of the future, as I begin to wade through my forties? As I mentioned, I've got a tour of Australia and New Zealand to look forward to and brand-new shows coming out on Channel 4. On top of all that, I've just received my American work visa for an exciting new show I'm doing over there – it's nerve-racking but I feel like I'm at the beginning of an adventure and I wouldn't want it any other way. So many questions. Will I break America? Will I have a mid-life crisis? Will I write another book? Who knows? Who can we look to who has all these answers?

Wait a minute – I know someone. Get that rump-ologist back – tell her to warm up her fingers, I want her to have another go on my arse.

Acknowledgements

Firstly my family: Paul, Mum, Dad, Gary, Carly, Bev, Joyce, Barbara and Ron Drayton.

Everyone at Off The Kerb, especially long-suffering Danny, who has been throughout the writing of this book not only my agent but my wingman, my shrink, my cheerleader, my conscience.

Rowland White, Karen Whitlock and everyone at Penguin.

And of course the people who allow me to keep having these wonderful moments – you!

Pictures Permissions

Inset 1

p.1 Alan Carr, Justin Lee Collins and Mariah Carey /
     EMPICS Entertainment

p.5 Alan Carr, Justin Lee Collins and Steven Segal / Ian
     West / Press Association Images

p.5 Alan Carr, Justin Lee Collins and Rob Lowe / Ian West /
     Press Association Images

p.6 Alan Carr as Kim Kardashian / Nicky Johnston / Heat
     Magazine

p.7 Alan Carr as Madonna / Simon Webb / Heat Magazine

p.7 Alan Carr, Justin Lee Collins and Kanye West /
     EMPICS Entertainment

p.8 Alan Carr and David Gest / EMPICS Entertainment

p.8 Alan Carr and David Hasselhoff / EMPICS
     Entertainment

Inset 2

p.1 Alan Carr collecting his BAFTA / BAFTA / Stephen
     Butler

p.3 Alan Carr and his partner Paul 'in bed' / Lorenzo Agius

p.6 Alan Carr's *New Year Specstacular* 2011 / Open Mike
     Productions Ltd.

p.6 Alan Carr and Bruce Forsyth / Open Mike Productions
     Ltd.

P.6 Alan Carr and Lionel Richie / Open Mike Productions Ltd.

p.7 Alan Carr and Bradley Cooper / Open Mike
     Productions Ltd.

p.7 Alan Carr and Justin Bieber / Open Mike Productions Ltd.

p.7 Alan Carr and Taylor Swift / Open Mike Productions Ltd.

p.7 Alan Carr and Lady Gaga / Open Mike Productions Ltd.

Image Credits

1. Alan, Justin Lee Collins (JLC) and Mariah Carey: Picture by: EMPICS Entertainment

2. Alan and Carol Vorderman in a plane: Alan's personal photographs

3. Alan's partner Paul: Alan's personal photographs

4. Alan and Paul in Vietnam: Alan's personal photographs

5. Alan and his dog Joyce as a puppy: Alan's personal photographs

6. Alan and Paul zip-wiring: Alan's personal photographs

7. Alan as Jeremy Clarkson: Alan's personal photographs

8. Alan, JLC and Steven Segal on the FNP: Picture by: Ian West/Press Association Images

9. Alan, JLC and Rob Lowe – FNP football sketch: Picture by: Ian West/Press Association Images

10. Alan as Kim Kardashian © Heat Magazine

11. Alan as Madonna © Heat Magazine

12. Alan, JLC and Kanye West on the FNP: Picture by: EMPICS Entertainment